ASTONISHING
X-MEN

EXALTED

NISHING X-MEN VOL. 9: EXALTED. Contains material originally published in magazine form as ASTONISHING X-MEN #44-47 and ASTONISHING X-MEN: GHOST BOXES #1. First printing 2012. ISBN# 978-0-
6178-3. Published by MARVEL WORLDWIDE, INC., a subsidiary of MARVEL ENTERTAINMENT, LLC. OFFICE OF PUBLICATION: 135 West 50th Street, New York, NY 10020. Copyright © 2008, 2011 and 2012 Marvel
cters, Inc. All rights reserved. $16.99 per copy in the U.S. and $18.99 in Canada (GST #R127032852); Canadian Agreement #40668537. All characters featured in this issue and the distinctive names and likenesses
of, and all related indicia are trademarks of Marvel Characters, Inc. No similarity between any of the names, characters, persons, and/or institutions in this magazine with those of any living or dead person or
tion is intended, and any such similarity which may exist is purely coincidental. Printed in the U.S.A. ALAN FINE, EVP - Office of the President, Marvel Worldwide, Inc. and EVP & CMO Marvel Characters B.V.; DAN
LEY, Publisher & President - Print, Animation & Digital Divisions; JOE QUESADA, Chief Creative Officer; TOM BREVOORT, SVP of Publishing; DAVID BOGART, SVP of Operations & Procurement, Publishing; RUWAN
ILLEKE, SVP & Associate Publisher, Publishing; C.B. CEBULSKI, SVP of Creator & Content Development; DAVID GABRIEL, SVP of Publishing Sales & Circulation; MICHAEL PASCIULLO, SVP of Brand Planning &
munications; JIM O'KEEFE, VP of Operations & Logistics; DAN CARR, Executive Director of Publishing Technology; SUSAN CRESPI, Editorial Operations Manager; ALEX MORALES, Publishing Operations Manager; STAN
Chairman Emeritus. For information regarding advertising in Marvel Comics or on Marvel.com, please contact Niza Disla, Director of Marvel Partnerships, at ndisla@marvel.com. For Marvel subscription inquiries,
e call 800-217-9158. Manufactured between 9/5/2012 and 10/8/2012 by R.R. DONNELLEY, INC., SALEM, VA, USA.

87654321

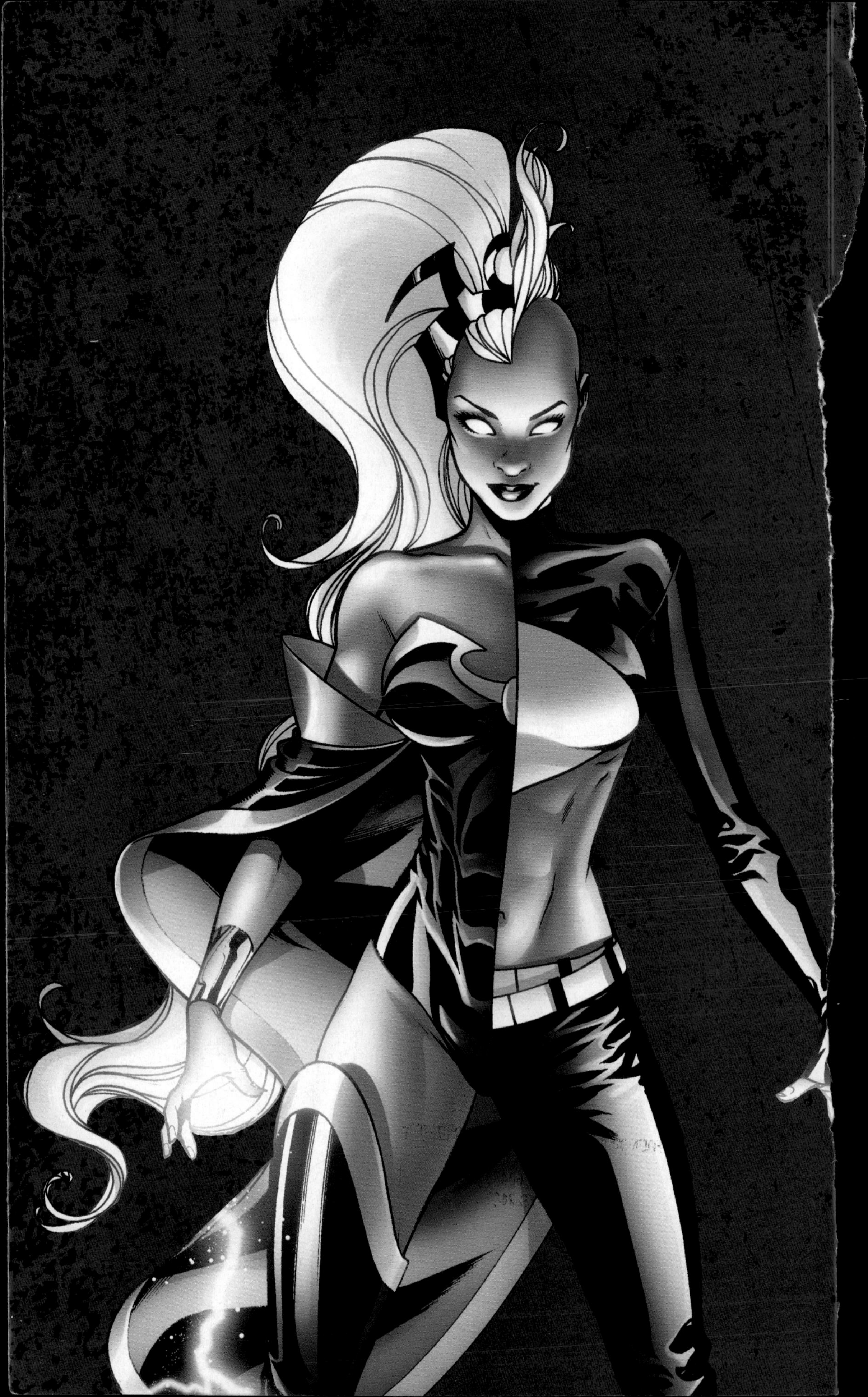

EXALTED

Writer: **Greg Pak**

Artist: **Mike McKone**

Color Artist: **Rachelle Rosenberg**

Cover Art: **Mike McKone & Rachelle Rosenberg**

Associate Editor: **Daniel Ketchum**

Editor: **Nick Lowe**

GHOST BOXES #1

Writer: **Warren Ellis**

Artist: **Adi Granov**

Letterer: **VC's Joe Caramagna**

Assistant Editors: **Daniel Ketchum & Will Panzo**

Editor: **Axel Alonso**

COLLECTION EDITOR: JENNIFER GRÜNWALD • ASSISTANT EDITORS: ALEX STARBUCK & NELSON RIBEIRO
DITOR, SPECIAL PROJECTS: MARK D. BEAZLEY • SENIOR EDITOR, SPECIAL PROJECTS: JEFF YOUNGQUIST • SENIOR VICE PRESIDENT OF SALES: DAVID GABRIEL
SVP OF BRAND PLANNING & COMMUNICATIONS: MICHAEL PASCIULLO

EDITOR IN CHIEF: AXEL ALONSO • CHIEF CREATIVE OFFICER: JOE QUESADA • PUBLISHER: DAN BUCKLEY • EXECUTIVE PRODUCER: ALAN FINE

ASTONISHING X-MEN

The X-Men have split in half. Separating over a
philosophical difference pertaining to their responsibilities
to the younger generation of mutants, Wolverine, Kitty
Pryde and Beast have left San Francisco to start a mutant
school in Westchester, while Cyclops continues to conduct
his team of X-Men as a mutant army on Utopia.

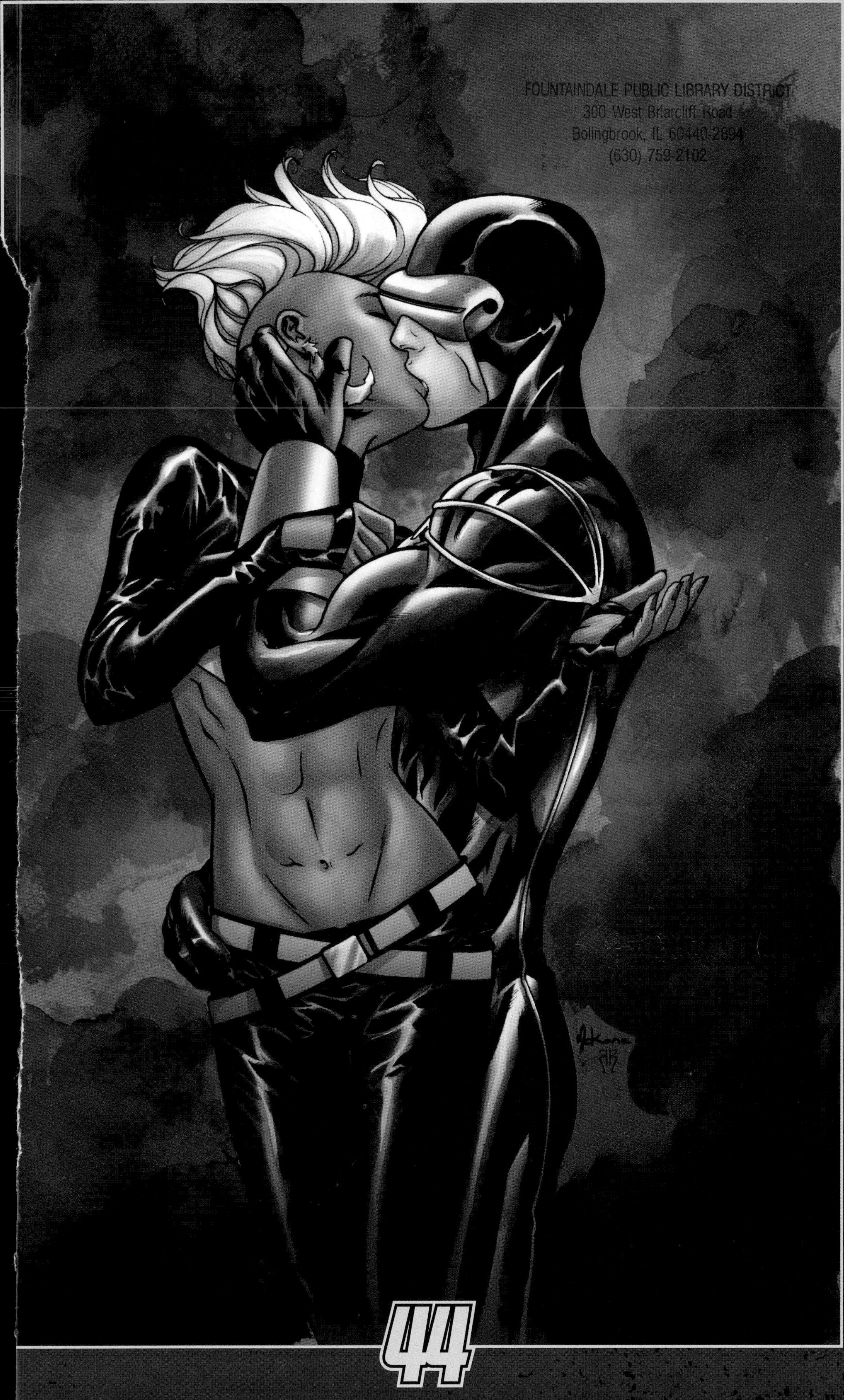
44

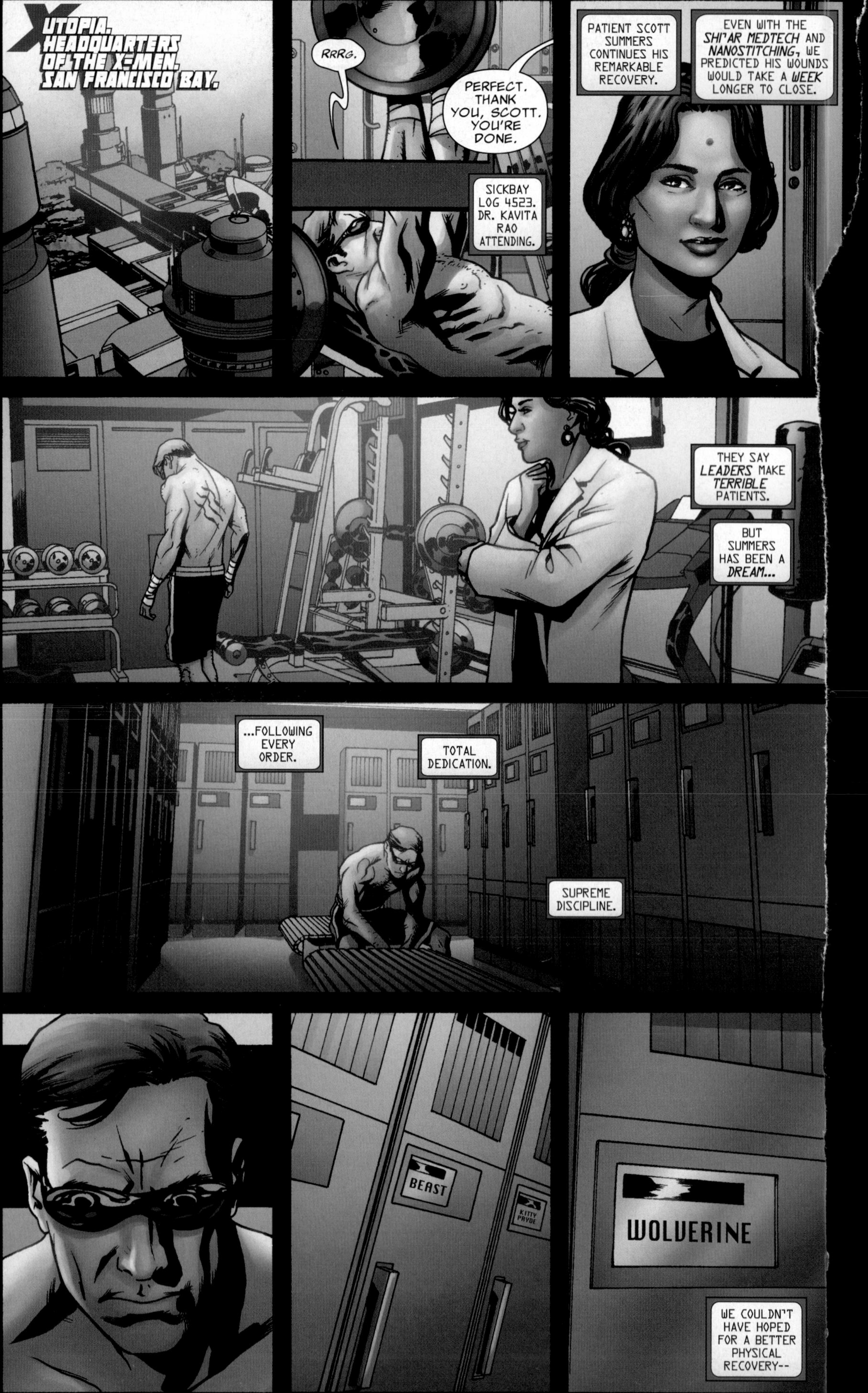
UTOPIA. HEADQUARTERS OF THE X-MEN. SAN FRANCISCO BAY.
RRRG.
PERFECT. THANK YOU, SCOTT. YOU'RE DONE.
SICKBAY LOG 4523. DR. KAVITA RAO ATTENDING.
PATIENT SCOTT SUMMERS CONTINUES HIS REMARKABLE RECOVERY.
EVEN WITH THE SHI'AR MEDTECH AND NANOSTITCHING, WE PREDICTED HIS WOUNDS WOULD TAKE A WEEK LONGER TO CLOSE.
THEY SAY LEADERS MAKE TERRIBLE PATIENTS.
BUT SUMMERS HAS BEEN A DREAM...
...FOLLOWING EVERY ORDER.
TOTAL DEDICATION.
SUPREME DISCIPLINE.
BEAST
KITTY PRYDE
WOLVERINE
WE COULDN'T HAVE HOPED FOR A BETTER PHYSICAL RECOVERY--

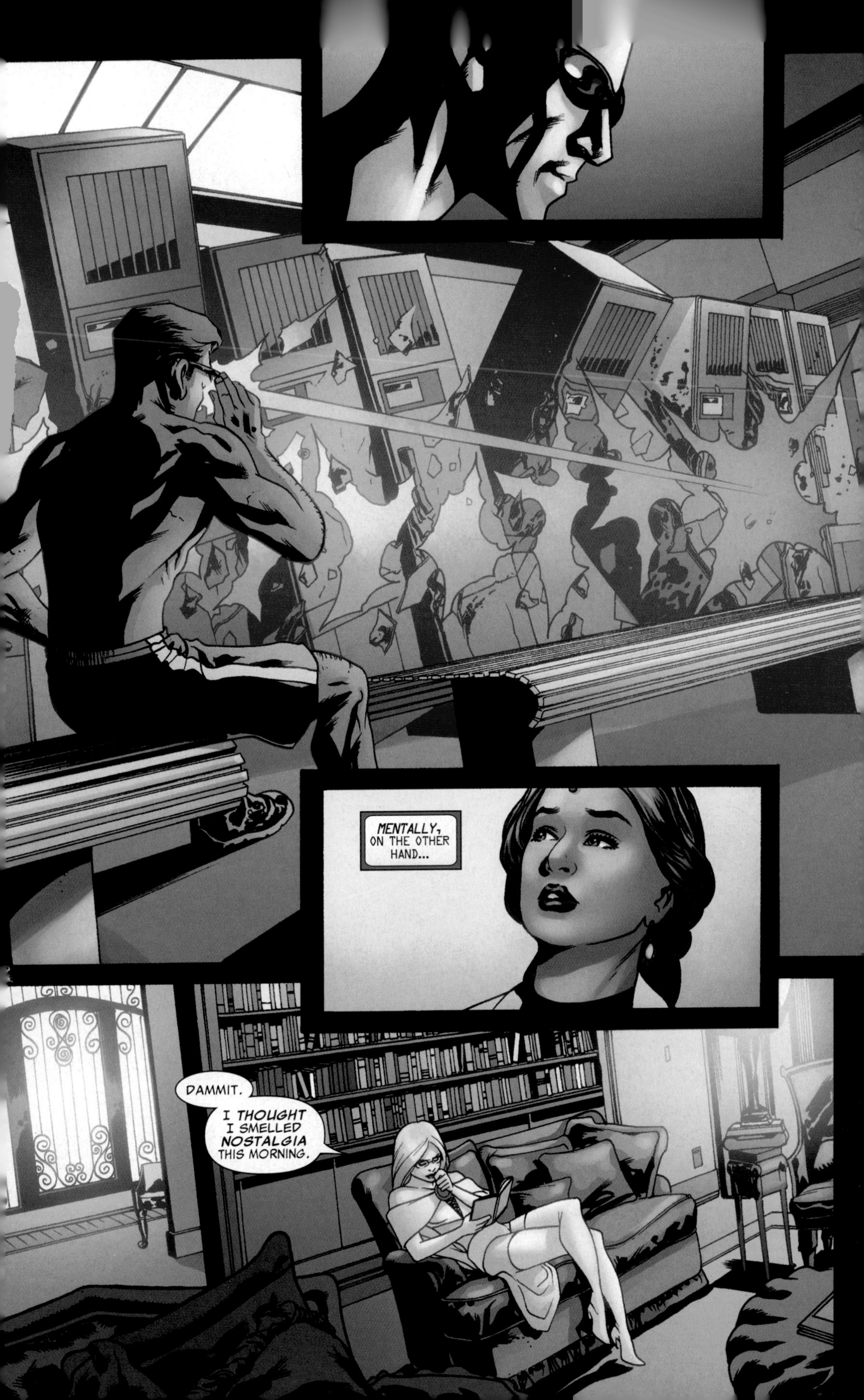

MENTALLY, ON THE OTHER HAND...
DAMMIT.
I THOUGHT I SMELLED NOSTALGIA THIS MORNING.

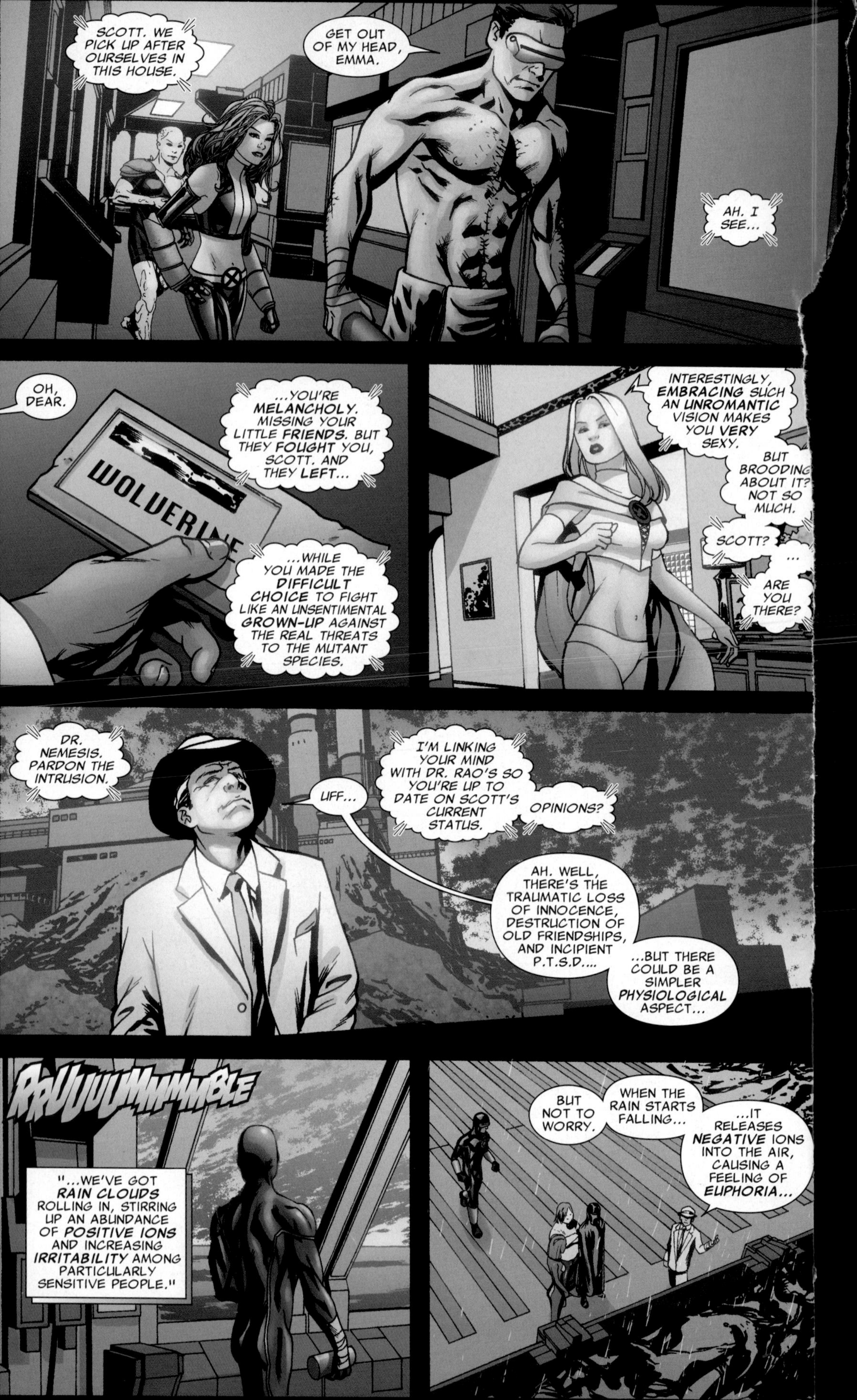
SCOTT. WE PICK UP AFTER OURSELVES IN THIS HOUSE.
GET OUT OF MY HEAD, EMMA.
AH. I SEE...
OH, DEAR.
...YOU'RE MELANCHOLY. MISSING YOUR LITTLE FRIENDS. BUT THEY FOUGHT YOU, SCOTT. AND THEY LEFT...
WOLVERINE
...WHILE YOU MADE THE DIFFICULT CHOICE TO FIGHT LIKE AN UNSENTIMENTAL GROWN-UP AGAINST THE REAL THREATS TO THE MUTANT SPECIES.
INTERESTINGLY, EMBRACING SUCH AN UNROMANTIC VISION MAKES YOU VERY SEXY.
BUT BROODING ABOUT IT? NOT SO MUCH.
SCOTT?
...
ARE YOU THERE?
DR. NEMESIS. PARDON THE INTRUSION.
UFF...
I'M LINKING YOUR MIND WITH DR. RAO'S SO YOU'RE UP TO DATE ON SCOTT'S CURRENT STATUS.
OPINIONS?
AH. WELL, THERE'S THE TRAUMATIC LOSS OF INNOCENCE, DESTRUCTION OF OLD FRIENDSHIPS, AND INCIPIENT P.T.S.D....
...BUT THERE COULD BE A SIMPLER PHYSIOLOGICAL ASPECT...
RRUUUUMMMMMBLE
"...WE'VE GOT RAIN CLOUDS ROLLING IN, STIRRING UP AN ABUNDANCE OF POSITIVE IONS AND INCREASING IRRITABILITY AMONG PARTICULARLY SENSITIVE PEOPLE."
BUT NOT TO WORRY.
WHEN THE RAIN STARTS FALLING...
...IT RELEASES NEGATIVE IONS INTO THE AIR, CAUSING A FEELING OF EUPHORIA...

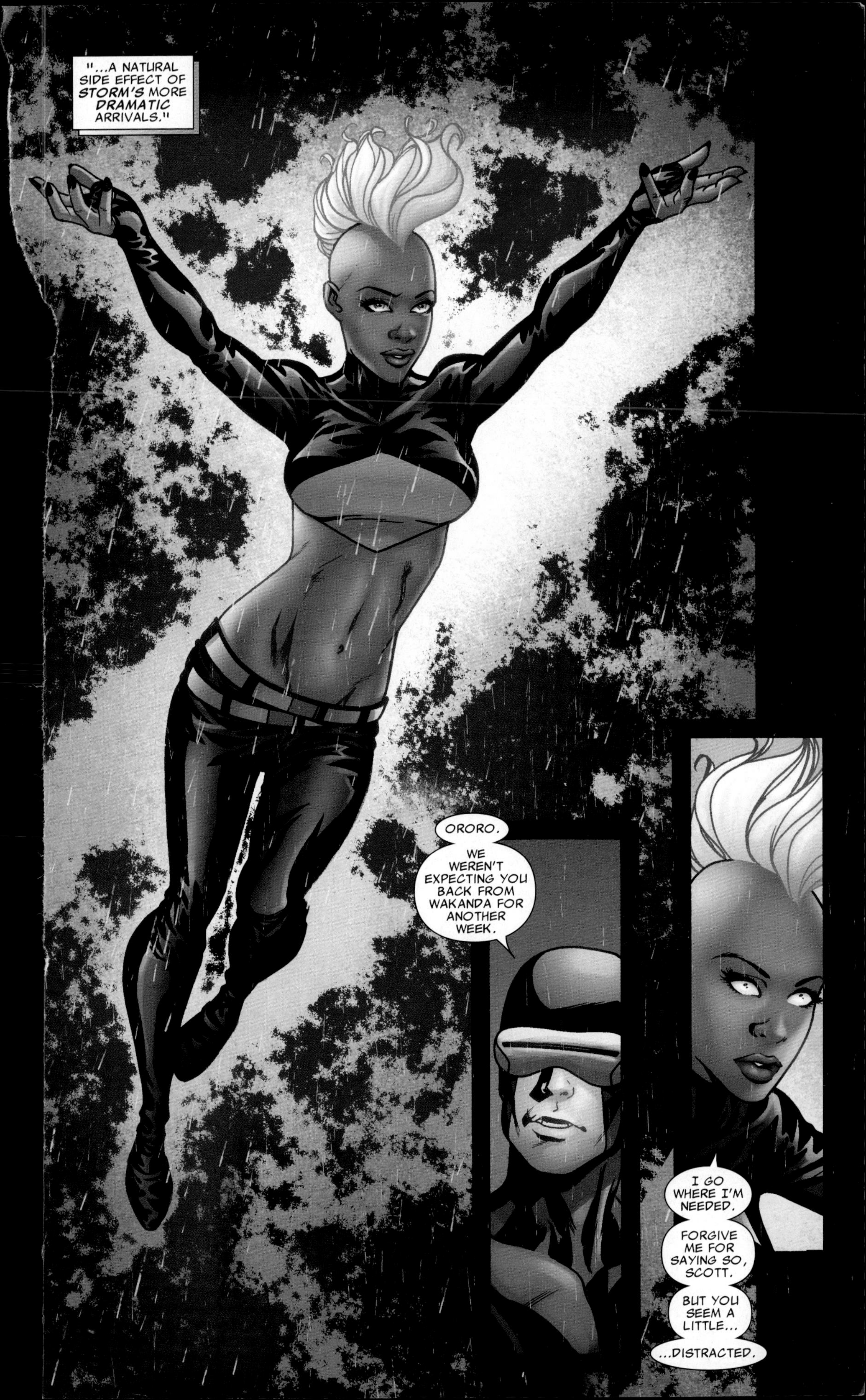
"...A NATURAL SIDE EFFECT OF STORM'S MORE DRAMATIC ARRIVALS."
ORORO.
WE WEREN'T EXPECTING YOU BACK FROM WAKANDA FOR ANOTHER WEEK.
I GO WHERE I'M NEEDED.
FORGIVE ME FOR SAYING SO, SCOTT.
BUT YOU SEEM A LITTLE...
...DISTRACTED.

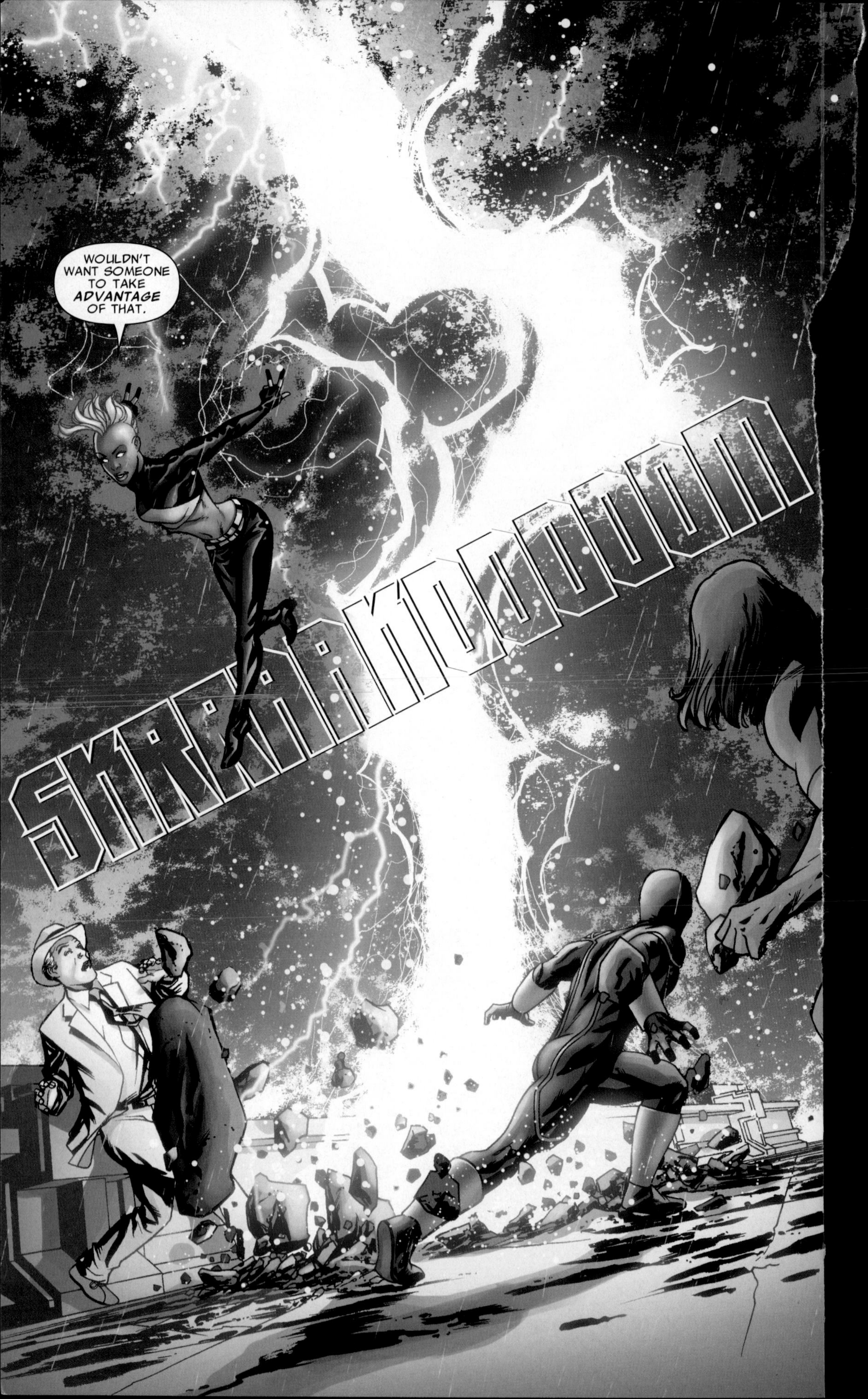
WOULDN'T WANT SOMEONE TO TAKE ADVANTAGE OF THAT.
SKRAAAKDOOOOOM

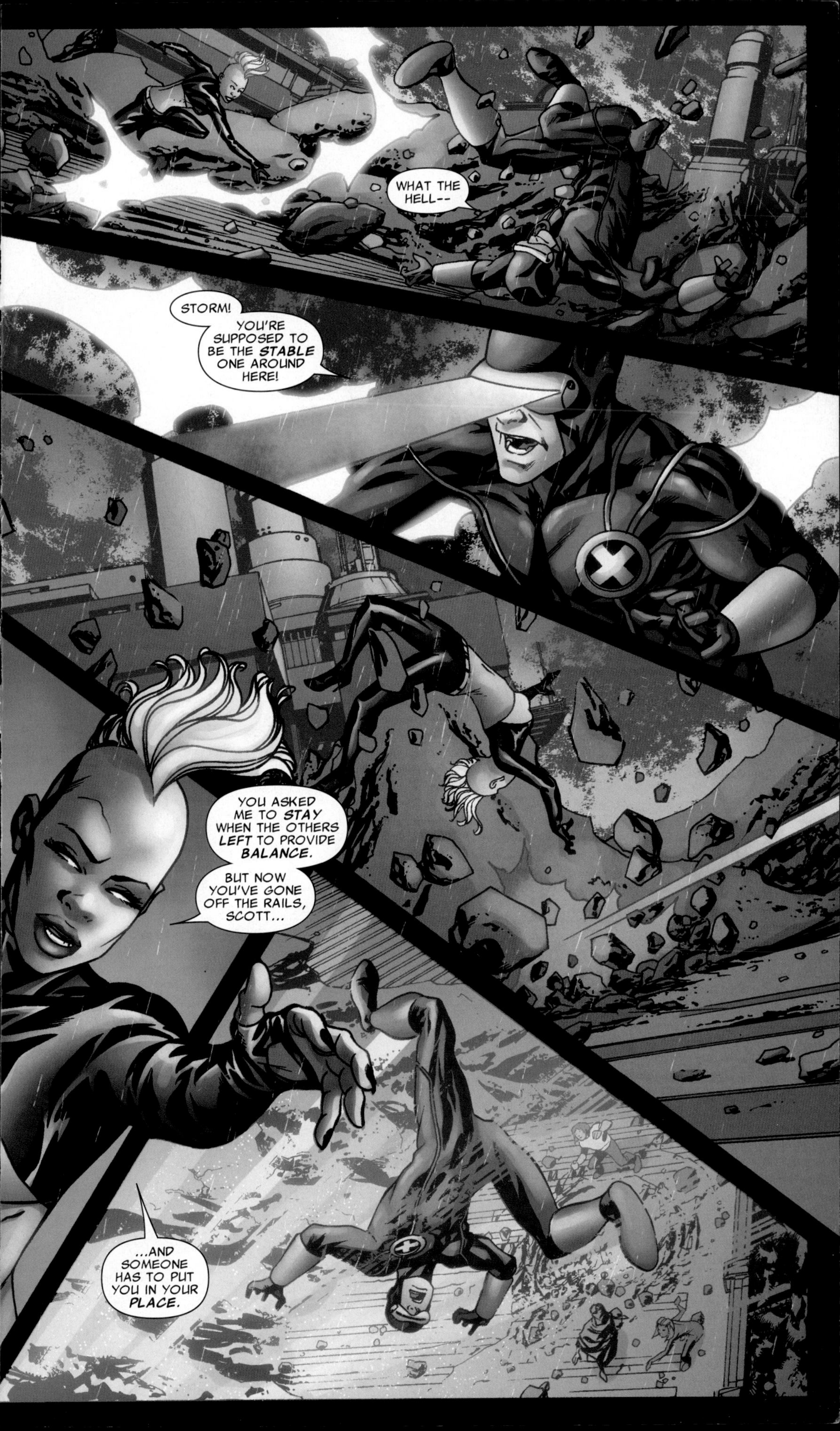
WHAT THE HELL--
STORM! YOU'RE SUPPOSED TO BE THE STABLE ONE AROUND HERE!
YOU ASKED ME TO STAY WHEN THE OTHERS LEFT TO PROVIDE BALANCE.
BUT NOW YOU'VE GONE OFF THE RAILS, SCOTT...
...AND SOMEONE HAS TO PUT YOU IN YOUR PLACE.

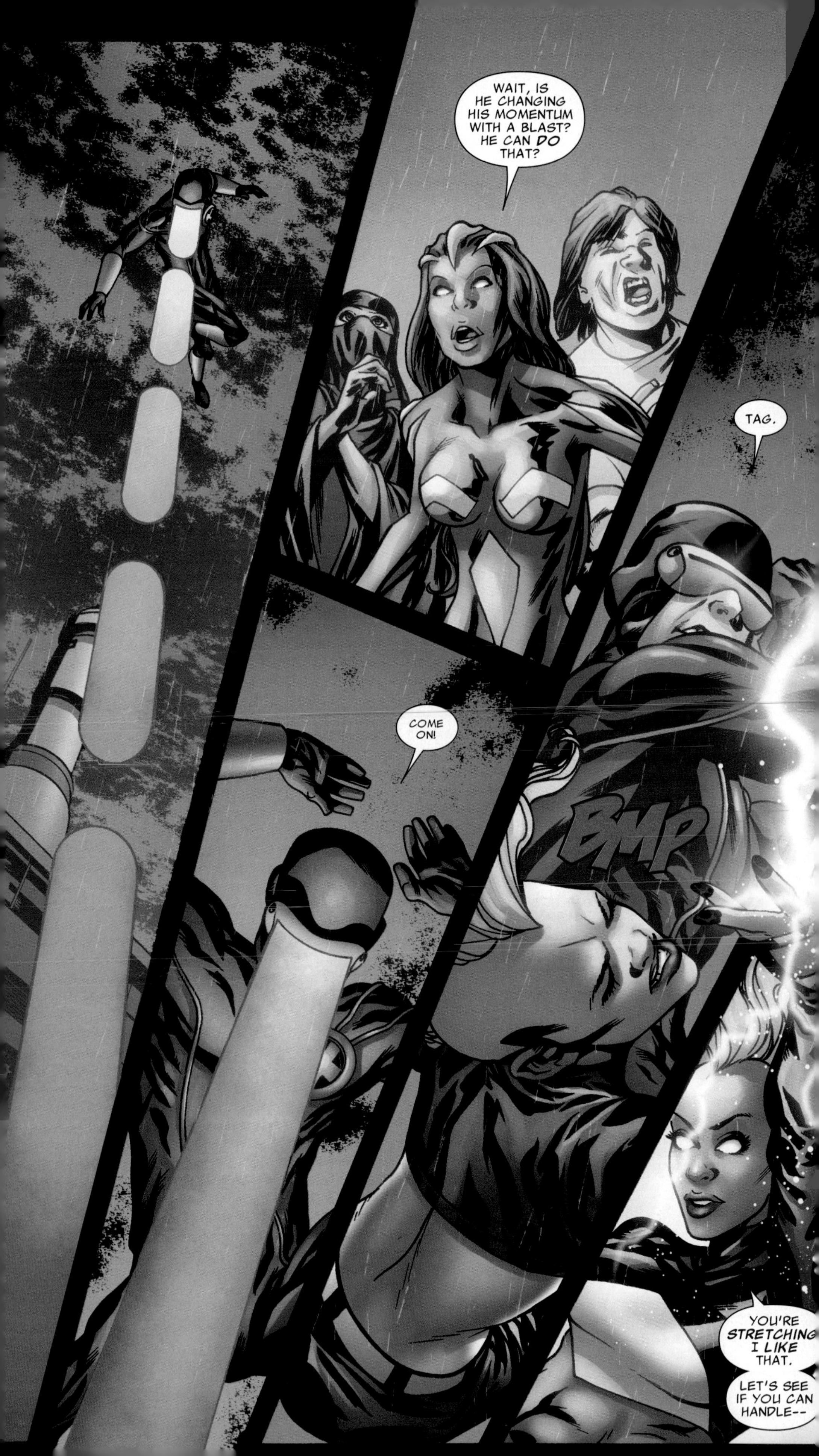
WAIT, IS HE CHANGING HIS MOMENTUM WITH A BLAST? HE CAN DO THAT?
COME ON!
TAG.
BMP
YOU'RE STRETCHING. I LIKE THAT.
LET'S SEE IF YOU CAN HANDLE--

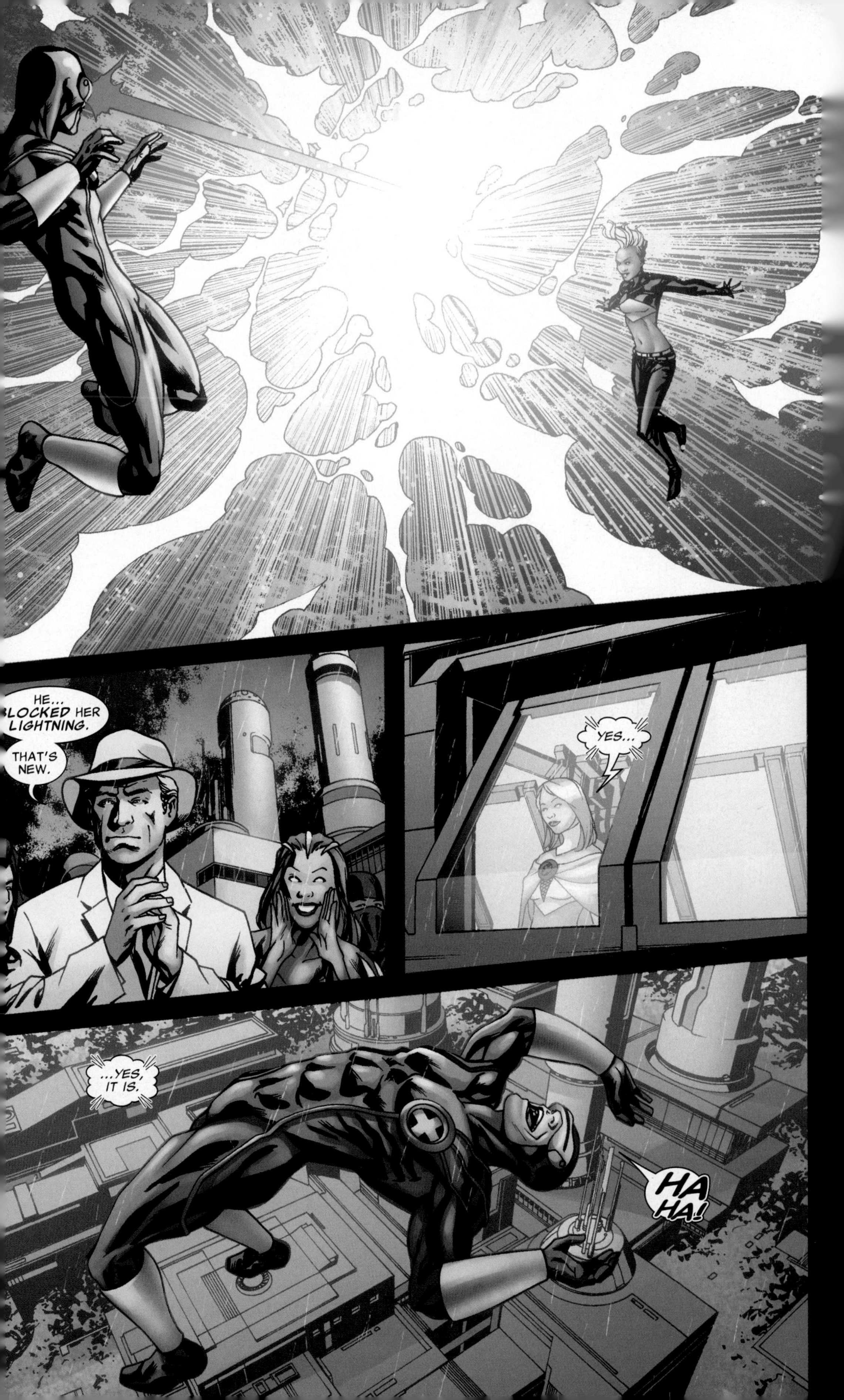
HE... BLOCKED HER LIGHTNING.
THAT'S NEW.
YES...
...YES, IT IS.
HA HA!

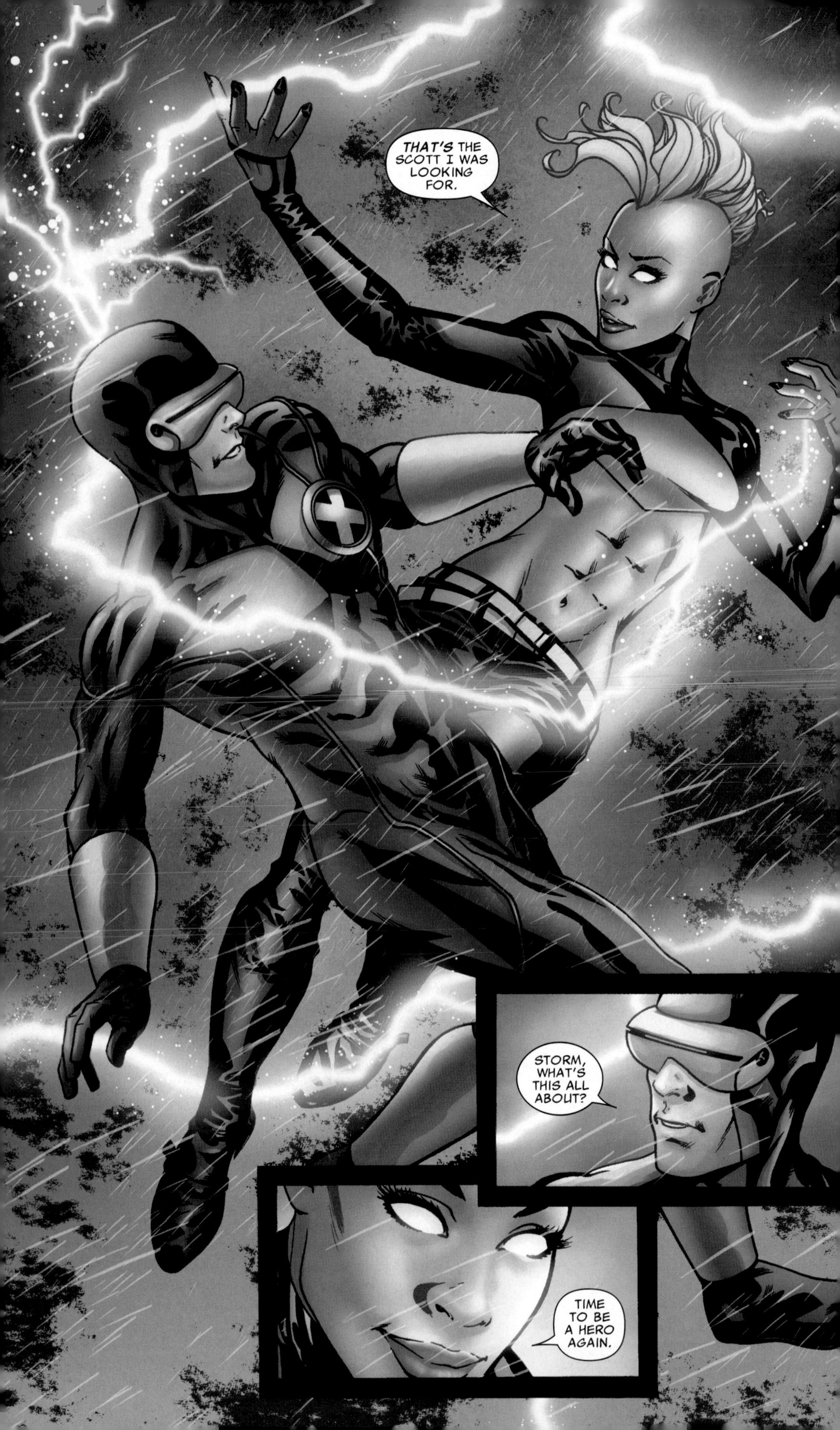
THAT'S THE SCOTT I WAS LOOKING FOR.
STORM, WHAT'S THIS ALL ABOUT?
TIME TO BE A HERO AGAIN.

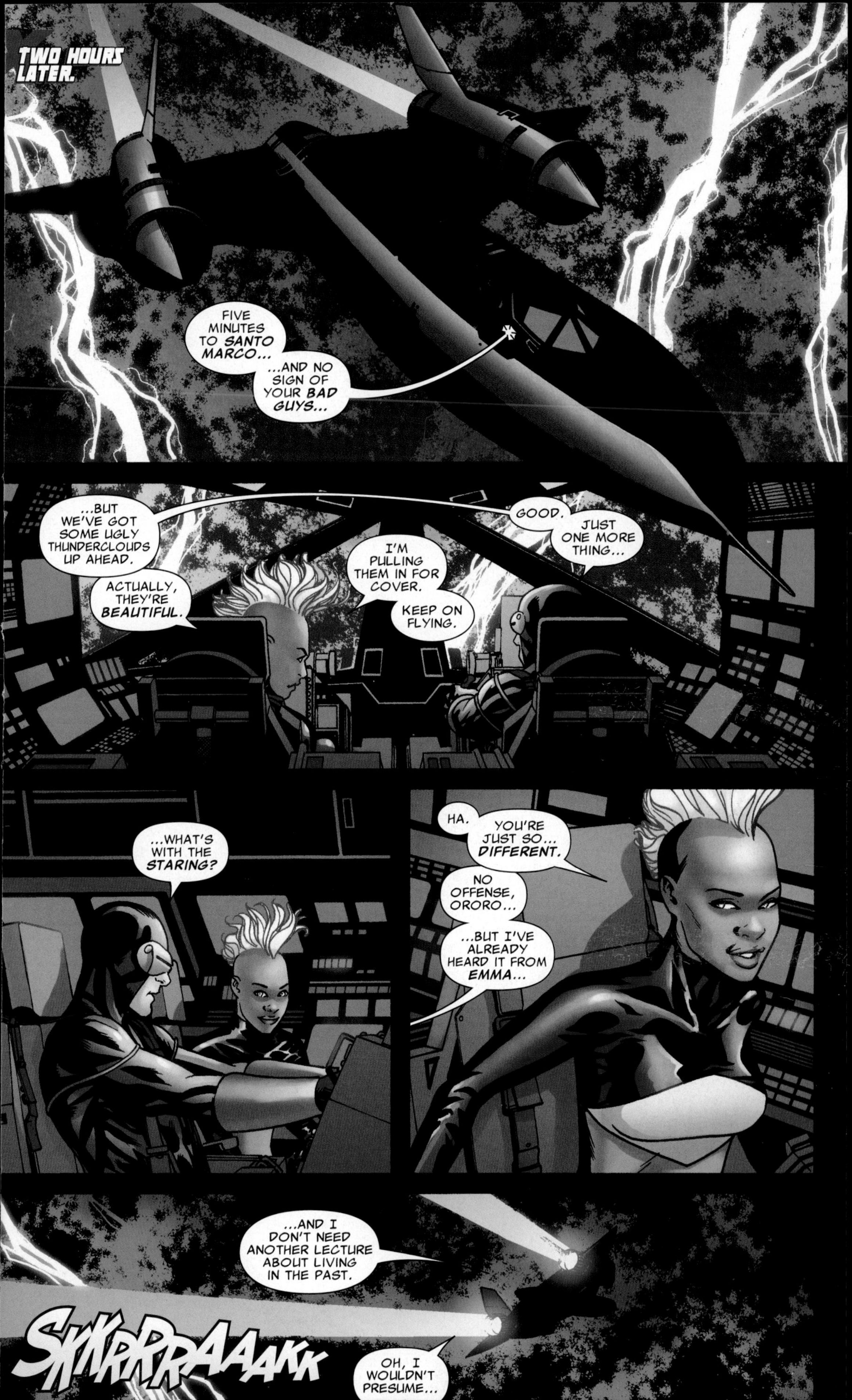
TWO HOURS LATER.
FIVE MINUTES TO SANTO MARCO...
...AND NO SIGN OF YOUR BAD GUYS...
...BUT WE'VE GOT SOME UGLY THUNDERCLOUDS UP AHEAD.
ACTUALLY, THEY'RE BEAUTIFUL.
I'M PULLING THEM IN FOR COVER.
KEEP ON FLYING.
GOOD.
JUST ONE MORE THING...
...WHAT'S WITH THE STARING?
HA.
YOU'RE JUST SO... DIFFERENT.
NO OFFENSE, ORORO...
...BUT I'VE ALREADY HEARD IT FROM EMMA...
...AND I DON'T NEED ANOTHER LECTURE ABOUT LIVING IN THE PAST.
SKKRRRAAAKK
OH, I WOULDN'T PRESUME...

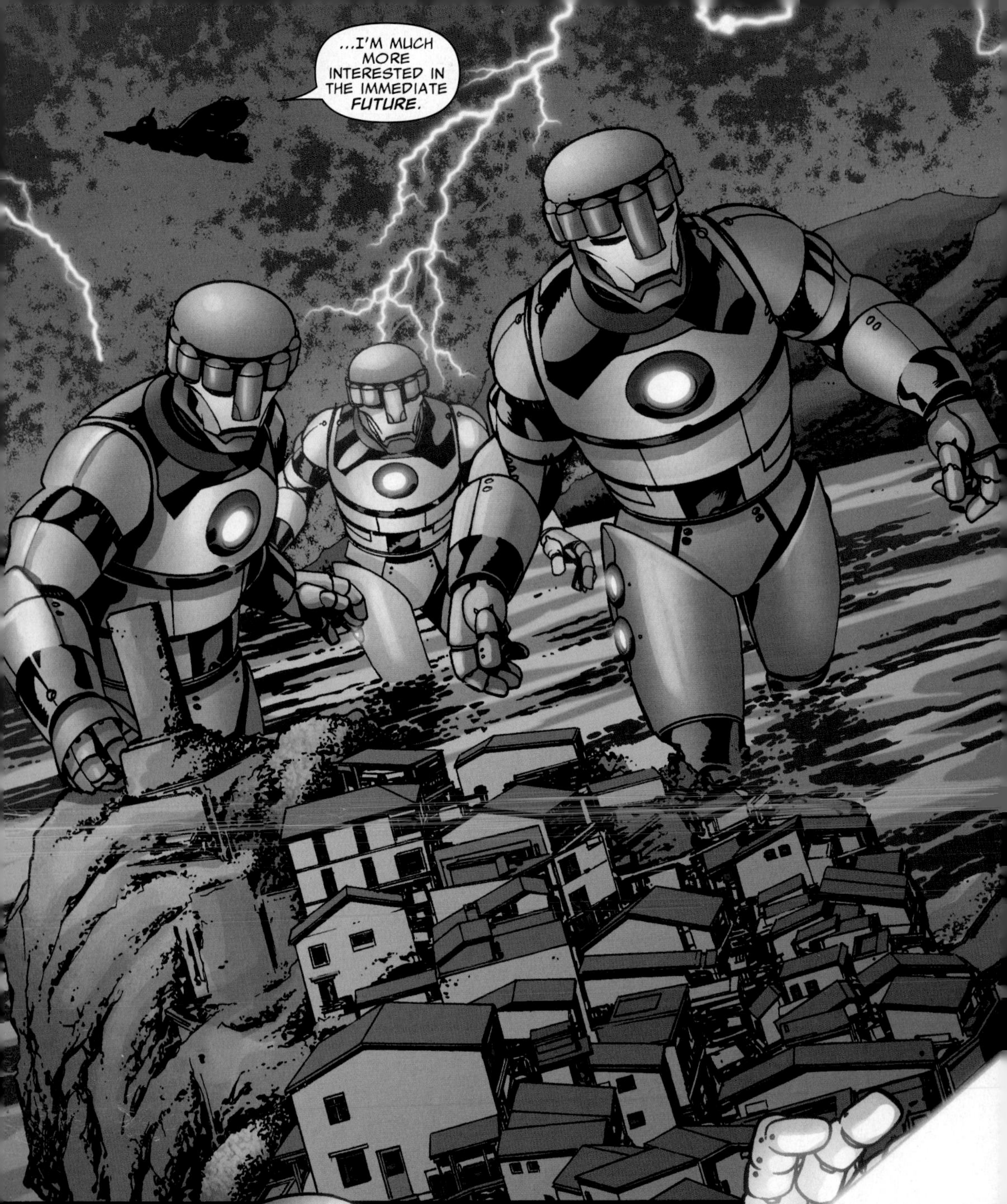
...I'M MUCH MORE INTERESTED IN THE IMMEDIATE FUTURE.
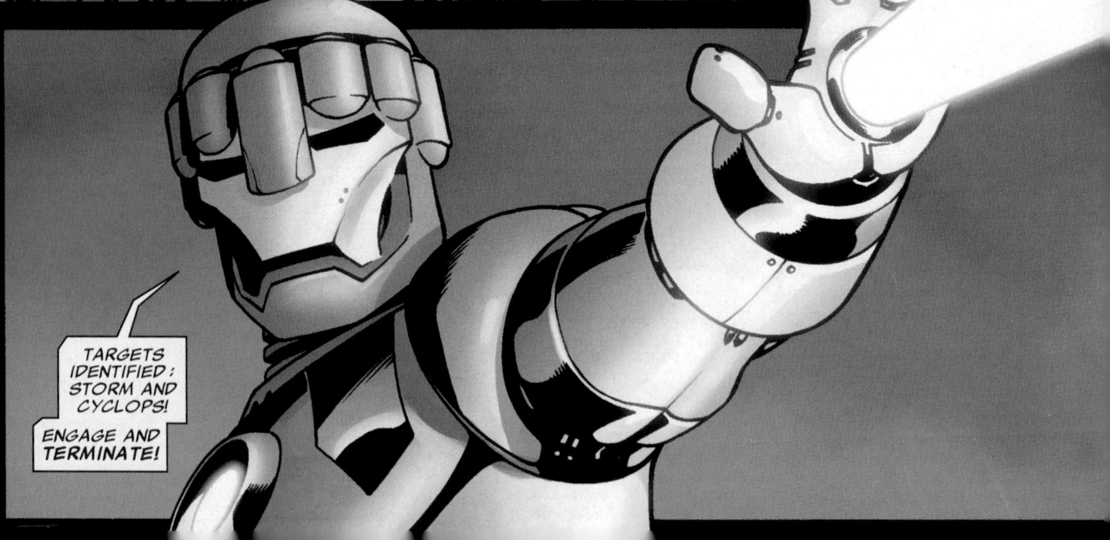
TARGETS IDENTIFIED: STORM AND CYCLOPS!
ENGAGE AND TERMINATE!

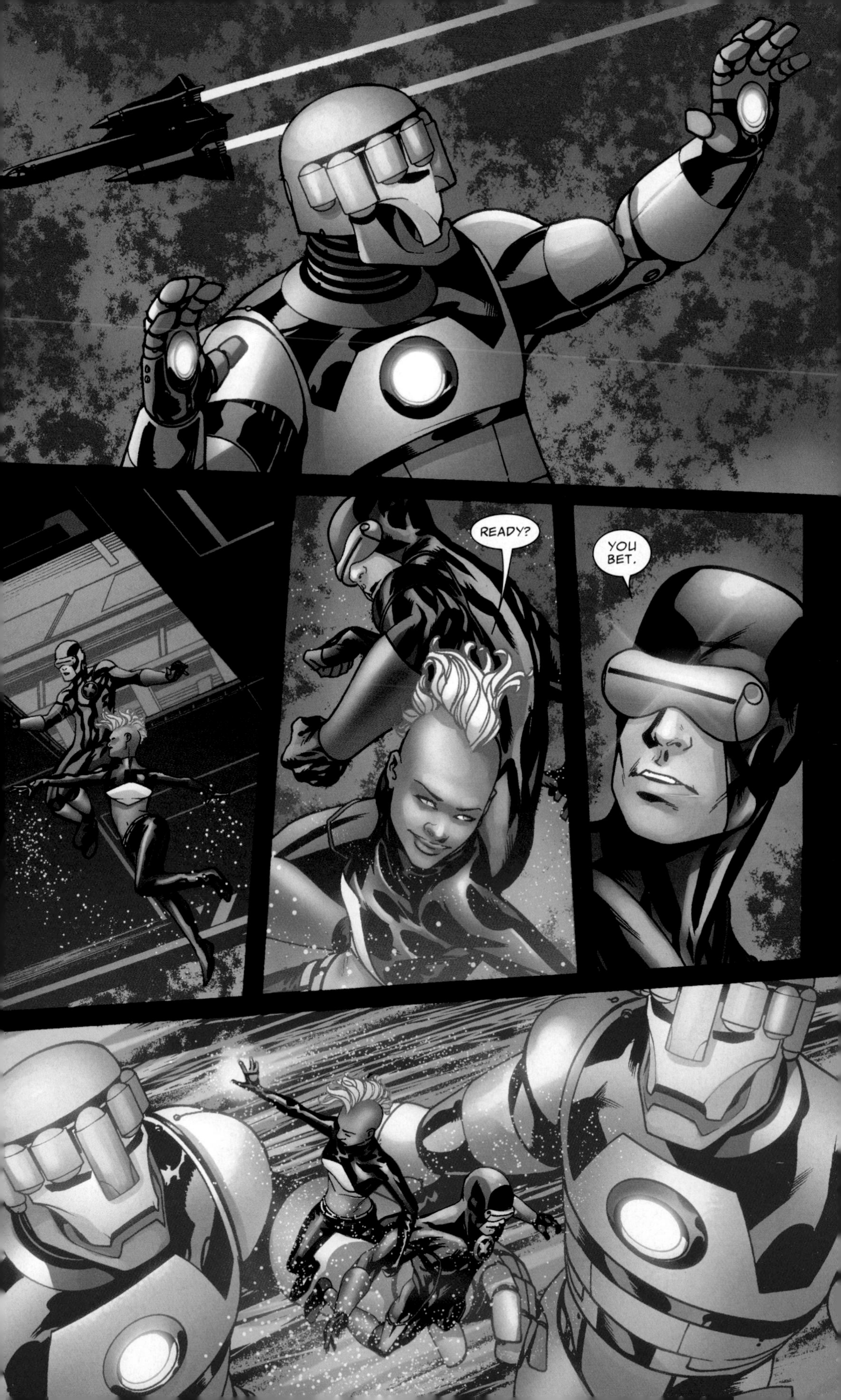
READY?
YOU BET.

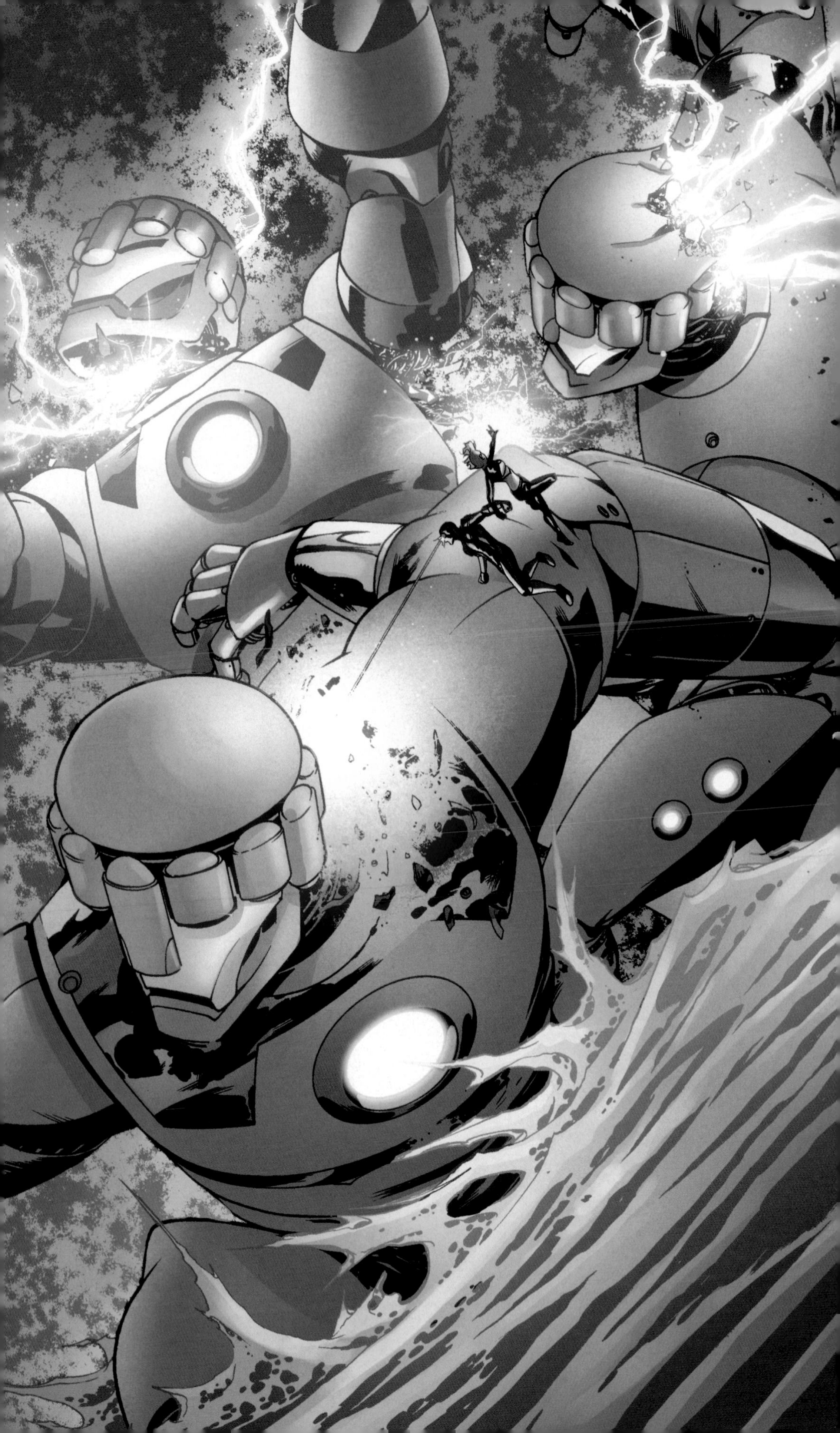

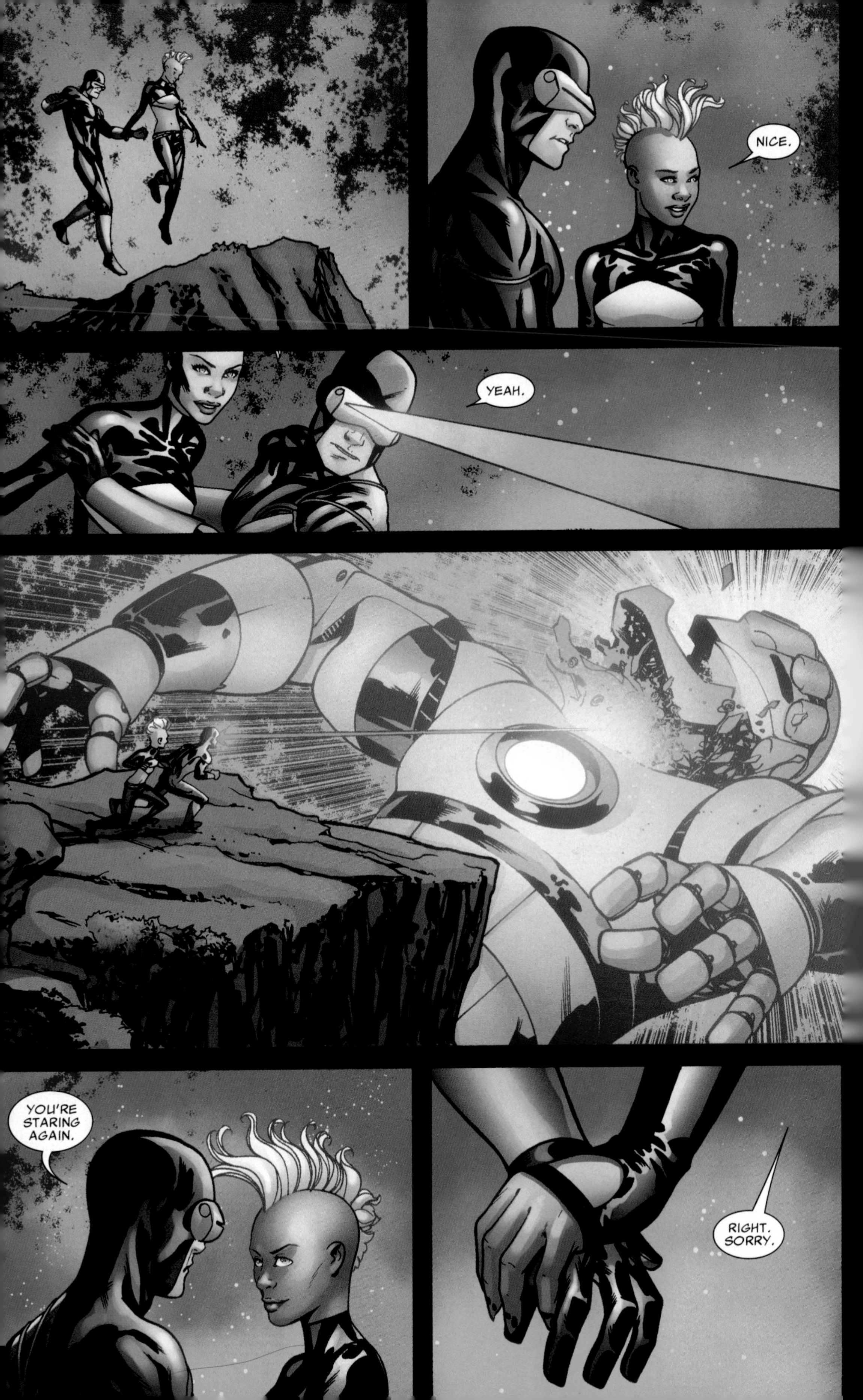
NICE.
YEAH.
YOU'RE STARING AGAIN.
RIGHT. SORRY.

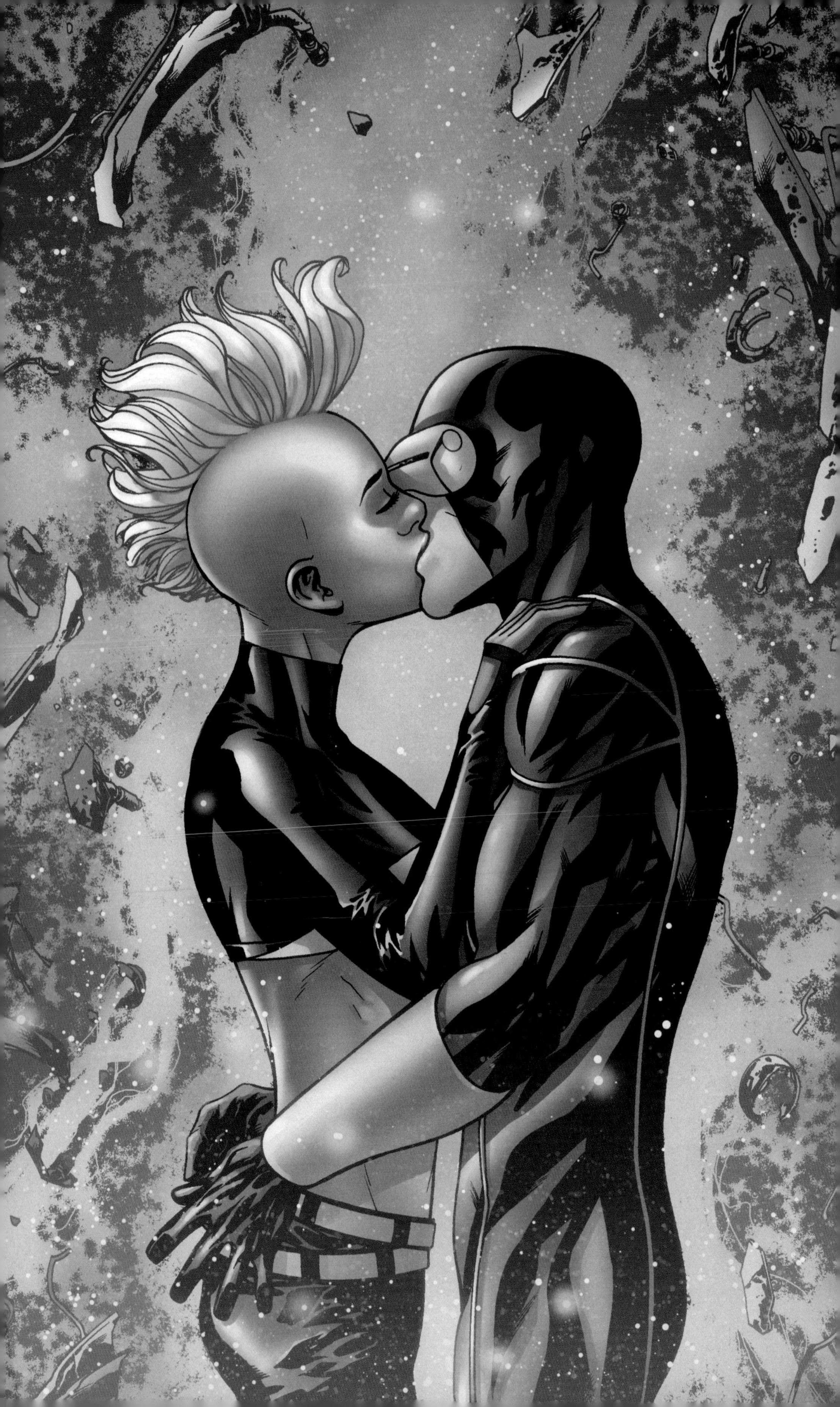

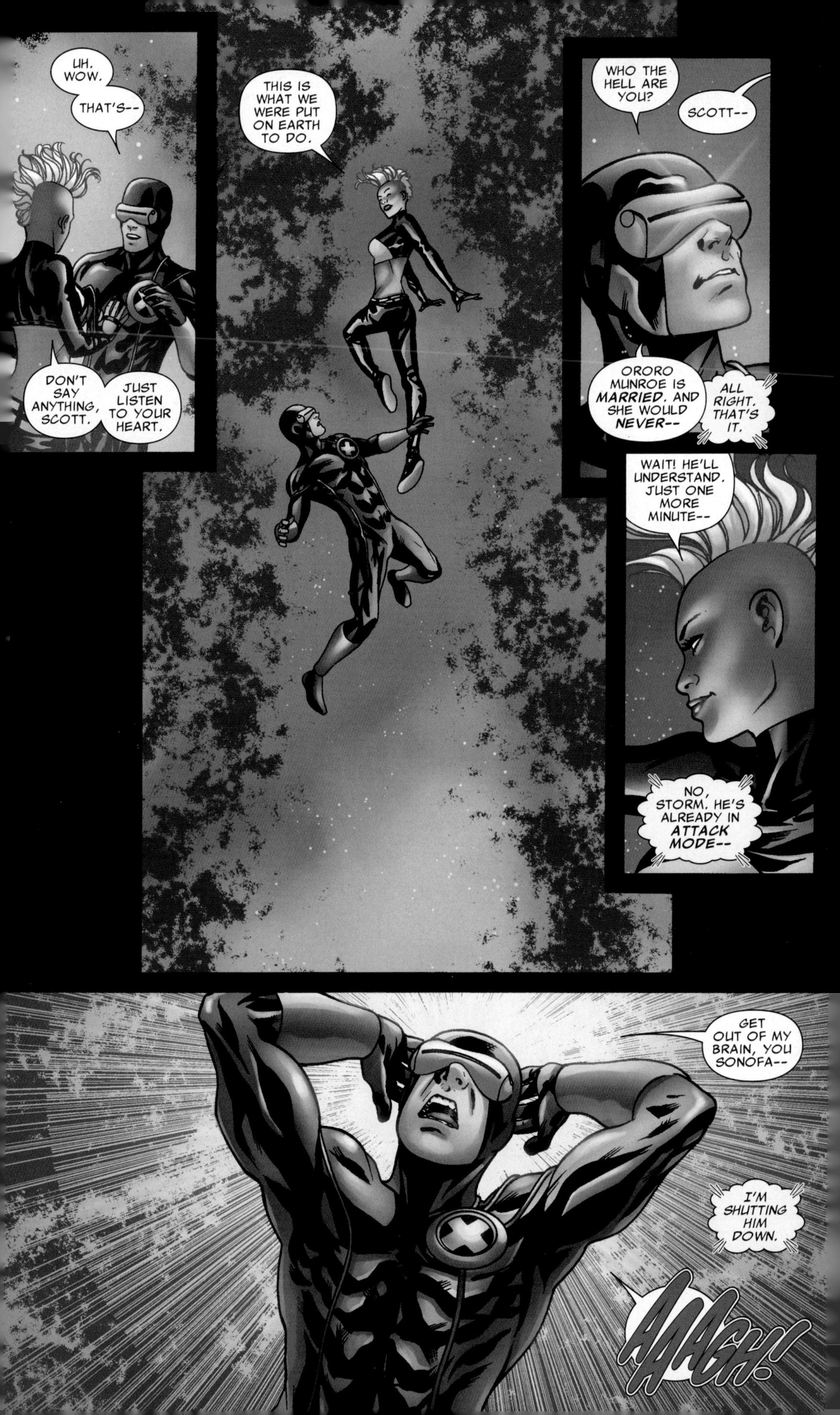
UH. WOW.
THAT'S--
THIS IS WHAT WE WERE PUT ON EARTH TO DO.
WHO THE HELL ARE YOU?
SCOTT--
DON'T SAY ANYTHING, SCOTT.
JUST LISTEN TO YOUR HEART.
ORORO MUNROE IS MARRIED. AND SHE WOULD NEVER--
ALL RIGHT, THAT'S IT.
WAIT! HE'LL UNDERSTAND. JUST ONE MORE MINUTE--
NO, STORM. HE'S ALREADY IN ATTACK MODE--
GET OUT OF MY BRAIN, YOU SONOFA--
I'M SHUTTING HIM DOWN.
AAAGH!

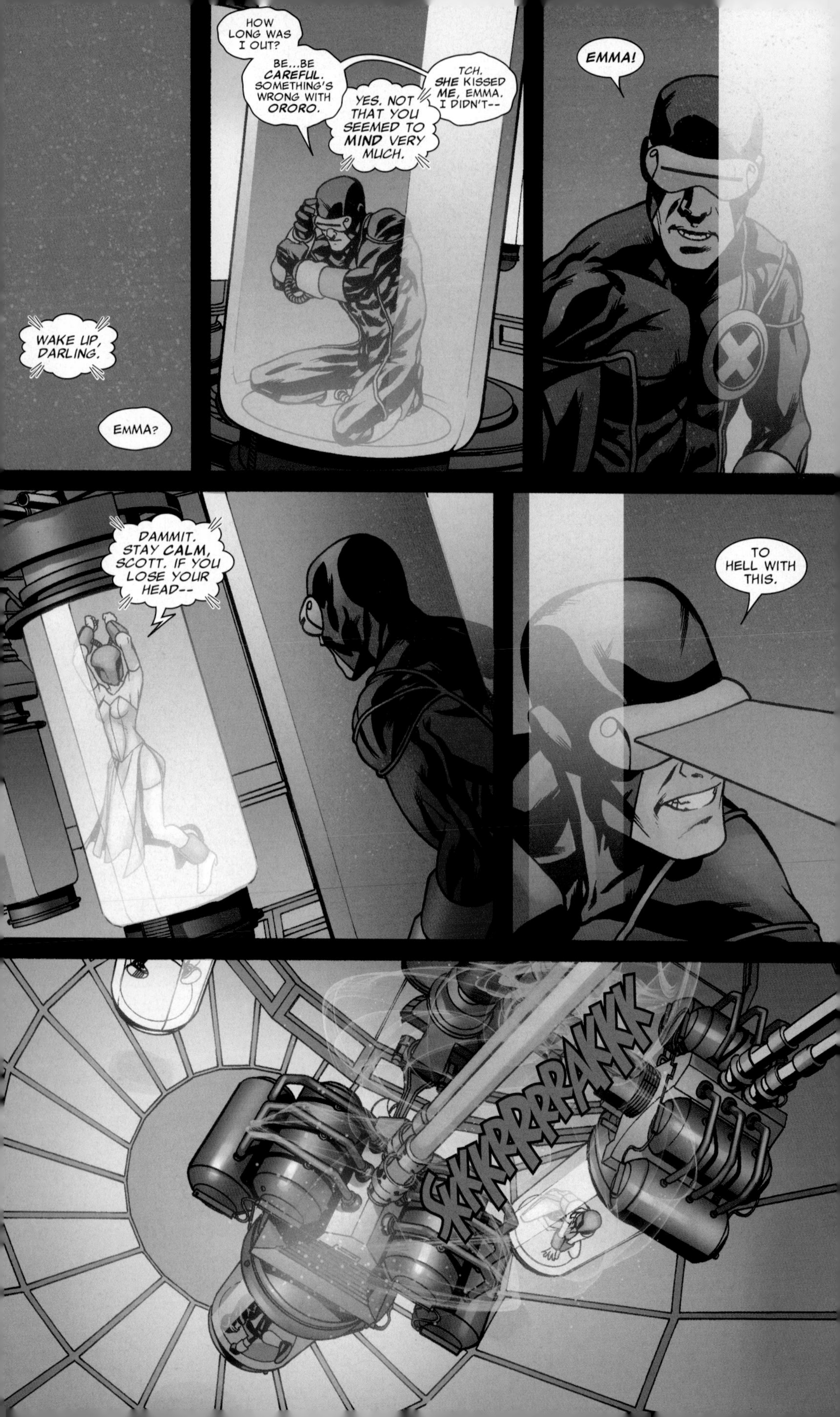
WAKE UP, DARLING.
EMMA?
HOW LONG WAS I OUT?
BE...BE CAREFUL. SOMETHING'S WRONG WITH ORORO.
YES. NOT THAT YOU SEEMED TO MIND VERY MUCH.
TCH. SHE KISSED ME, EMMA. I DIDN'T--
EMMA!
DAMMIT. STAY CALM, SCOTT. IF YOU LOSE YOUR HEAD--
TO HELL WITH THIS.
SKKKRRRAKKK

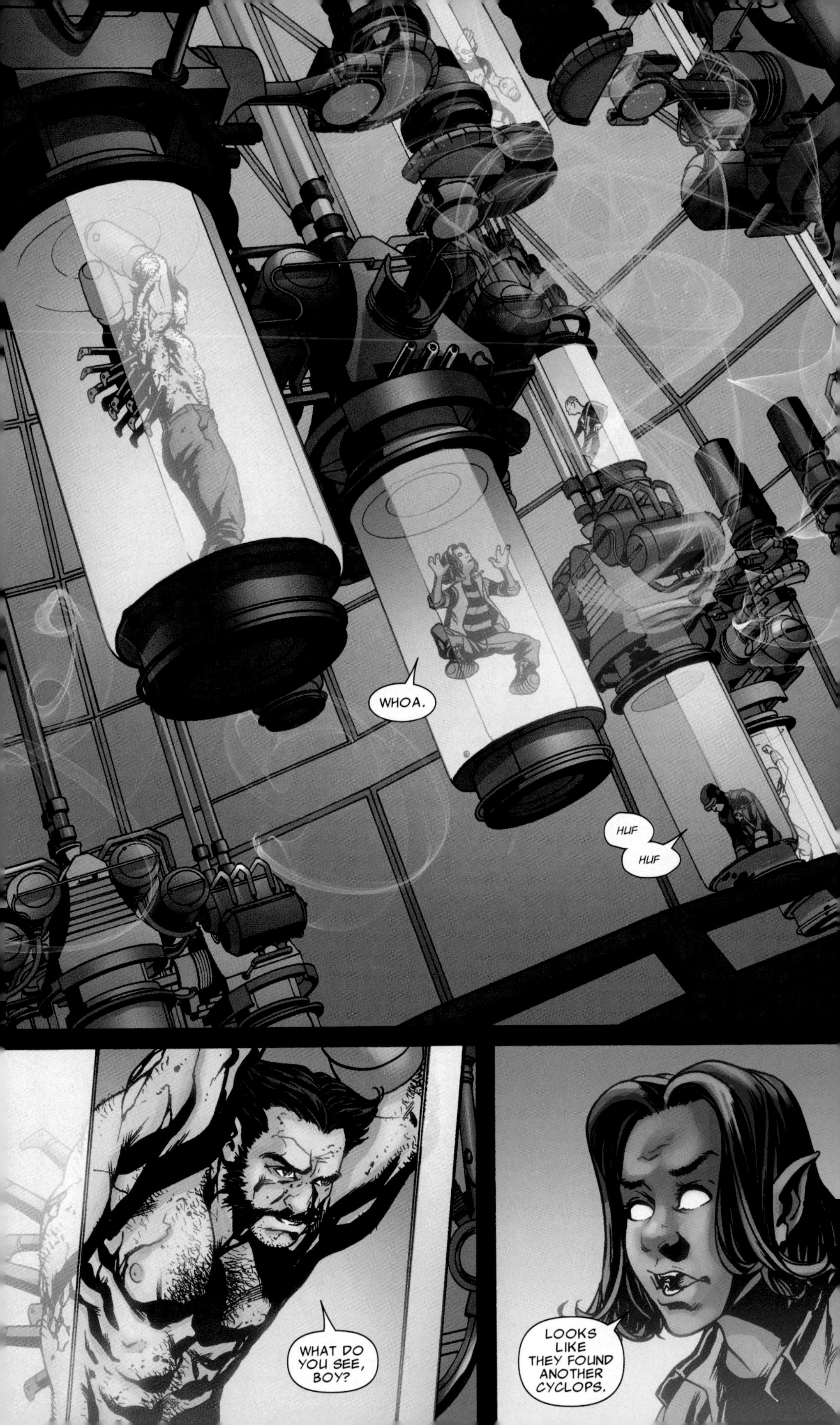
WHOA.
HUF
HUF
WHAT DO YOU SEE, BOY?
LOOKS LIKE THEY FOUND ANOTHER CYCLOPS.

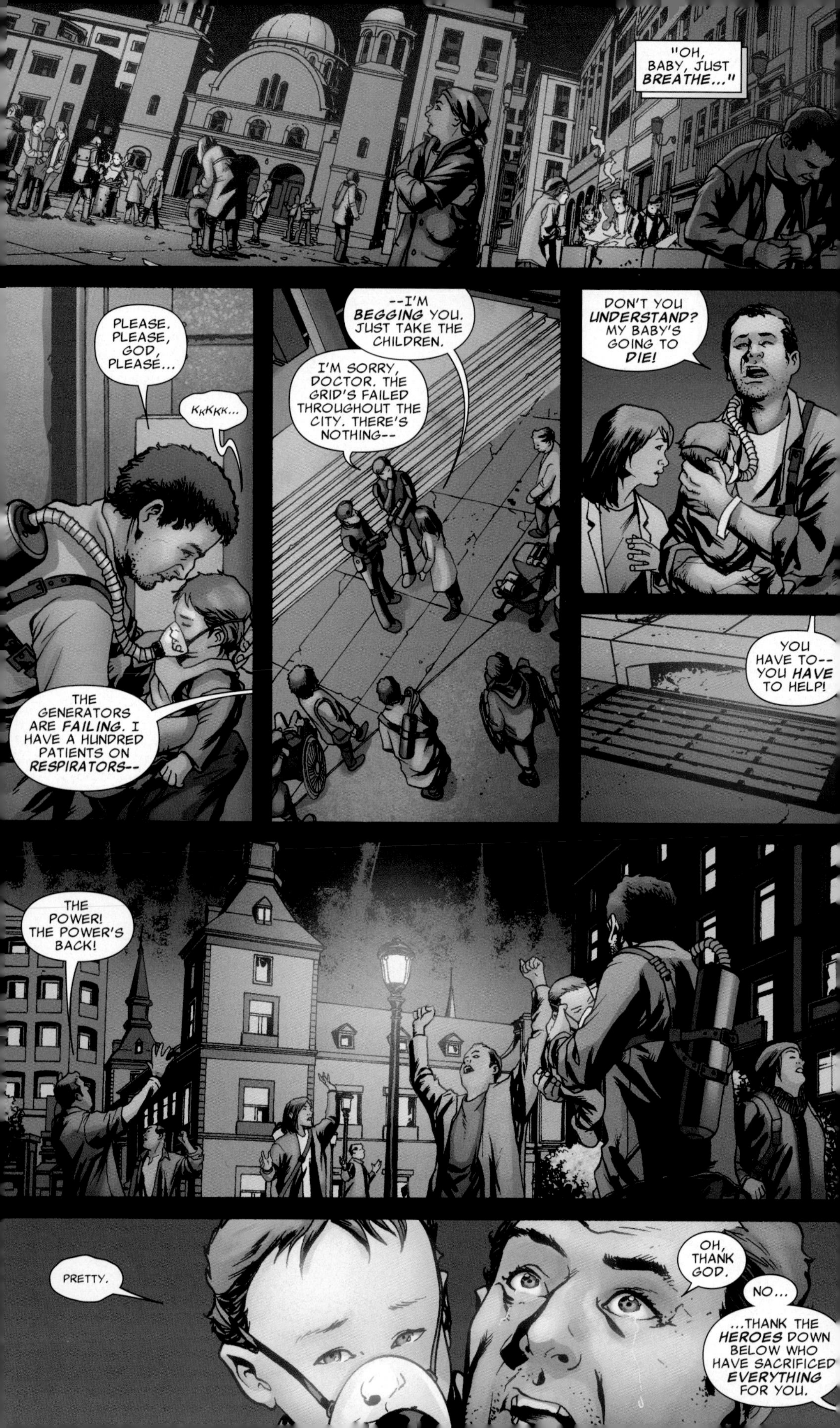
"OH, BABY, JUST BREATHE..."
PLEASE. PLEASE, GOD, PLEASE...
KKKKK...
THE GENERATORS ARE FAILING. I HAVE A HUNDRED PATIENTS ON RESPIRATORS--
--I'M BEGGING YOU. JUST TAKE THE CHILDREN.
I'M SORRY, DOCTOR. THE GRID'S FAILED THROUGHOUT THE CITY. THERE'S NOTHING--
DON'T YOU UNDERSTAND? MY BABY'S GOING TO DIE!
YOU HAVE TO-- YOU HAVE TO HELP!
THE POWER! THE POWER'S BACK!
PRETTY.
OH, THANK GOD.
NO...
...THANK THE HEROES DOWN BELOW WHO HAVE SACRIFICED EVERYTHING FOR YOU.

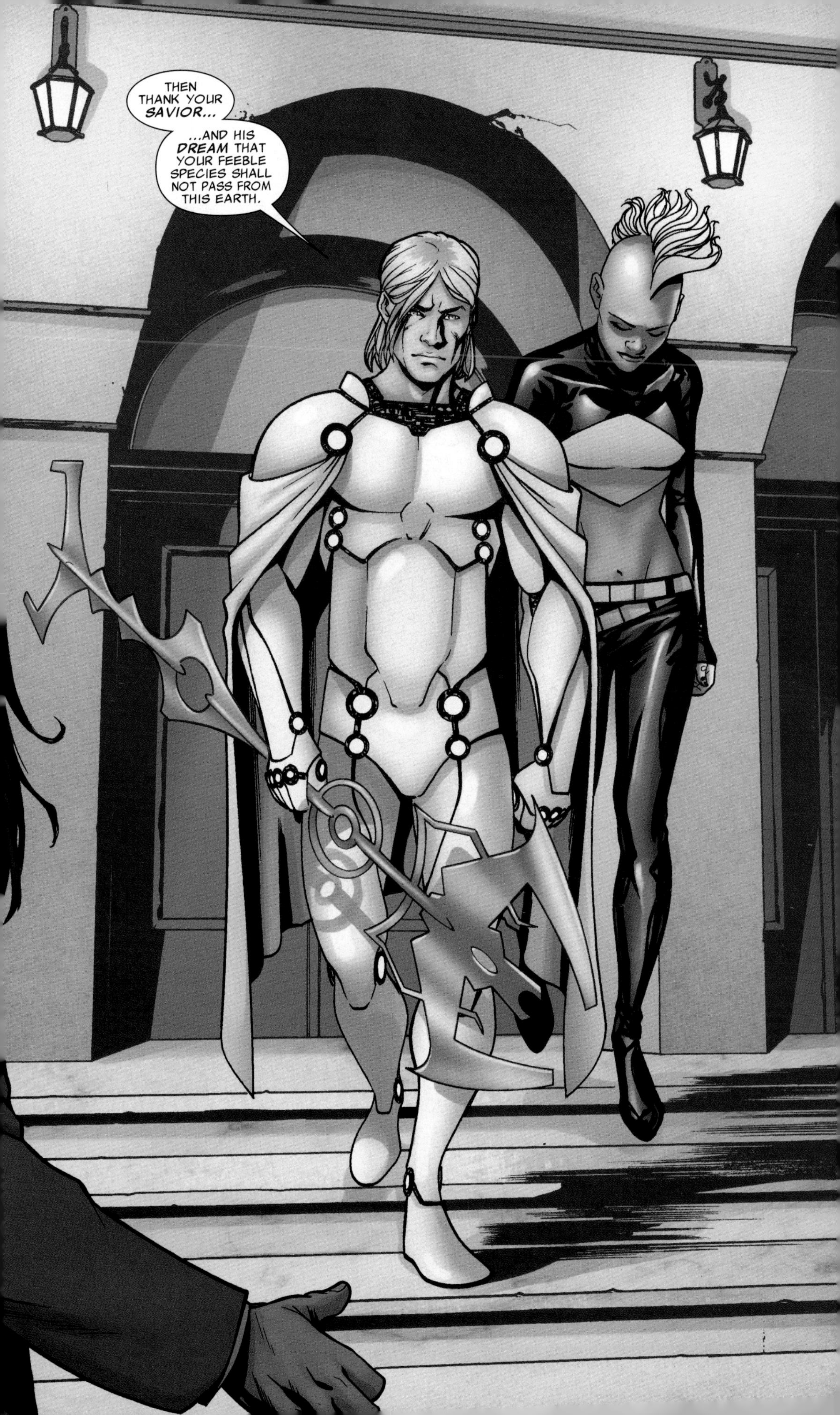
THEN THANK YOUR SAVIOR...
...AND HIS DREAM THAT YOUR FEEBLE SPECIES SHALL NOT PASS FROM THIS EARTH.

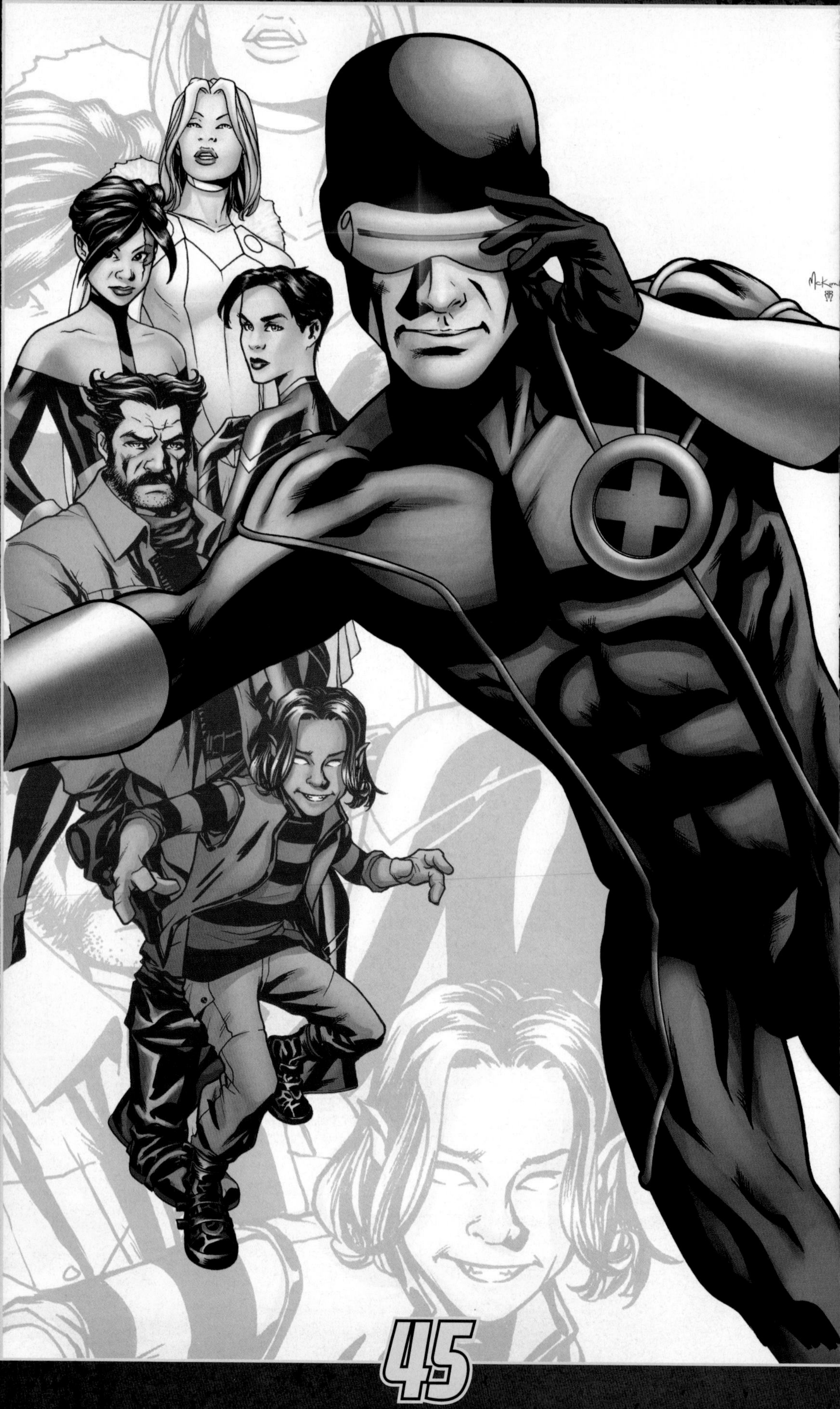
45

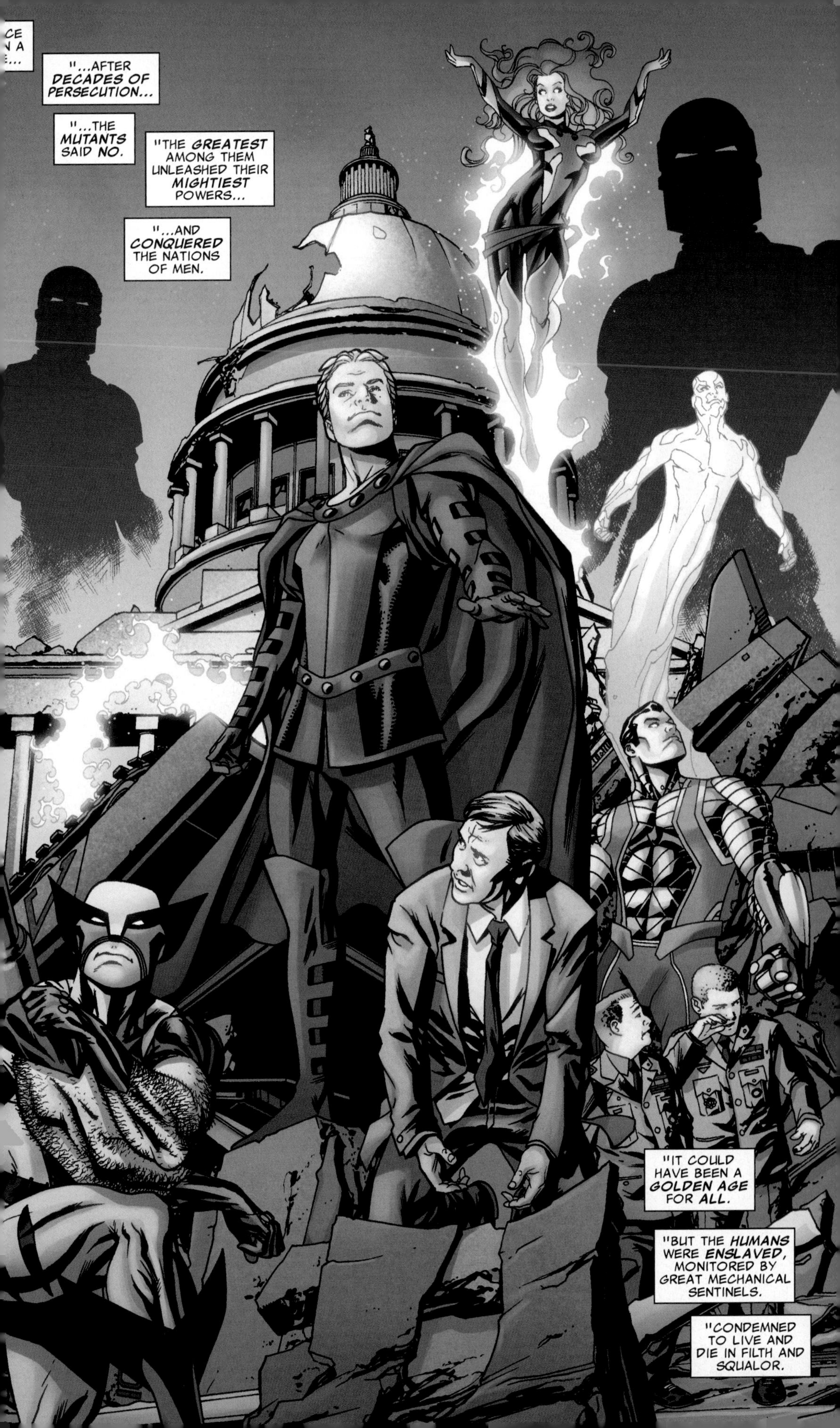
"...AFTER DECADES OF PERSECUTION...
"...THE MUTANTS SAID NO.
"THE GREATEST AMONG THEM UNLEASHED THEIR MIGHTIEST POWERS...
"...AND CONQUERED THE NATIONS OF MEN.
"IT COULD HAVE BEEN A GOLDEN AGE FOR ALL.
"BUT THE HUMANS WERE ENSLAVED, MONITORED BY GREAT MECHANICAL SENTINELS.
"CONDEMNED TO LIVE AND DIE IN FILTH AND SQUALOR.

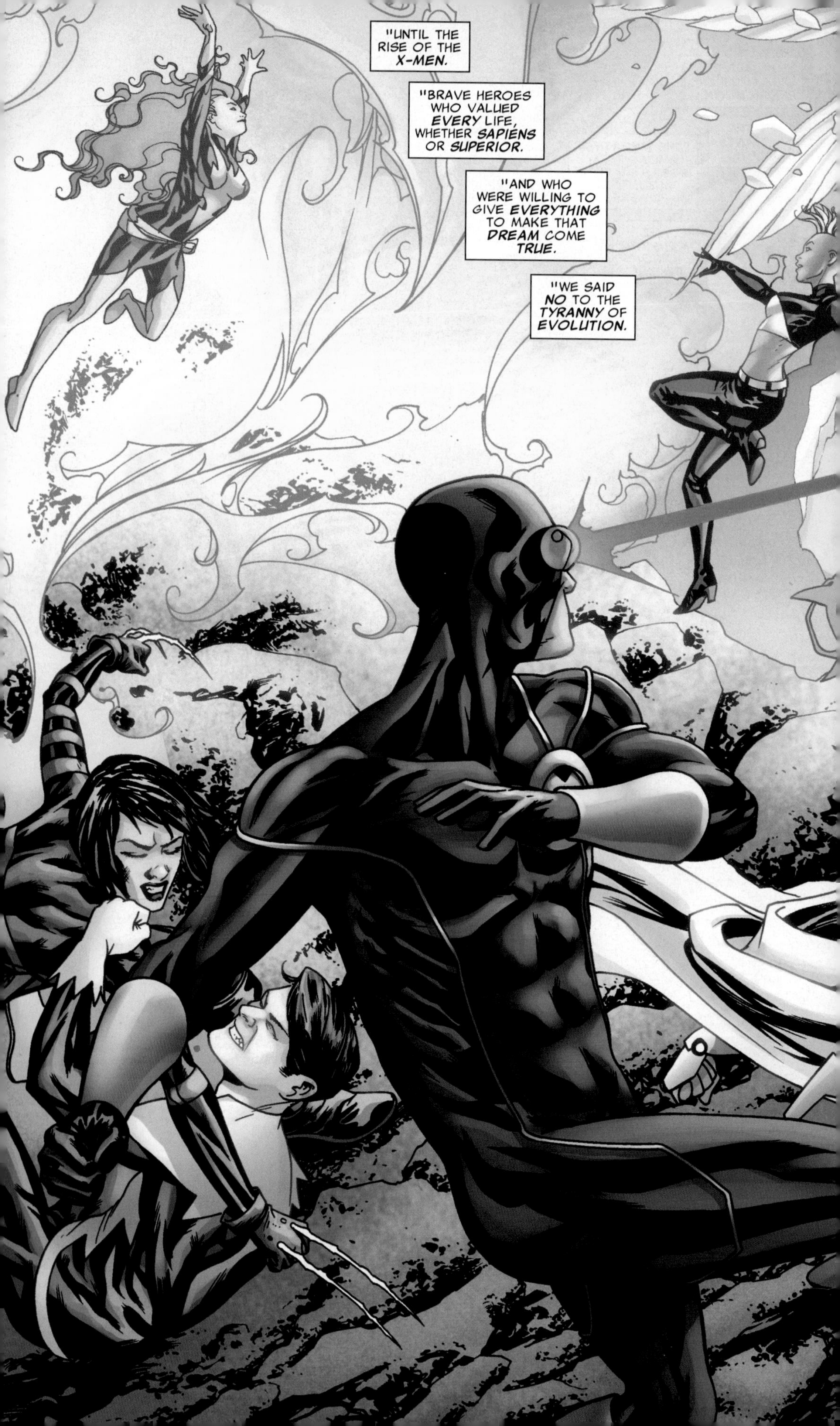
"UNTIL THE RISE OF THE *X-MEN.*
"BRAVE HEROES WHO VALUED *EVERY* LIFE, WHETHER *SAPIENS* OR *SUPERIOR.*
"AND WHO WERE WILLING TO GIVE *EVERYTHING* TO MAKE THAT *DREAM* COME *TRUE.*
"WE SAID *NO* TO THE *TYRANNY* OF *EVOLUTION.*

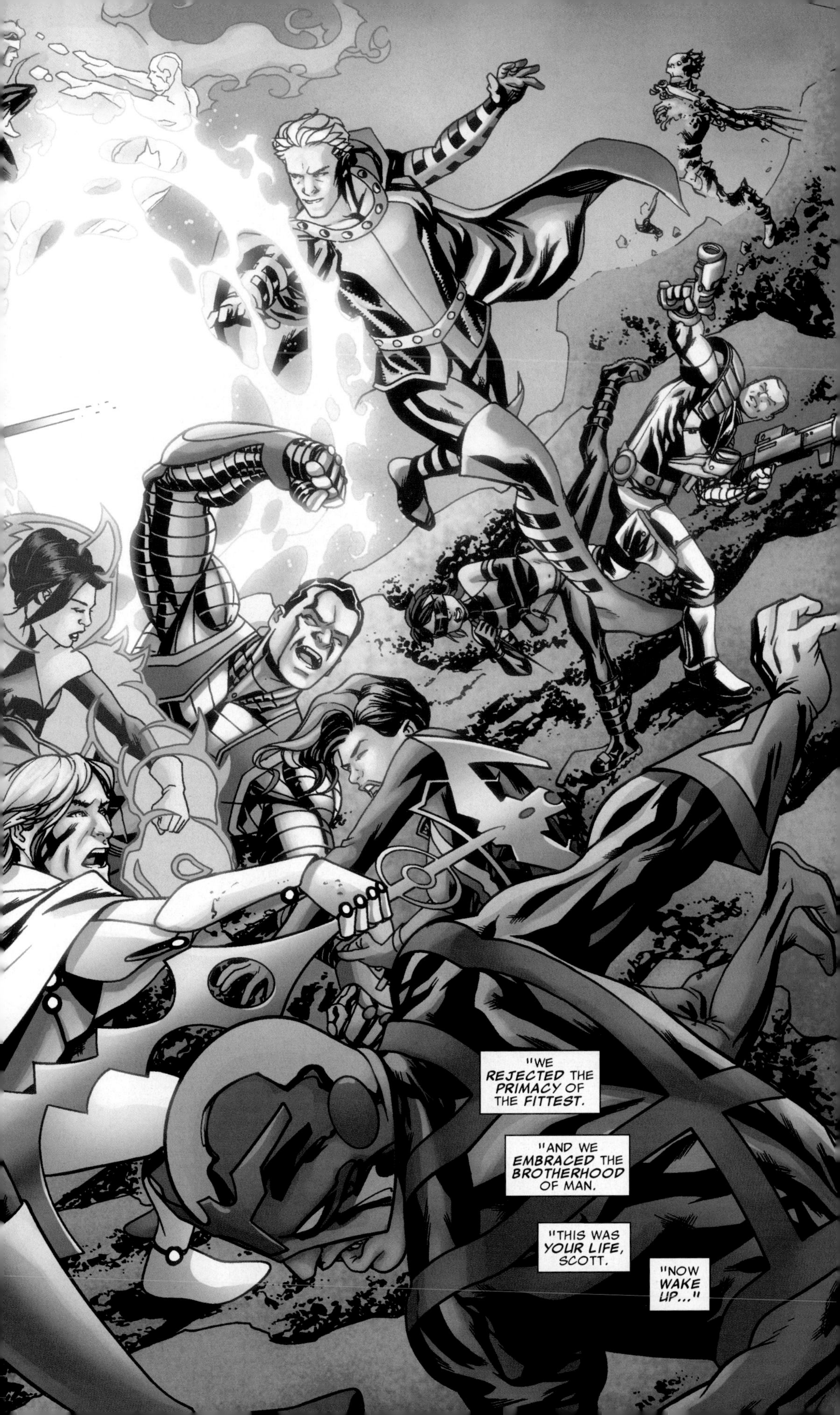
"WE REJECTED THE PRIMACY OF THE FITTEST.
"AND WE EMBRACED THE BROTHERHOOD OF MAN.
"THIS WAS YOUR LIFE, SCOTT.
"NOW WAKE UP..."

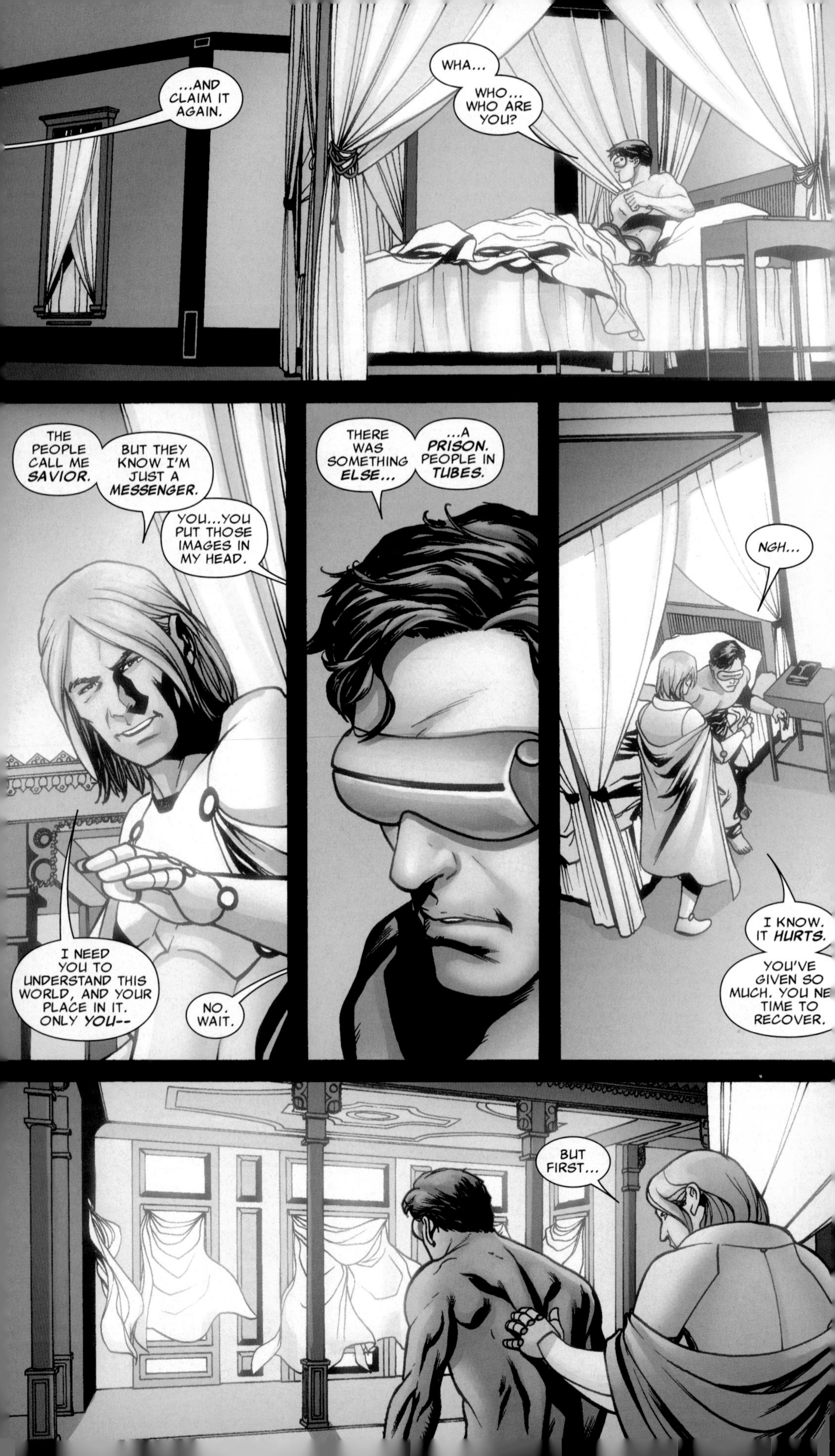
...AND CLAIM IT AGAIN.
WHA...
WHO... WHO ARE YOU?
THE PEOPLE CALL ME SAVIOR.
BUT THEY KNOW I'M JUST A MESSENGER.
YOU...YOU PUT THOSE IMAGES IN MY HEAD.
I NEED YOU TO UNDERSTAND THIS WORLD, AND YOUR PLACE IN IT. ONLY YOU--
NO. WAIT.
THERE WAS SOMETHING ELSE...
...A PRISON. PEOPLE IN TUBES.
NGH...
I KNOW. IT HURTS.
YOU'VE GIVEN SO MUCH. YOU NE
TIME TO RECOVER.
BUT FIRST...

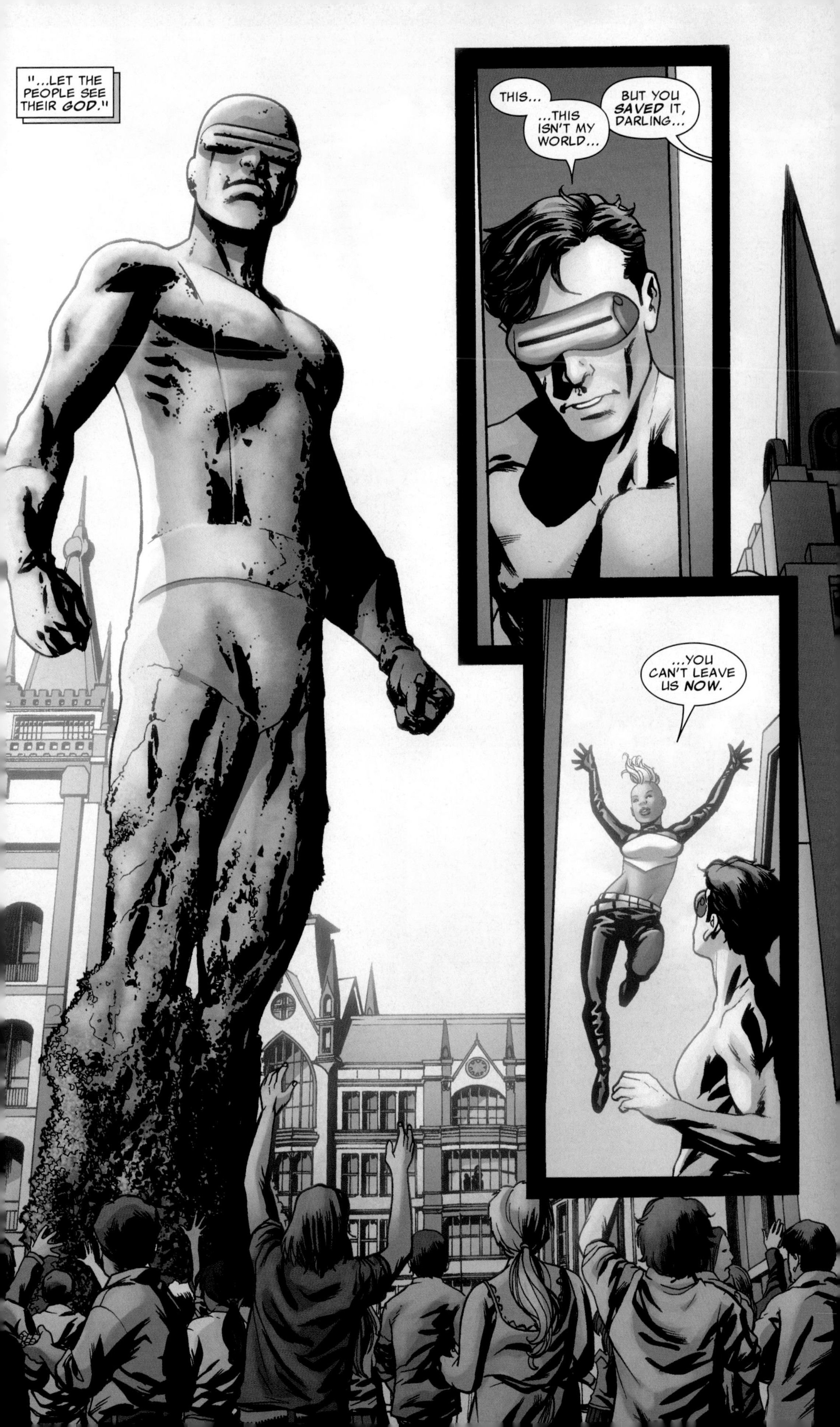
"...LET THE PEOPLE SEE THEIR GOD."
THIS...
...THIS ISN'T MY WORLD...
BUT YOU SAVED IT, DARLING...
...YOU CAN'T LEAVE US NOW.

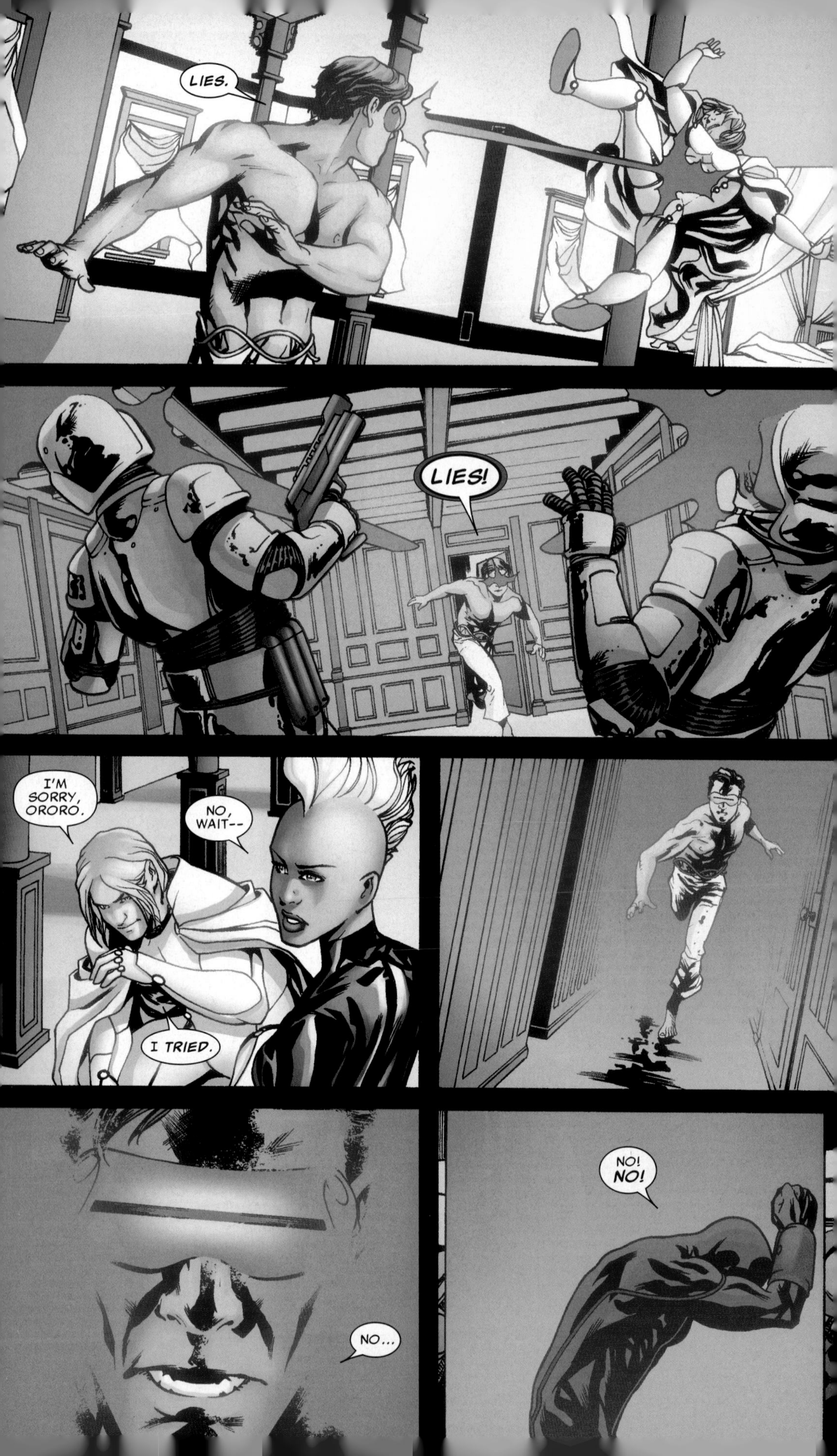

LIES.
LIES!
I'M SORRY, ORORO.
NO, WAIT--
I TRIED.
NO...
NO! NO!

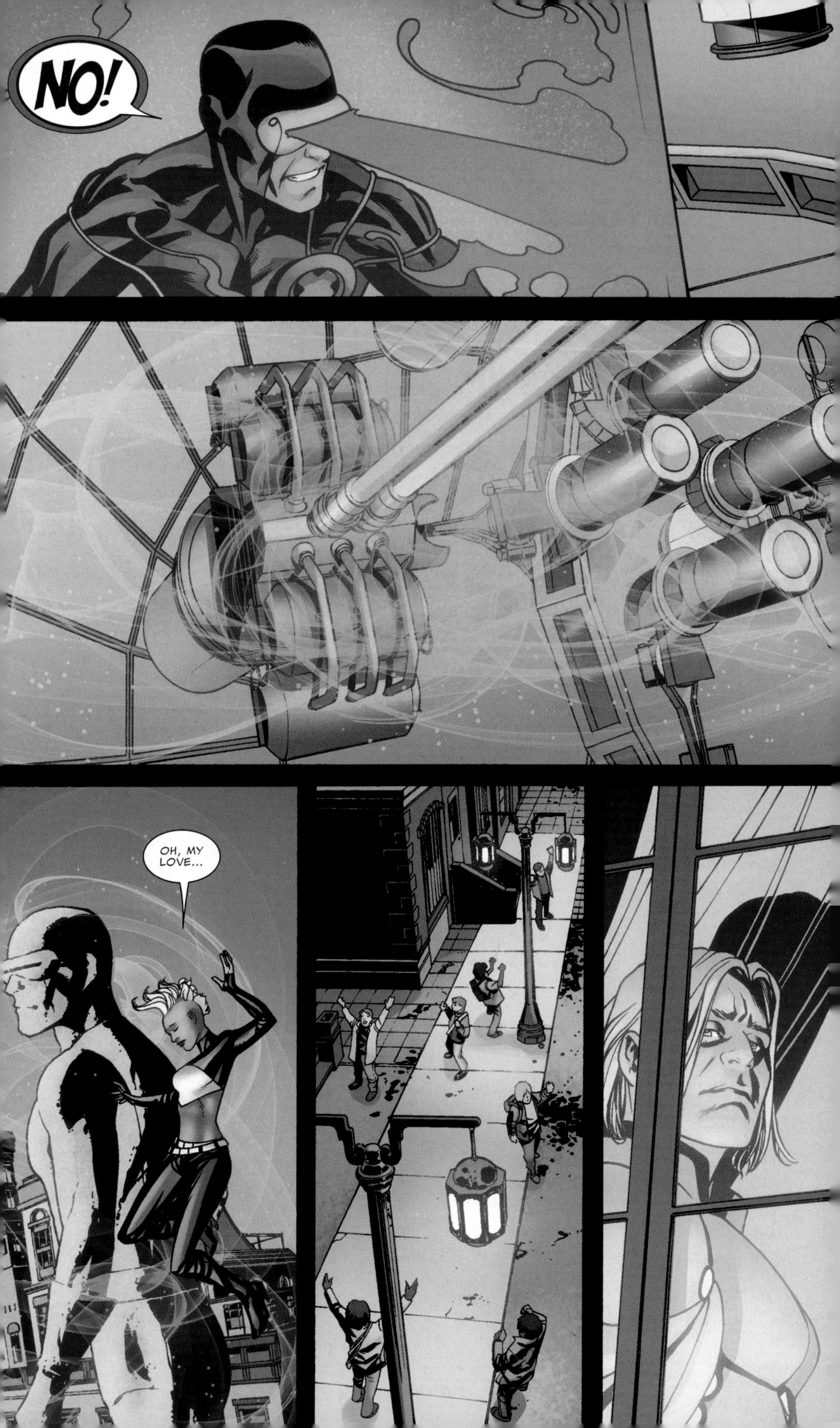
NO!
OH, MY LOVE...

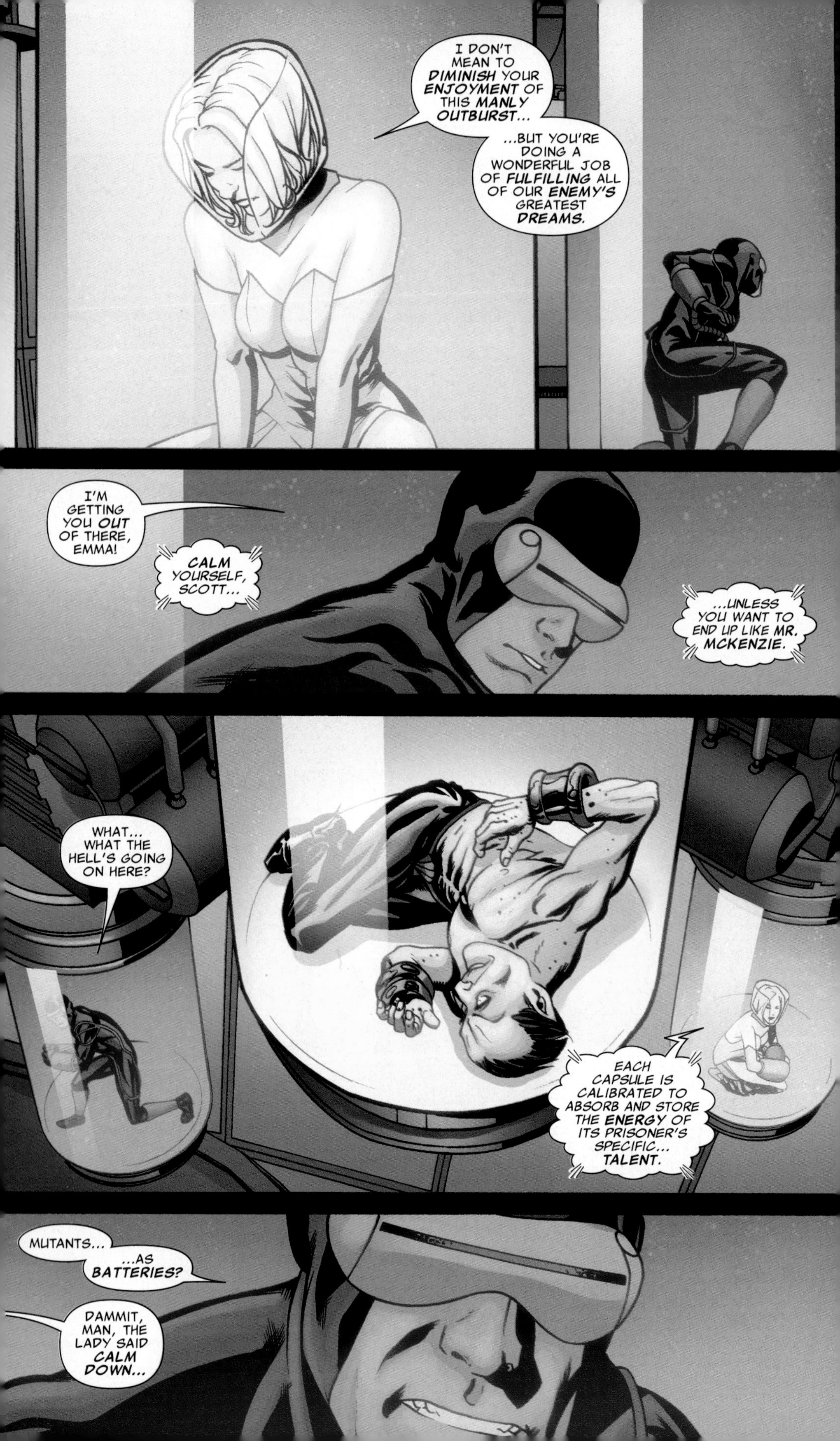

I DON'T MEAN TO DIMINISH YOUR ENJOYMENT OF THIS MANLY OUTBURST...
...BUT YOU'RE DOING A WONDERFUL JOB OF FULFILLING ALL OF OUR ENEMY'S GREATEST DREAMS.
I'M GETTING YOU OUT OF THERE, EMMA!
CALM YOURSELF, SCOTT...
...UNLESS YOU WANT TO END UP LIKE MR. MCKENZIE.
WHAT... WHAT THE HELL'S GOING ON HERE?
EACH CAPSULE IS CALIBRATED TO ABSORB AND STORE THE ENERGY OF ITS PRISONER'S SPECIFIC... TALENT.
MUTANTS...
...AS BATTERIES?
DAMMIT, MAN, THE LADY SAID CALM DOWN...

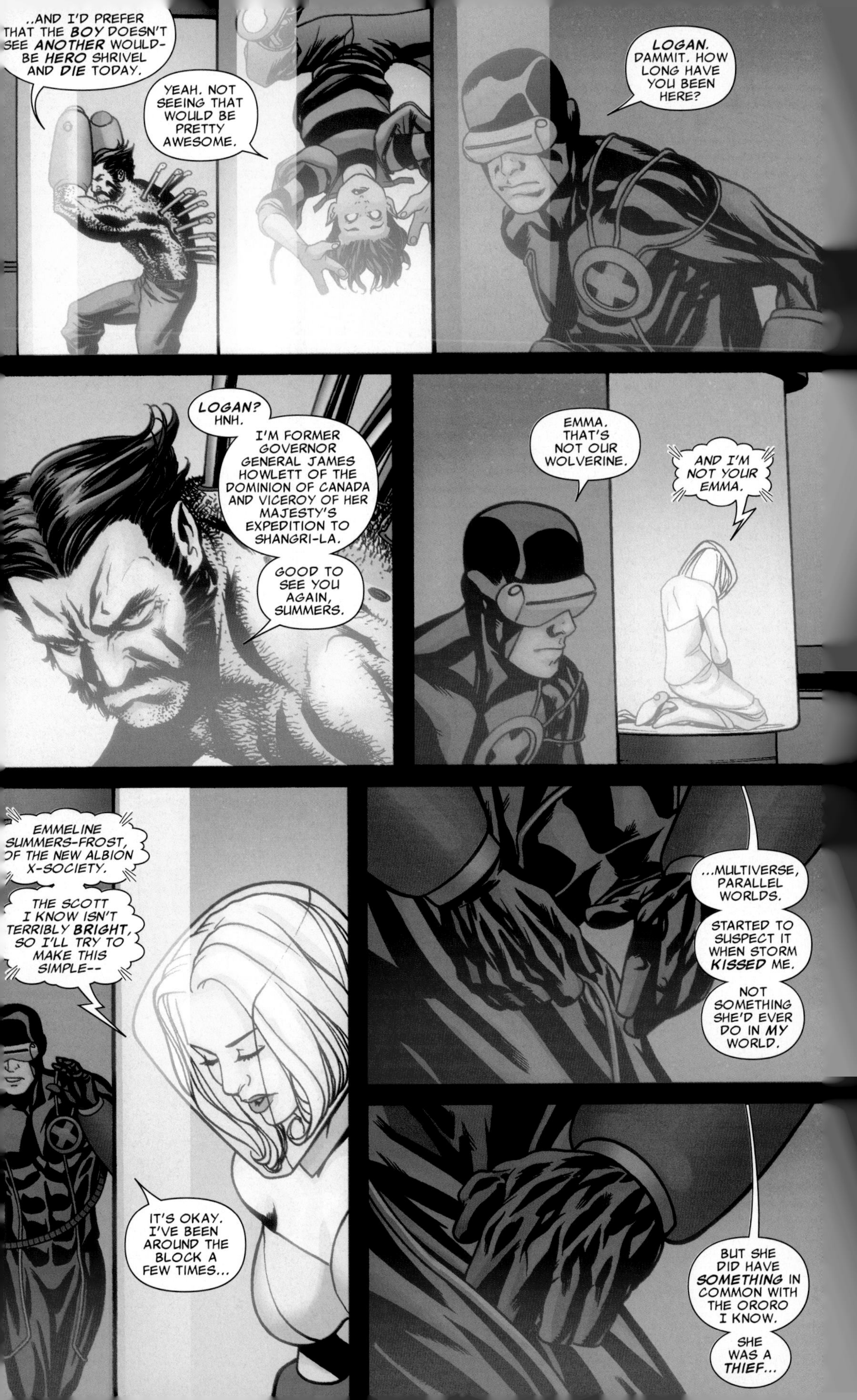

..AND I'D PREFER THAT THE BOY DOESN'T SEE ANOTHER WOULD-BE HERO SHRIVEL AND DIE TODAY.
YEAH. NOT SEEING THAT WOULD BE PRETTY AWESOME.
LOGAN. DAMMIT. HOW LONG HAVE YOU BEEN HERE?
LOGAN? HNH.
I'M FORMER GOVERNOR GENERAL JAMES HOWLETT OF THE DOMINION OF CANADA AND VICEROY OF HER MAJESTY'S EXPEDITION TO SHANGRI-LA.
GOOD TO SEE YOU AGAIN, SUMMERS.
EMMA. THAT'S NOT OUR WOLVERINE.
AND I'M NOT YOUR EMMA.
EMMELINE SUMMERS-FROST, OF THE NEW ALBION X-SOCIETY.
THE SCOTT I KNOW ISN'T TERRIBLY BRIGHT, SO I'LL TRY TO MAKE THIS SIMPLE--
IT'S OKAY. I'VE BEEN AROUND THE BLOCK A FEW TIMES...
...MULTIVERSE, PARALLEL WORLDS.
STARTED TO SUSPECT IT WHEN STORM KISSED ME.
NOT SOMETHING SHE'D EVER DO IN MY WORLD.
BUT SHE DID HAVE SOMETHING IN COMMON WITH THE ORORO I KNOW.
SHE WAS A THIEF...

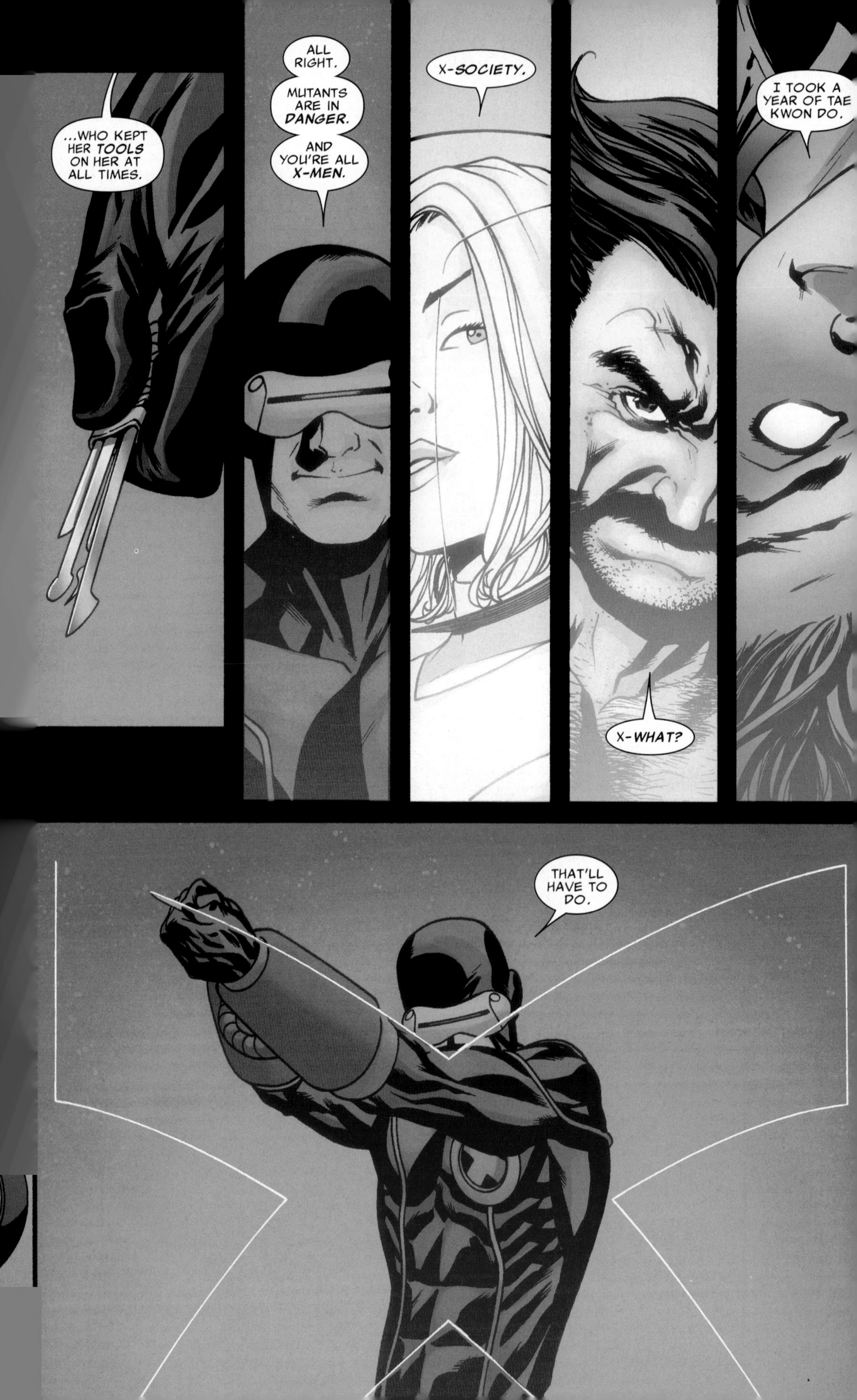
...WHO KEPT HER TOOLS ON HER AT ALL TIMES.
ALL RIGHT.
MUTANTS ARE IN DANGER.
AND YOU'RE ALL X-MEN.
X-SOCIETY.
X-WHAT?
I TOOK A YEAR OF TAE KWON DO.
THAT'LL HAVE TO DO.

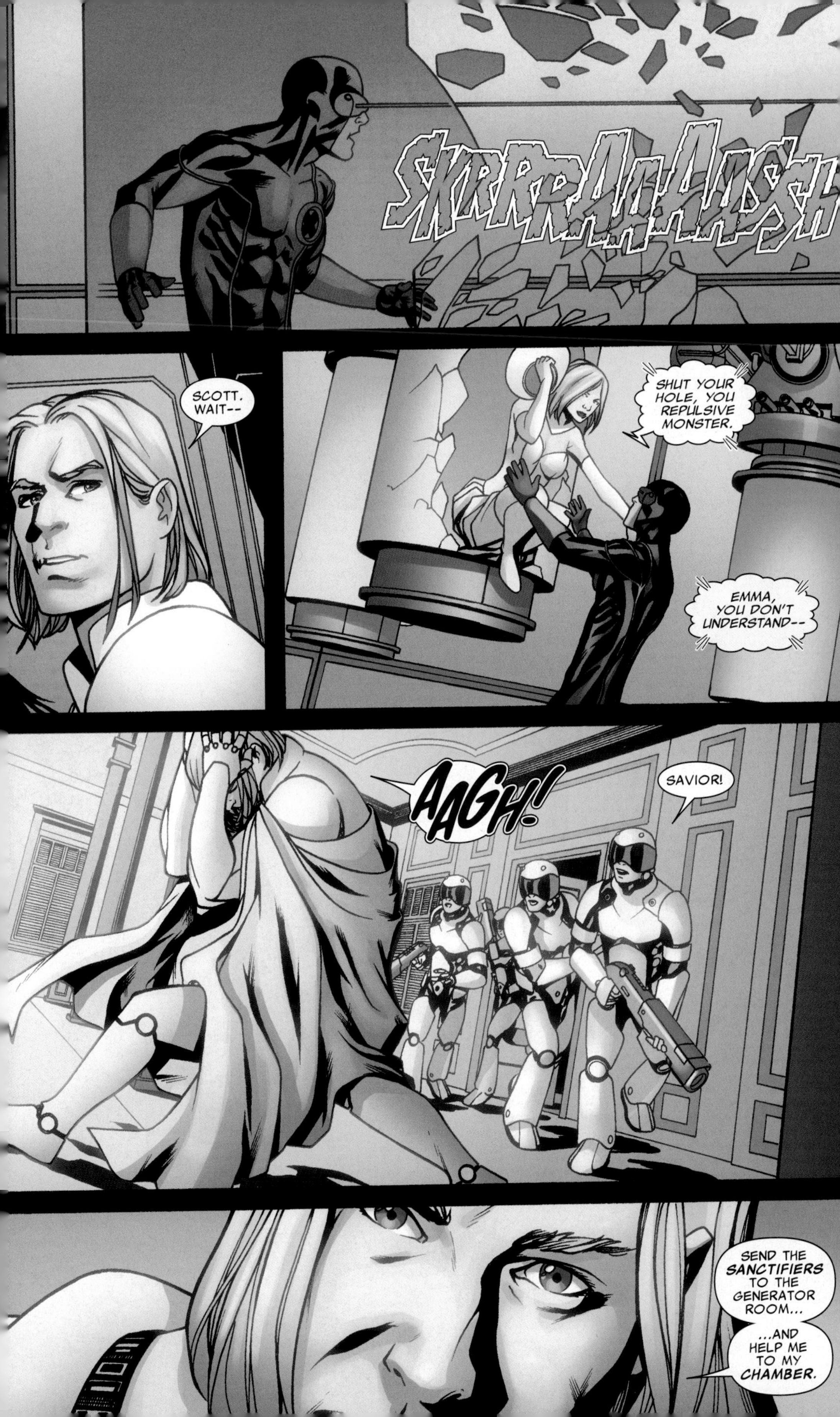
SKRRRAAAAASH
SCOTT. WAIT--
SHUT YOUR HOLE, YOU REPULSIVE MONSTER.
EMMA, YOU DON'T UNDERSTAND--
AAGH!
SAVIOR!
SEND THE SANCTIFIERS TO THE GENERATOR ROOM...
...AND HELP ME TO MY CHAMBER.

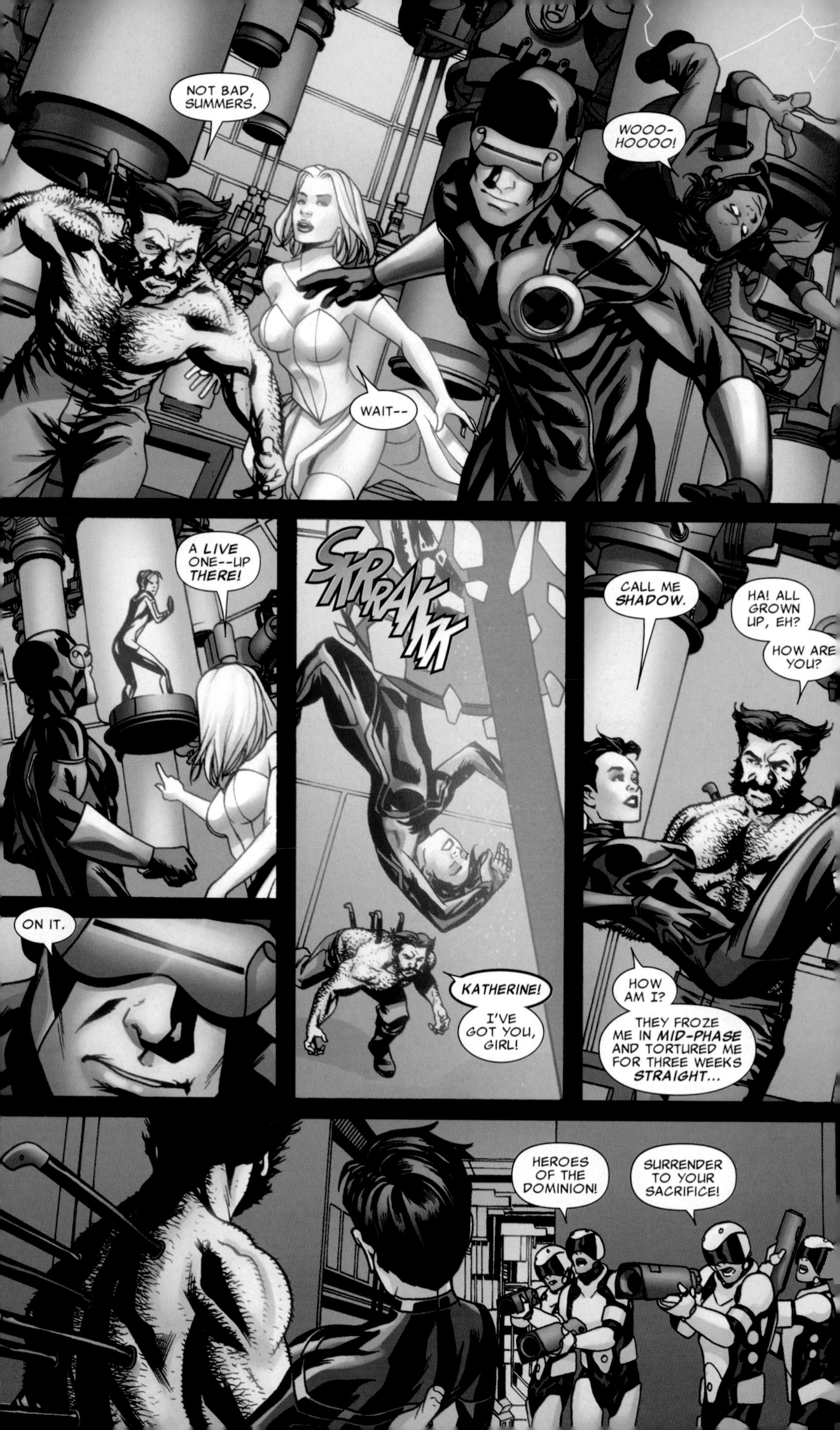
NOT BAD, SUMMERS.
WOOO-HOOOO!
WAIT--
A LIVE ONE--UP THERE!
ON IT.
SKRRAKKK
KATHERINE!
I'VE GOT YOU, GIRL!
CALL ME SHADOW.
HA! ALL GROWN UP, EH?
HOW ARE YOU?
HOW AM I?
THEY FROZE ME IN MID-PHASE AND TORTURED ME FOR THREE WEEKS STRAIGHT...
HEROES OF THE DOMINION!
SURRENDER TO YOUR SACRIFICE!

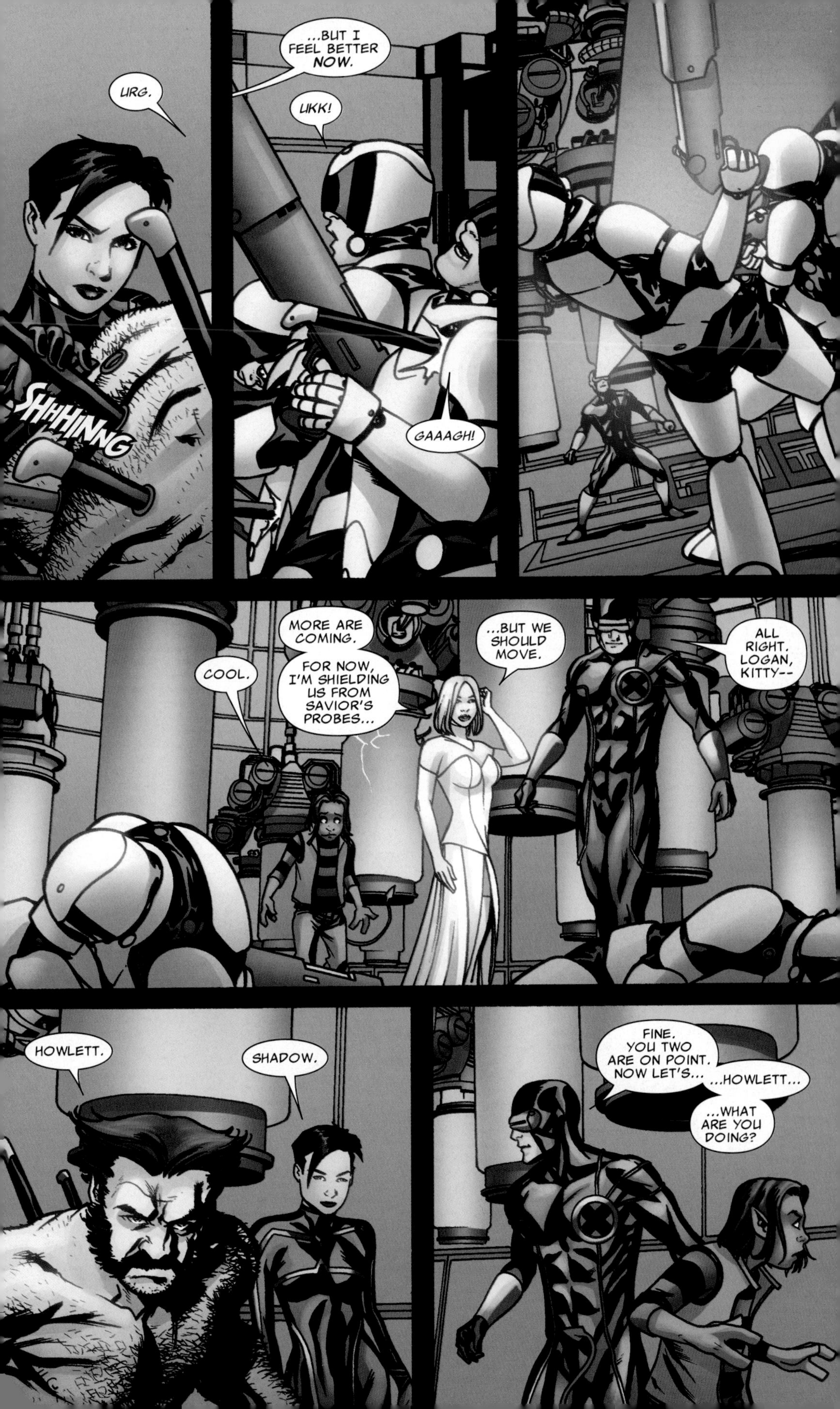
URG.
SHHHINNG
...BUT I FEEL BETTER NOW.
UKK!
GAAAGH!
MORE ARE COMING.
COOL.
FOR NOW, I'M SHIELDING US FROM SAVIOR'S PROBES...
...BUT WE SHOULD MOVE.
ALL RIGHT. LOGAN, KITTY--
HOWLETT.
SHADOW.
FINE. YOU TWO ARE ON POINT. NOW LET'S...
...HOWLETT...
...WHAT ARE YOU DOING?

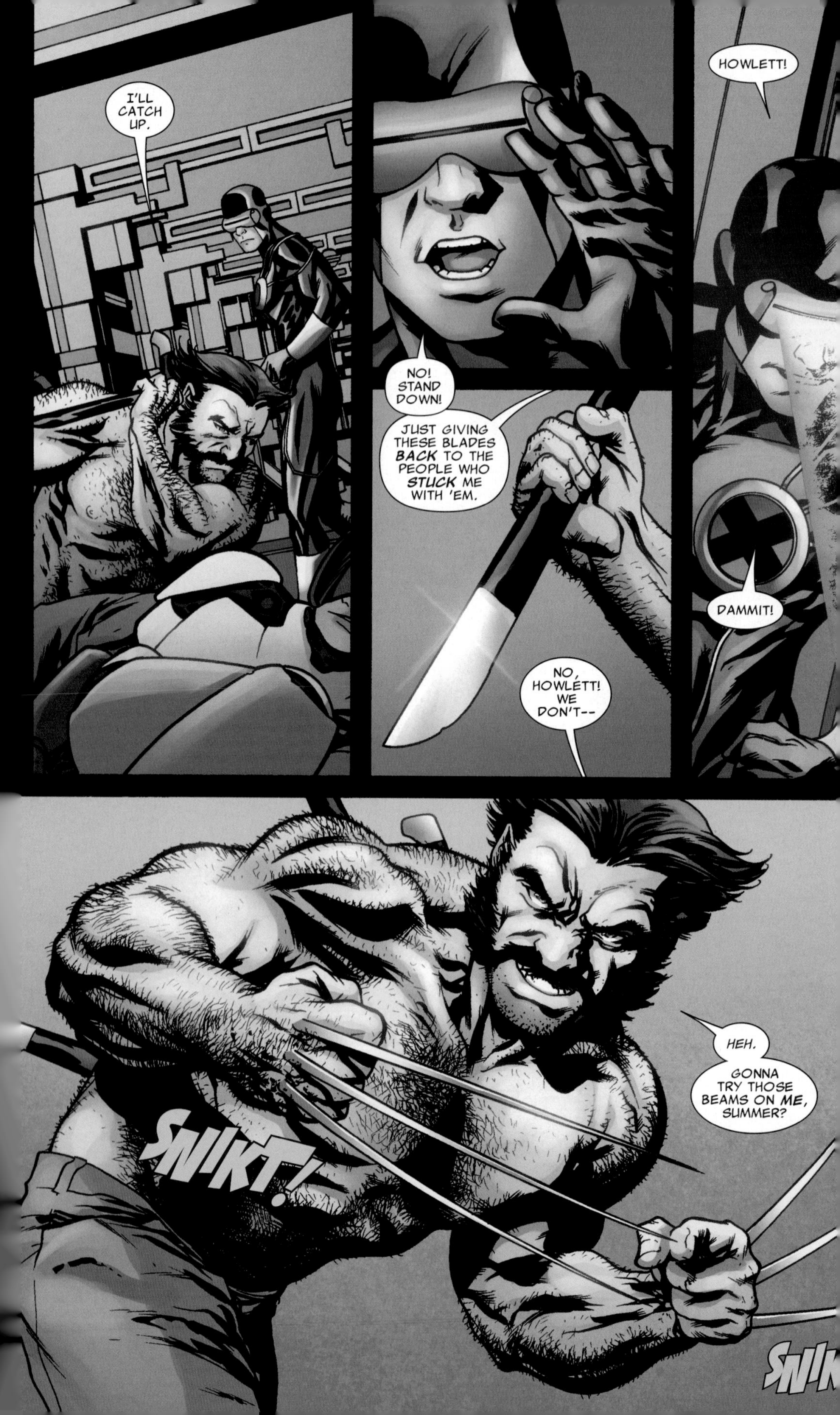
I'LL CATCH UP.
NO! STAND DOWN!
JUST GIVING THESE BLADES BACK TO THE PEOPLE WHO STUCK ME WITH 'EM.
NO, HOWLETT! WE DON'T--
HOWLETT!
DAMMIT!
SNIKT!
HEH.
GONNA TRY THOSE BEAMS ON ME, SUMMER?

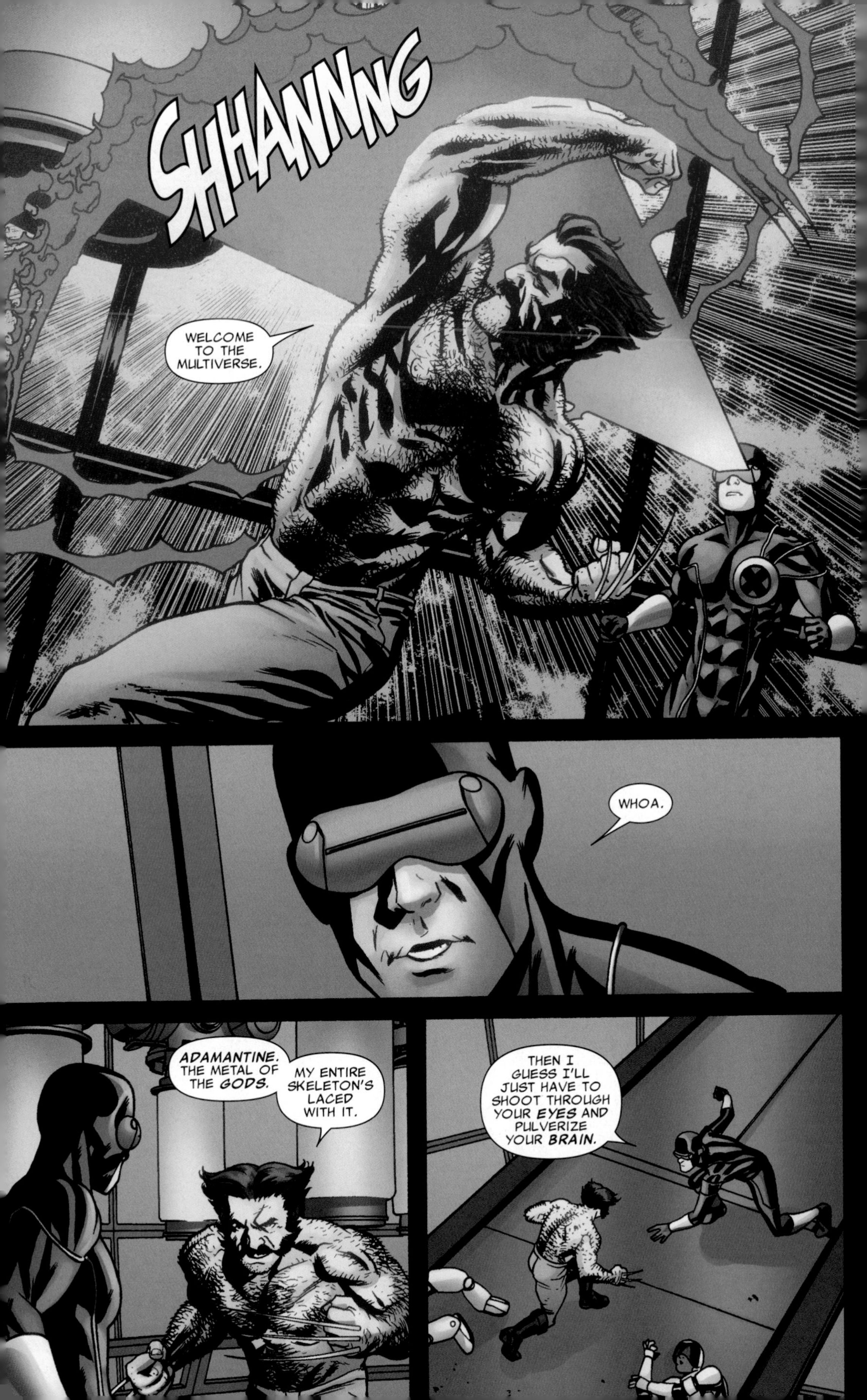
SHHANNNG
WELCOME TO THE MULTIVERSE.
WHOA.
ADAMANTINE. THE METAL OF THE GODS.
MY ENTIRE SKELETON'S LACED WITH IT.
THEN I GUESS I'LL JUST HAVE TO SHOOT THROUGH YOUR EYES AND PULVERIZE YOUR BRAIN.

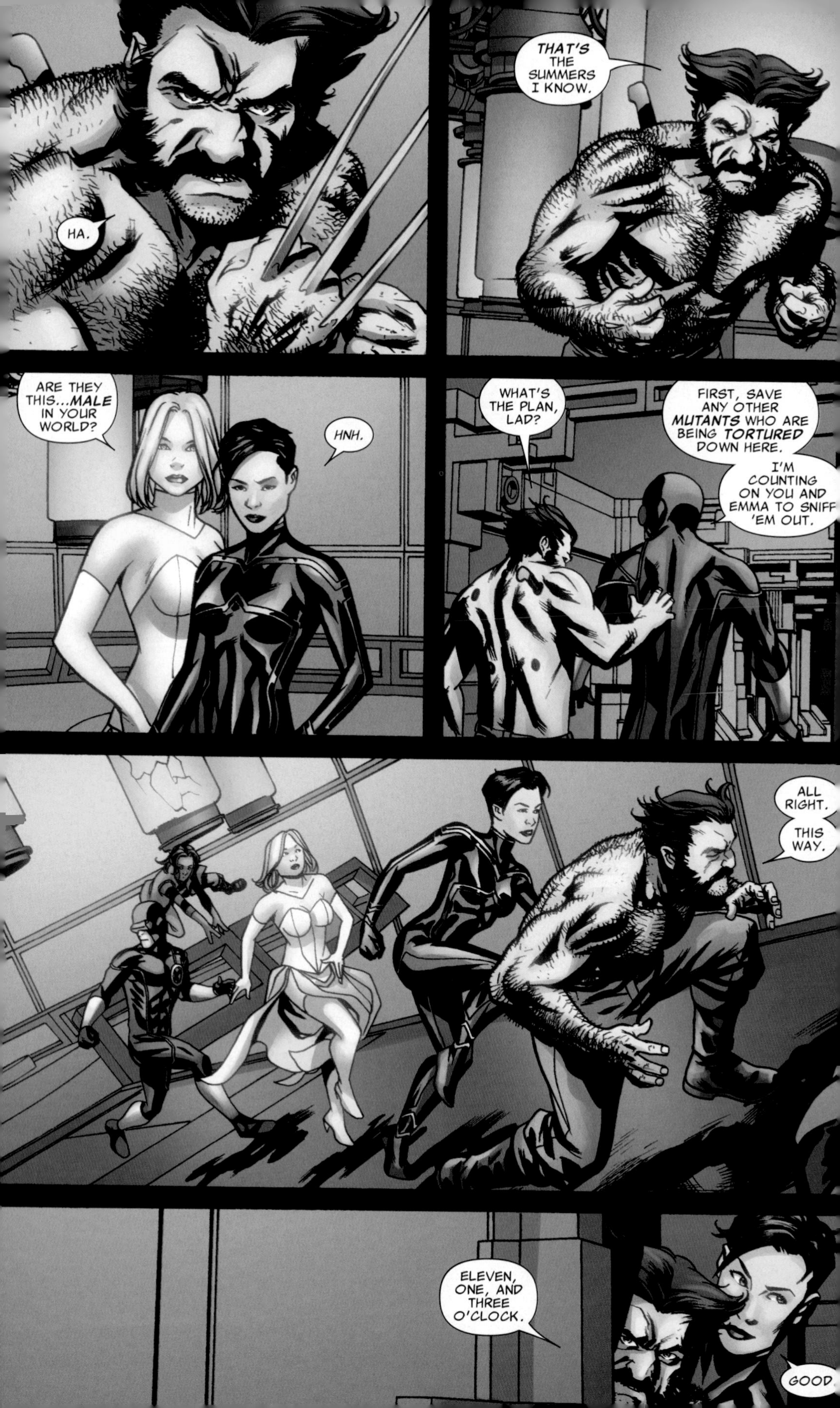
HA.
THAT'S THE SUMMERS I KNOW.
ARE THEY THIS...MALE IN YOUR WORLD?
HNH.
WHAT'S THE PLAN, LAD?
FIRST, SAVE ANY OTHER MUTANTS WHO ARE BEING TORTURED DOWN HERE.
I'M COUNTING ON YOU AND EMMA TO SNIFF 'EM OUT.
ALL RIGHT.
THIS WAY.
ELEVEN, ONE, AND THREE O'CLOCK.
GOOD.

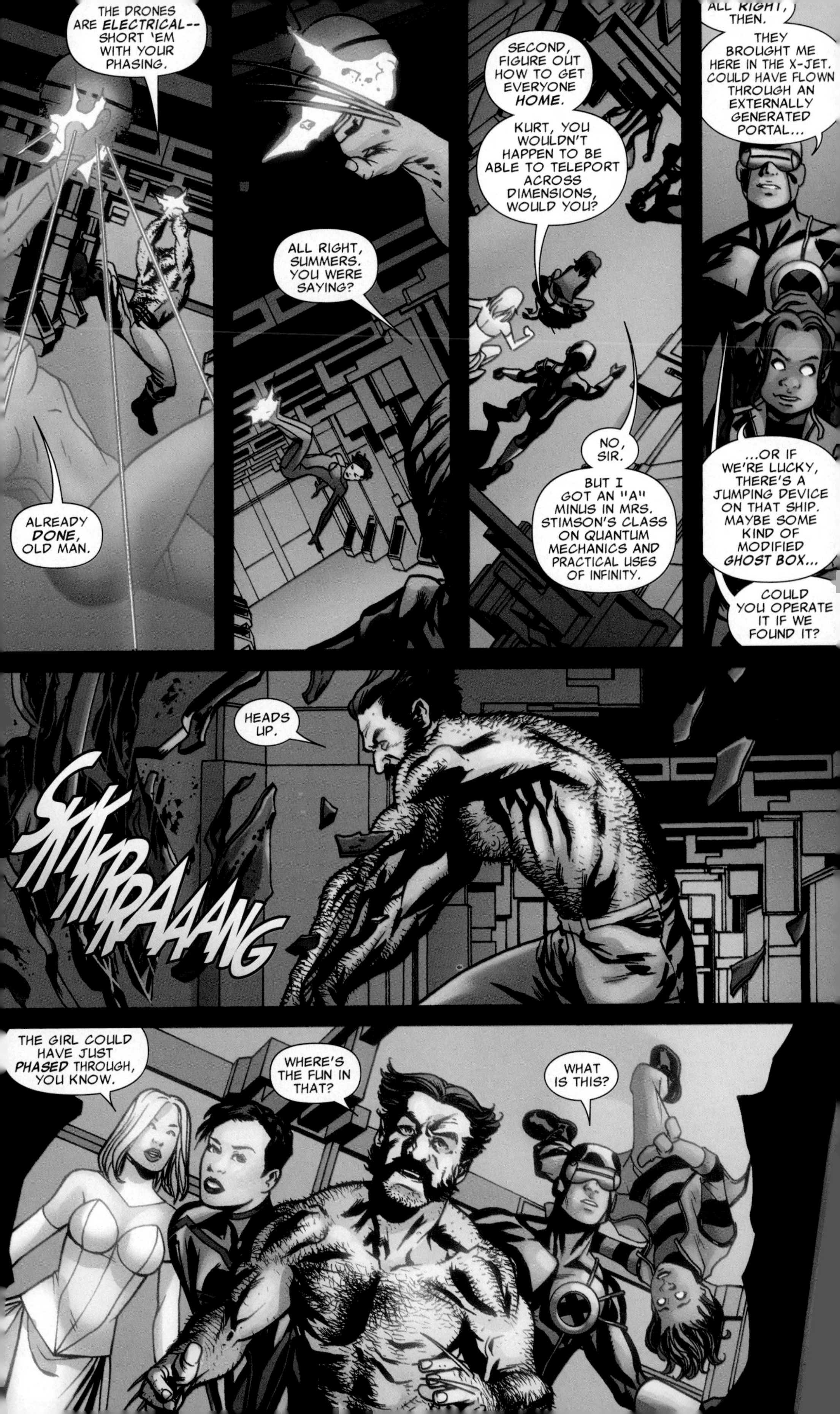
THE DRONES ARE ELECTRICAL-- SHORT 'EM WITH YOUR PHASING.
ALREADY DONE, OLD MAN.
ALL RIGHT, SUMMERS. YOU WERE SAYING?
SECOND, FIGURE OUT HOW TO GET EVERYONE HOME.
KURT, YOU WOULDN'T HAPPEN TO BE ABLE TO TELEPORT ACROSS DIMENSIONS, WOULD YOU?
NO, SIR.
BUT I GOT AN "A" MINUS IN MRS. STIMSON'S CLASS ON QUANTUM MECHANICS AND PRACTICAL USES OF INFINITY.
ALL RIGHT, THEN.
THEY BROUGHT ME HERE IN THE X-JET. COULD HAVE FLOWN THROUGH AN EXTERNALLY GENERATED PORTAL...
...OR IF WE'RE LUCKY, THERE'S A JUMPING DEVICE ON THAT SHIP. MAYBE SOME KIND OF MODIFIED GHOST BOX...
COULD YOU OPERATE IT IF WE FOUND IT?
HEADS UP.
SKKRAAANG
THE GIRL COULD HAVE JUST PHASED THROUGH, YOU KNOW.
WHERE'S THE FUN IN THAT?
WHAT IS THIS?

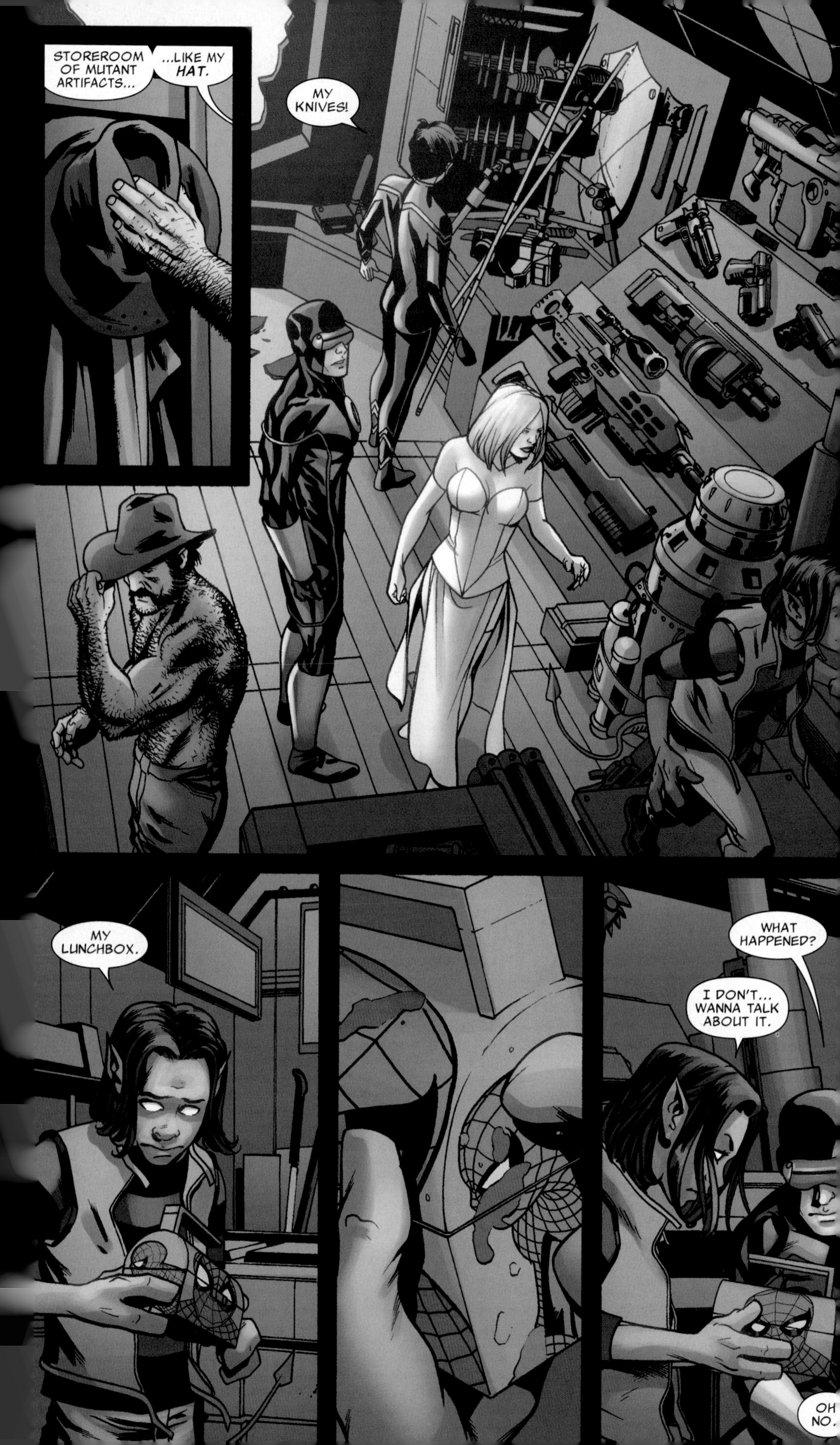
STOREROOM OF MUTANT ARTIFACTS...
...LIKE MY *HAT.*
MY KNIVES!
MY LUNCHBOX.
WHAT HAPPENED?
I DON'T... WANNA TALK ABOUT IT.
OH NO.

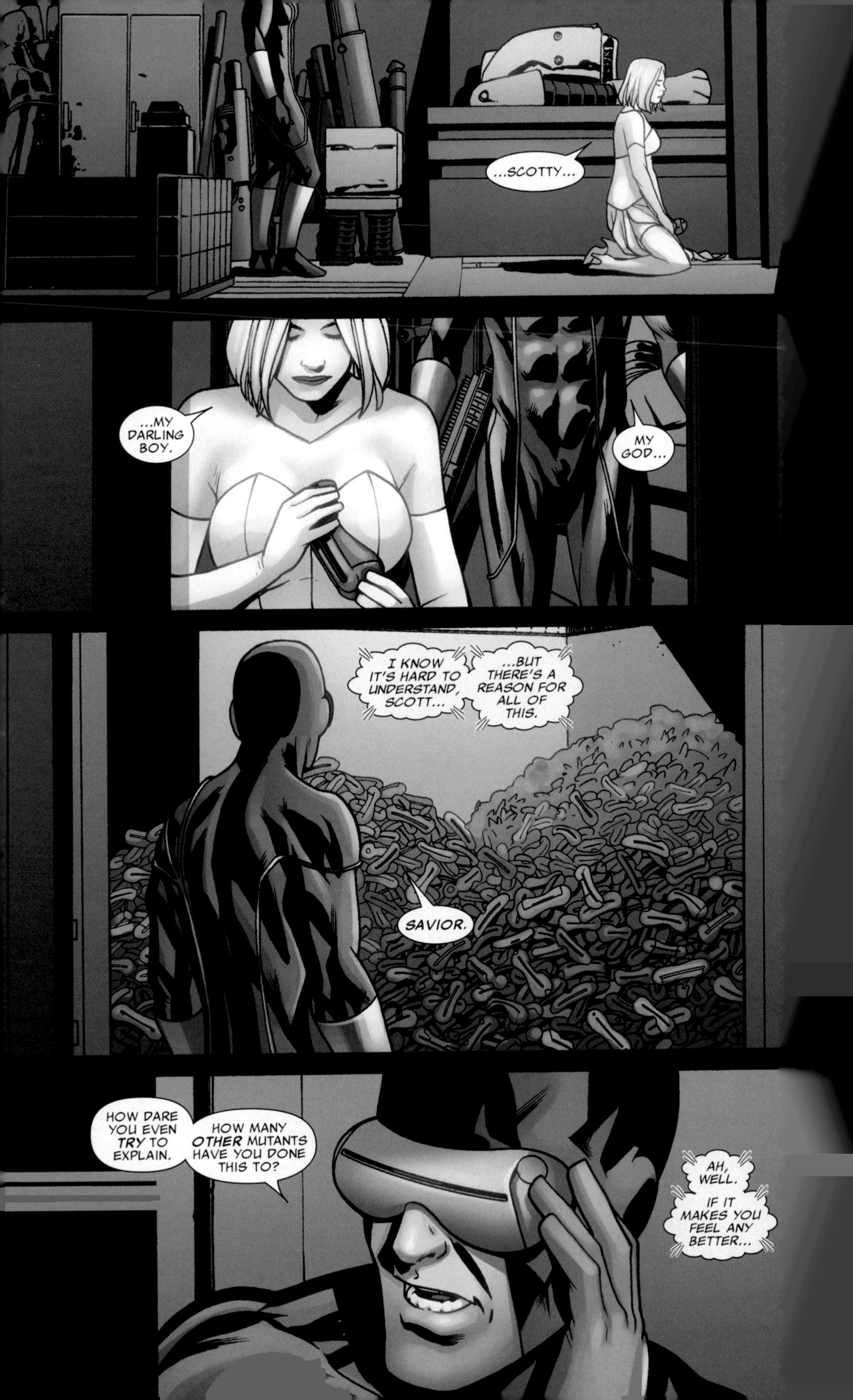
...SCOTTY...
...MY DARLING BOY.
MY GOD...
I KNOW IT'S HARD TO UNDERSTAND, SCOTT...
...BUT THERE'S A REASON FOR ALL OF THIS.
SAVIOR.
HOW DARE YOU EVEN TRY TO EXPLAIN.
HOW MANY OTHER MUTANTS HAVE YOU DONE THIS TO?
AH, WELL.
IF IT MAKES YOU FEEL ANY BETTER...

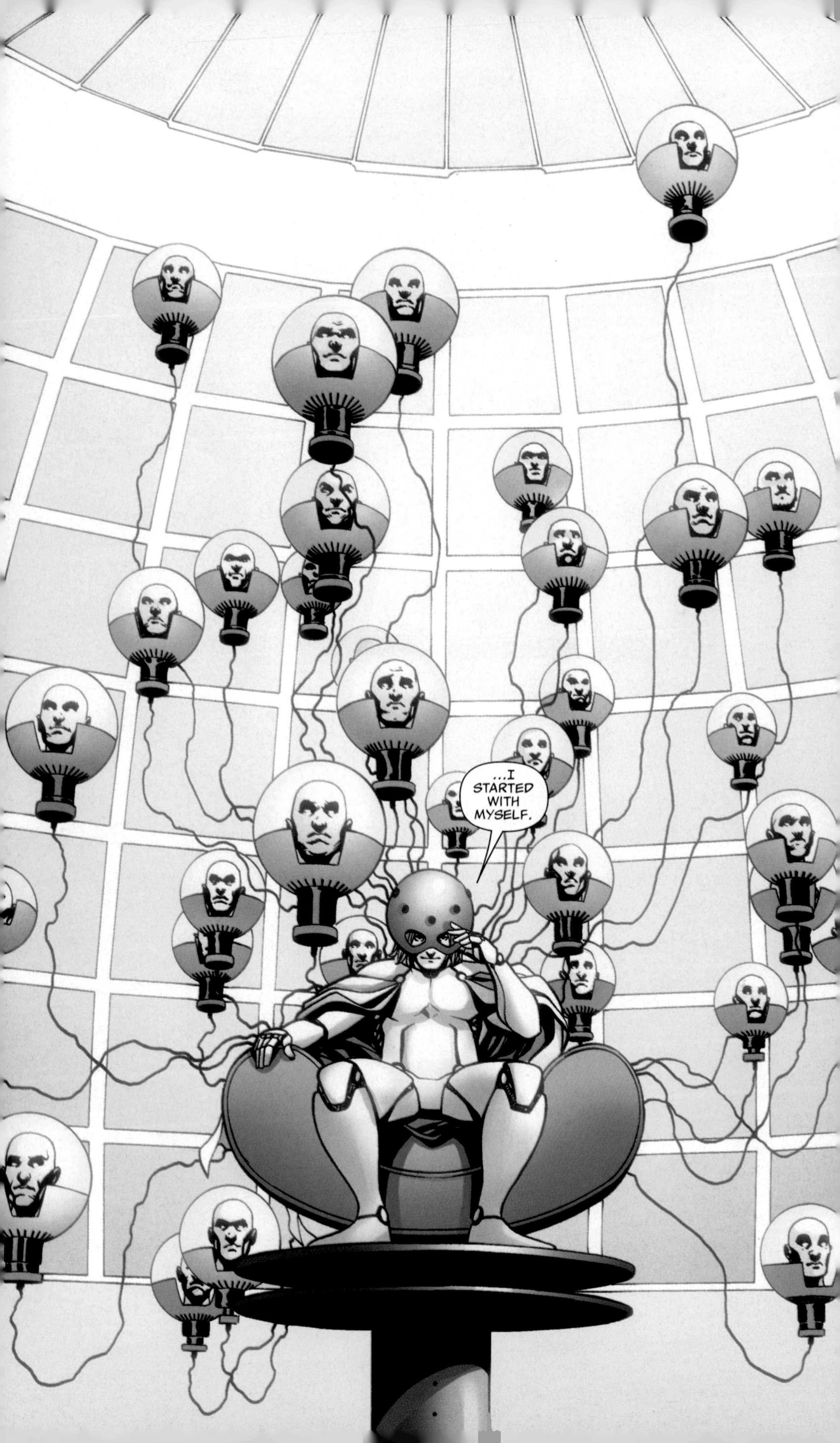
...I STARTED WITH MYSELF.

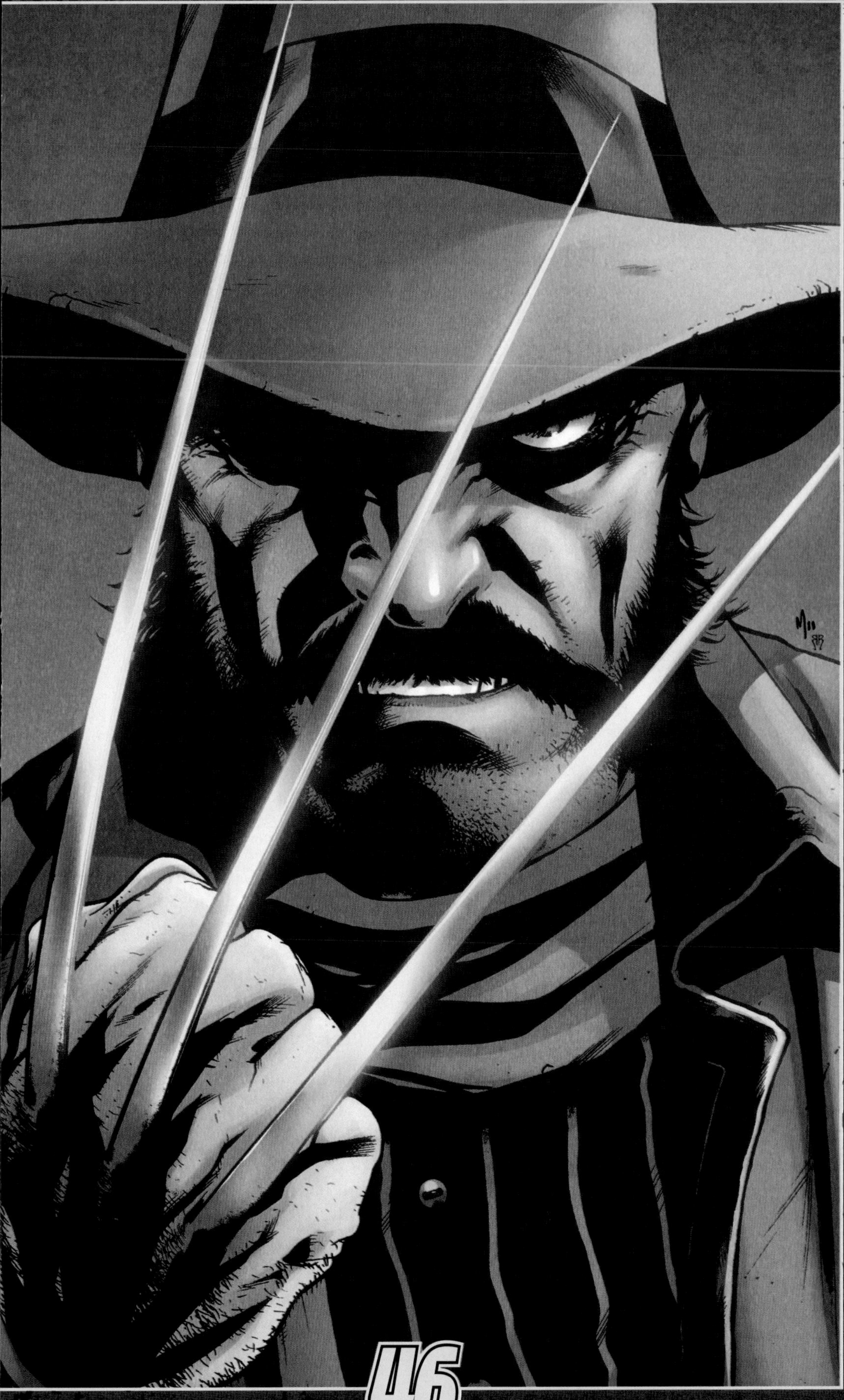

46

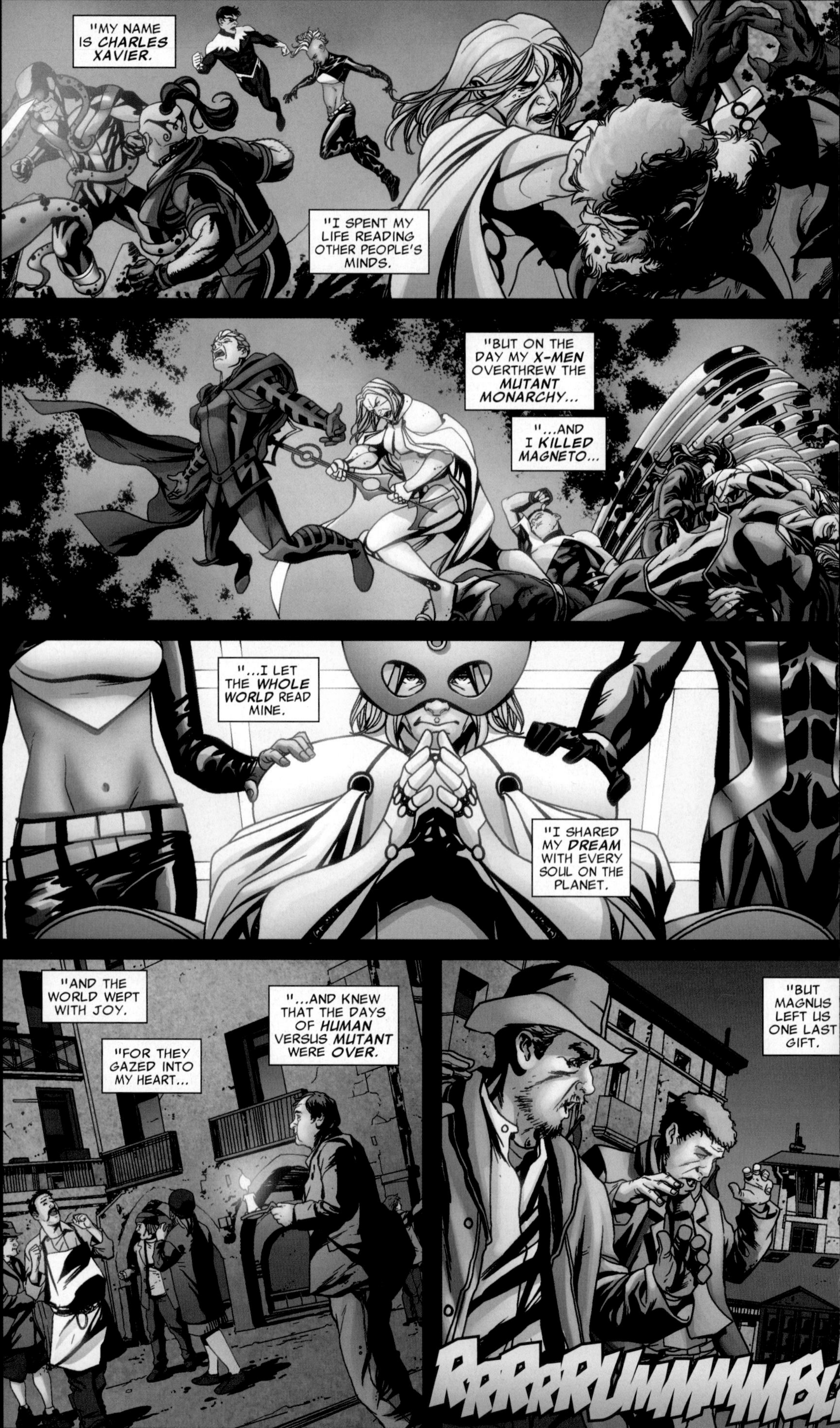
"MY NAME IS CHARLES XAVIER.
"I SPENT MY LIFE READING OTHER PEOPLE'S MINDS.
"BUT ON THE DAY MY X-MEN OVERTHREW THE MUTANT MONARCHY...
"...AND I KILLED MAGNETO...
"...I LET THE WHOLE WORLD READ MINE.
"I SHARED MY DREAM WITH EVERY SOUL ON THE PLANET.
"AND THE WORLD WEPT WITH JOY.
"FOR THEY GAZED INTO MY HEART...
"...AND KNEW THAT THE DAYS OF HUMAN VERSUS MUTANT WERE OVER.
"BUT MAGNUS LEFT US ONE LAST GIFT.
RRRRRUMMMMMBL

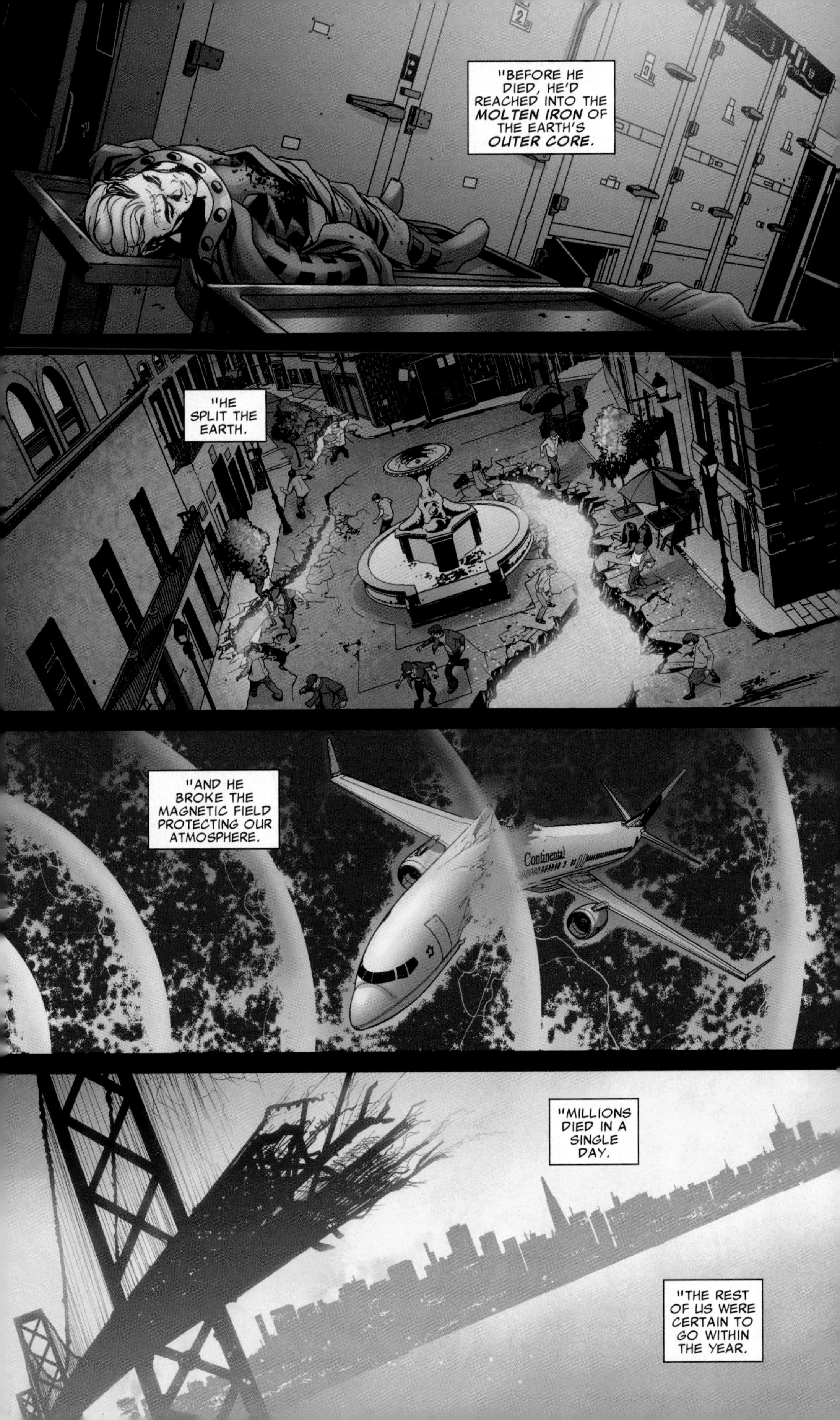
"BEFORE HE DIED, HE'D REACHED INTO THE MOLTEN IRON OF THE EARTH'S OUTER CORE.
"HE SPLIT THE EARTH.
"AND HE BROKE THE MAGNETIC FIELD PROTECTING OUR ATMOSPHERE.
Continental
"MILLIONS DIED IN A SINGLE DAY.
"THE REST OF US WERE CERTAIN TO GO WITHIN THE YEAR.

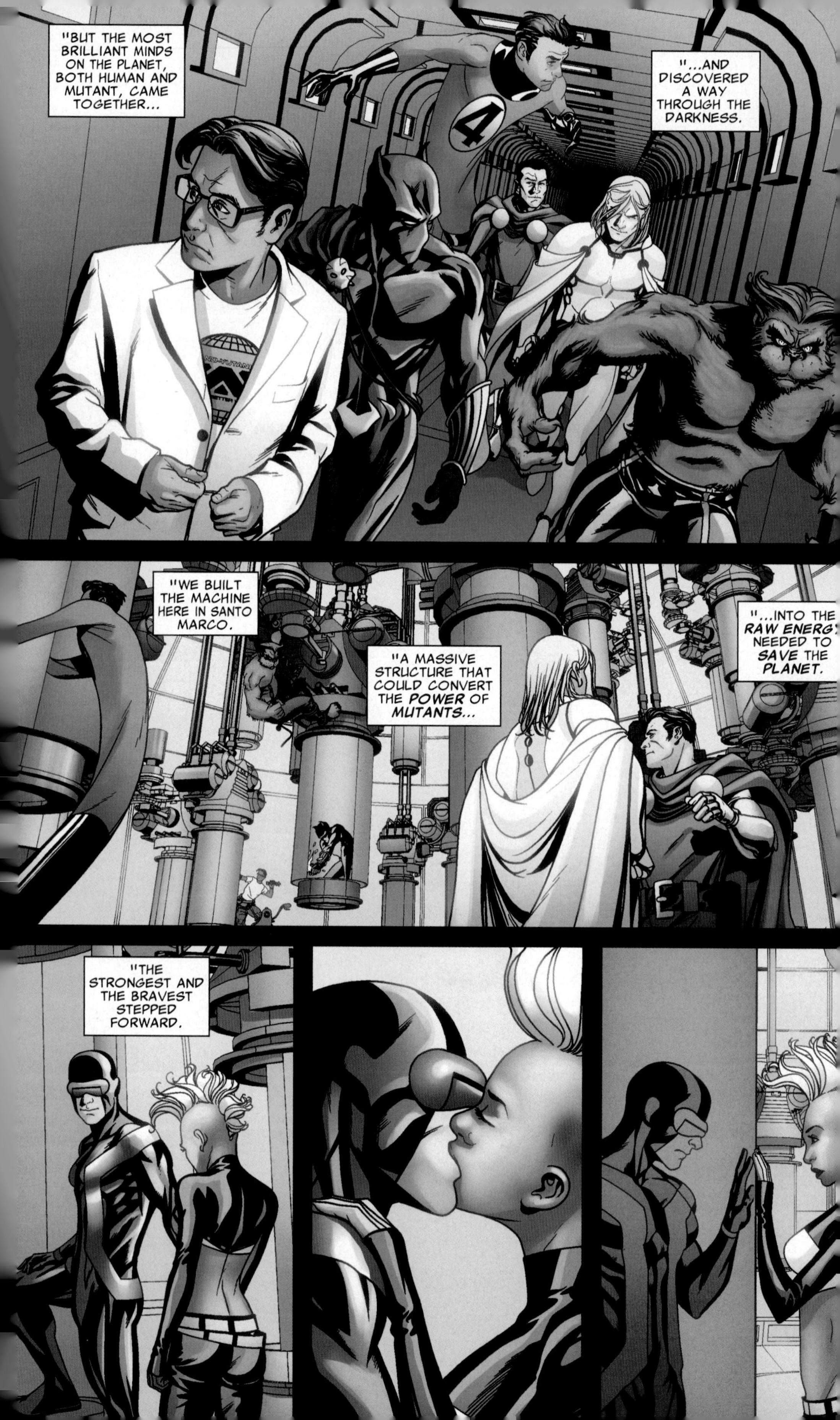
"BUT THE MOST BRILLIANT MINDS ON THE PLANET, BOTH HUMAN AND MUTANT, CAME TOGETHER...
"...AND DISCOVERED A WAY THROUGH THE DARKNESS.
"WE BUILT THE MACHINE HERE IN SANTO MARCO.
"A MASSIVE STRUCTURE THAT COULD CONVERT THE POWER OF MUTANTS...
"...INTO THE RAW ENERGY NEEDED TO SAVE THE PLANET.
"THE STRONGEST AND THE BRAVEST STEPPED FORWARD.

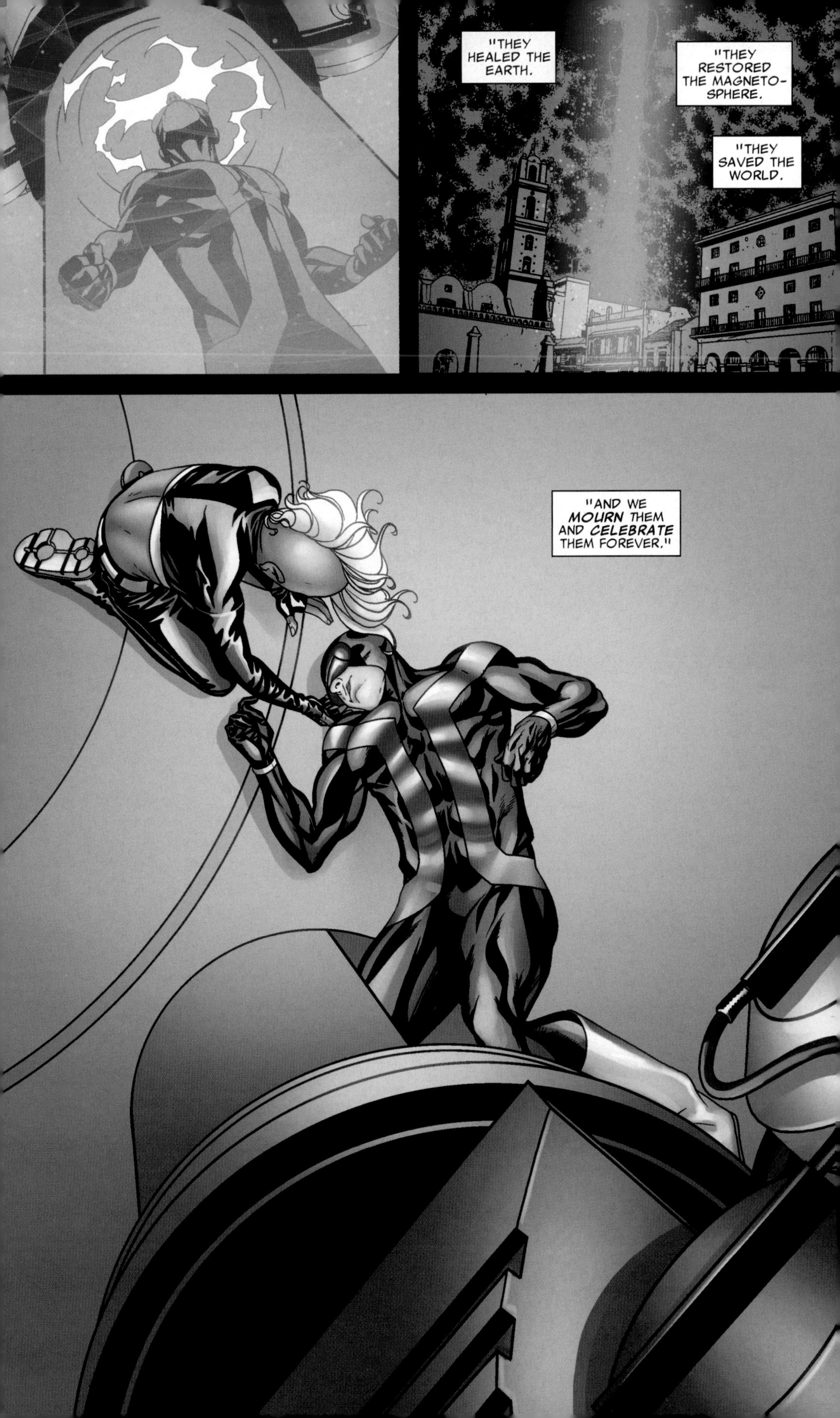
"THEY HEALED THE EARTH.
"THEY RESTORED THE MAGNETO-SPHERE.
"THEY SAVED THE WORLD.
"AND WE MOURN THEM AND CELEBRATE THEM FOREVER."

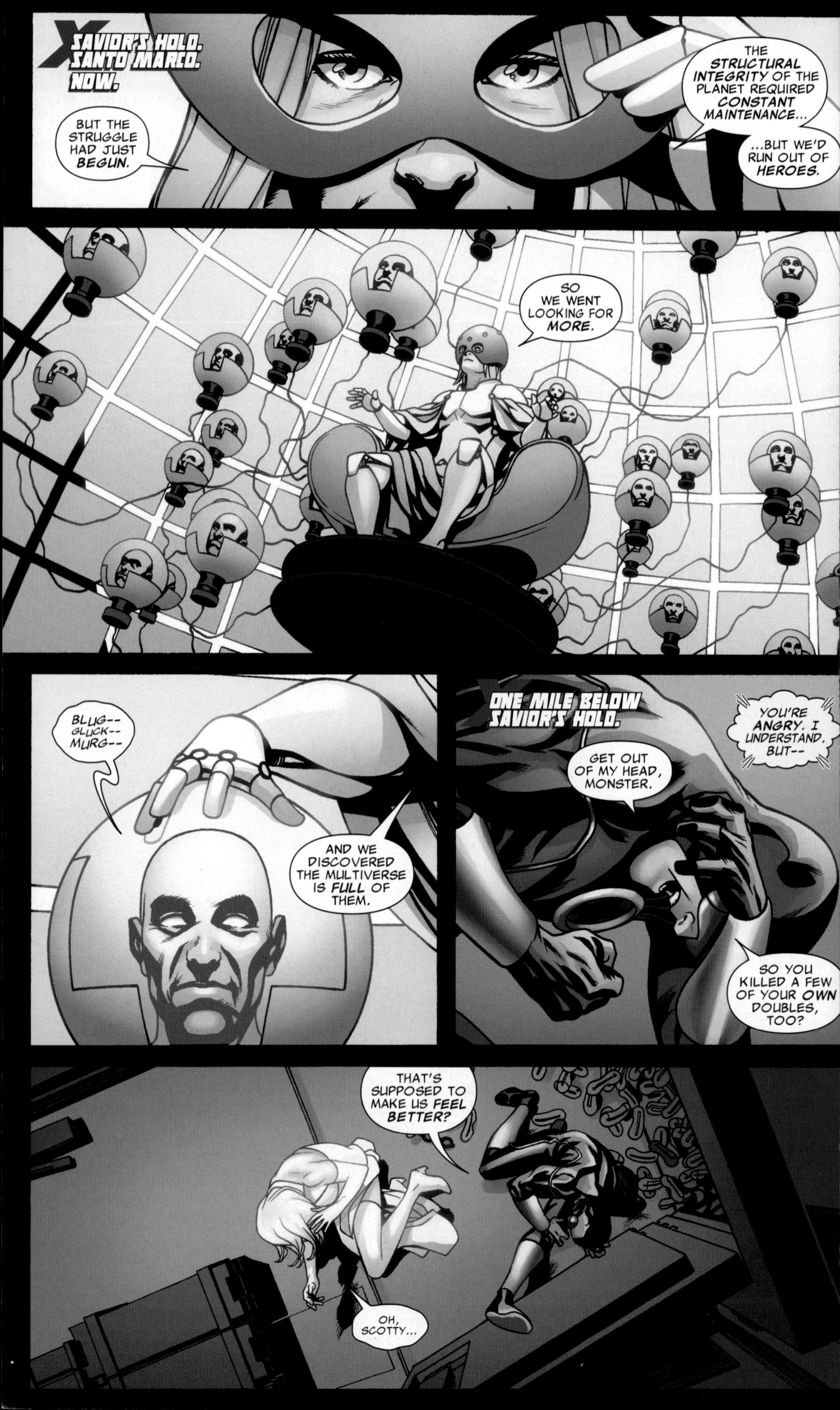
SAVIOR'S HOLD. SANTO MARCO. NOW.
BUT THE STRUGGLE HAD JUST BEGUN.
THE STRUCTURAL INTEGRITY OF THE PLANET REQUIRED CONSTANT MAINTENANCE...
...BUT WE'D RUN OUT OF HEROES.
SO WE WENT LOOKING FOR MORE.
BLUG-- GLUCK-- MURG--
AND WE DISCOVERED THE MULTIVERSE IS FULL OF THEM.
ONE MILE BELOW SAVIOR'S HOLD.
YOU'RE ANGRY. I UNDERSTAND. BUT--
GET OUT OF MY HEAD, MONSTER.
SO YOU KILLED A FEW OF YOUR OWN DOUBLES, TOO?
THAT'S SUPPOSED TO MAKE US FEEL BETTER?
OH, SCOTTY...

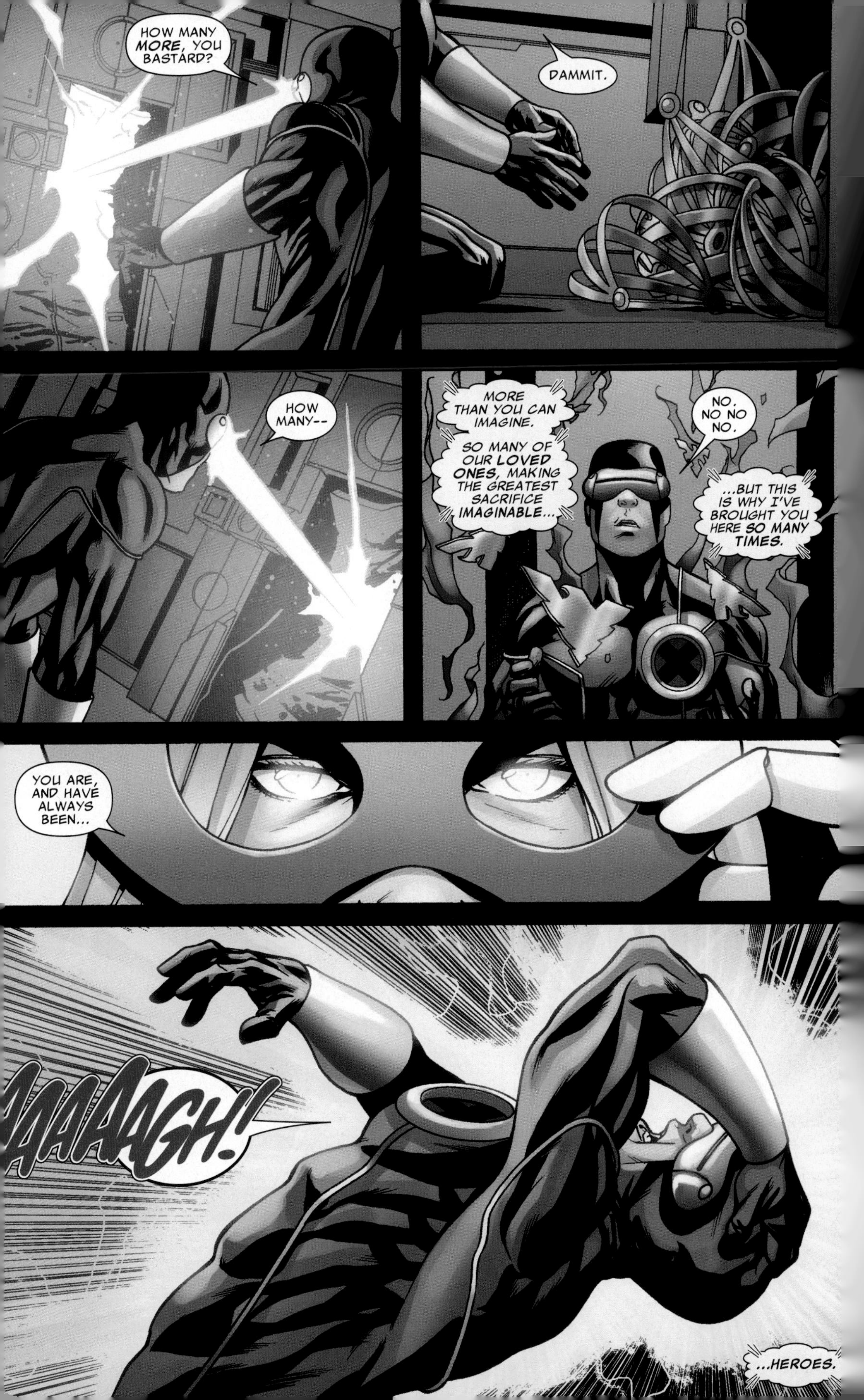
HOW MANY **MORE**, YOU BASTARD?
DAMMIT.
HOW MANY--
MORE THAN YOU CAN IMAGINE.
SO MANY OF OUR **LOVED ONES**, MAKING THE GREATEST SACRIFICE **IMAGINABLE**...
NO. NO NO NO.
...BUT THIS IS WHY I'VE BROUGHT YOU HERE **SO MANY TIMES**.
YOU ARE, AND HAVE ALWAYS BEEN...
AAAAAAGH!
...HEROES.

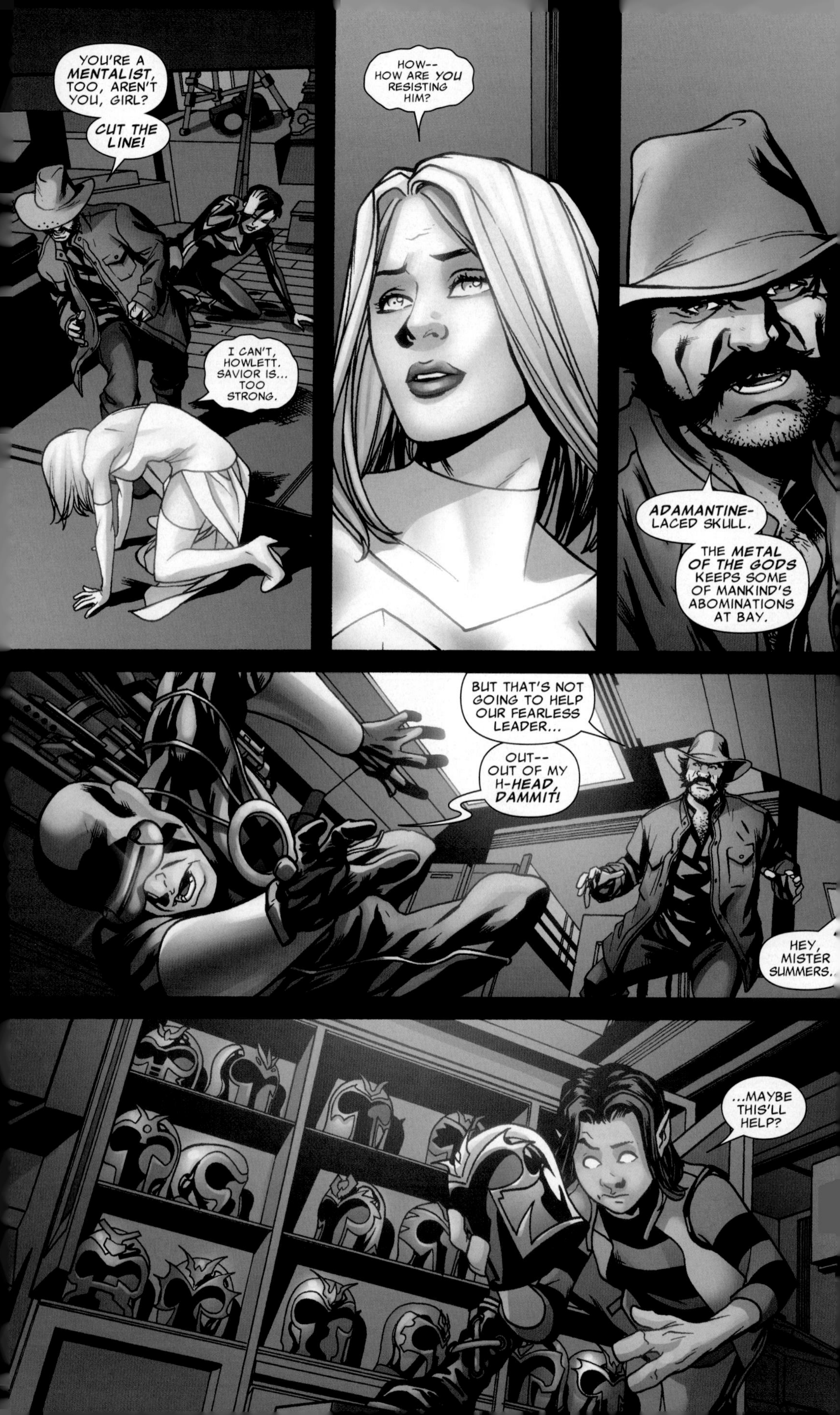
YOU'RE A MENTALIST, TOO, AREN'T YOU, GIRL?
CUT THE LINE!
I CAN'T, HOWLETT. SAVIOR IS... TOO STRONG.
HOW-- HOW ARE YOU RESISTING HIM?
ADAMANTINE-LACED SKULL.
THE METAL OF THE GODS KEEPS SOME OF MANKIND'S ABOMINATIONS AT BAY.
BUT THAT'S NOT GOING TO HELP OUR FEARLESS LEADER...
OUT-- OUT OF MY H-HEAD, DAMMIT!
HEY, MISTER SUMMERS.
...MAYBE THIS'LL HELP?

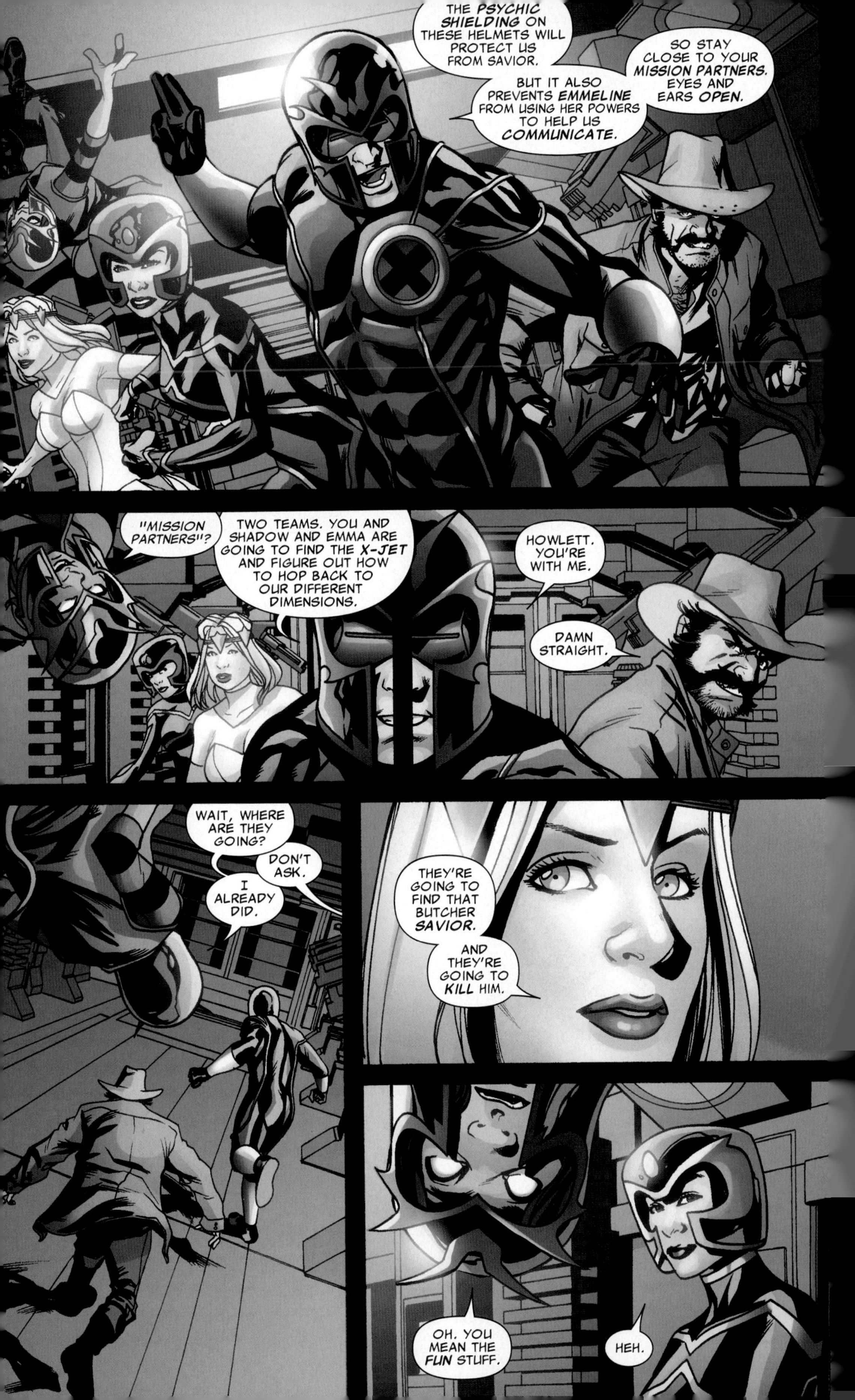
THE PSYCHIC SHIELDING ON THESE HELMETS WILL PROTECT US FROM SAVIOR.
BUT IT ALSO PREVENTS EMMELINE FROM USING HER POWERS TO HELP US COMMUNICATE.
SO STAY CLOSE TO YOUR MISSION PARTNERS. EYES AND EARS OPEN.
"MISSION PARTNERS"?
TWO TEAMS. YOU AND SHADOW AND EMMA ARE GOING TO FIND THE X-JET AND FIGURE OUT HOW TO HOP BACK TO OUR DIFFERENT DIMENSIONS.
HOWLETT. YOU'RE WITH ME.
DAMN STRAIGHT.
WAIT, WHERE ARE THEY GOING?
DON'T ASK.
I ALREADY DID.
THEY'RE GOING TO FIND THAT BUTCHER SAVIOR.
AND THEY'RE GOING TO KILL HIM.
OH. YOU MEAN THE FUN STUFF.
HEH.

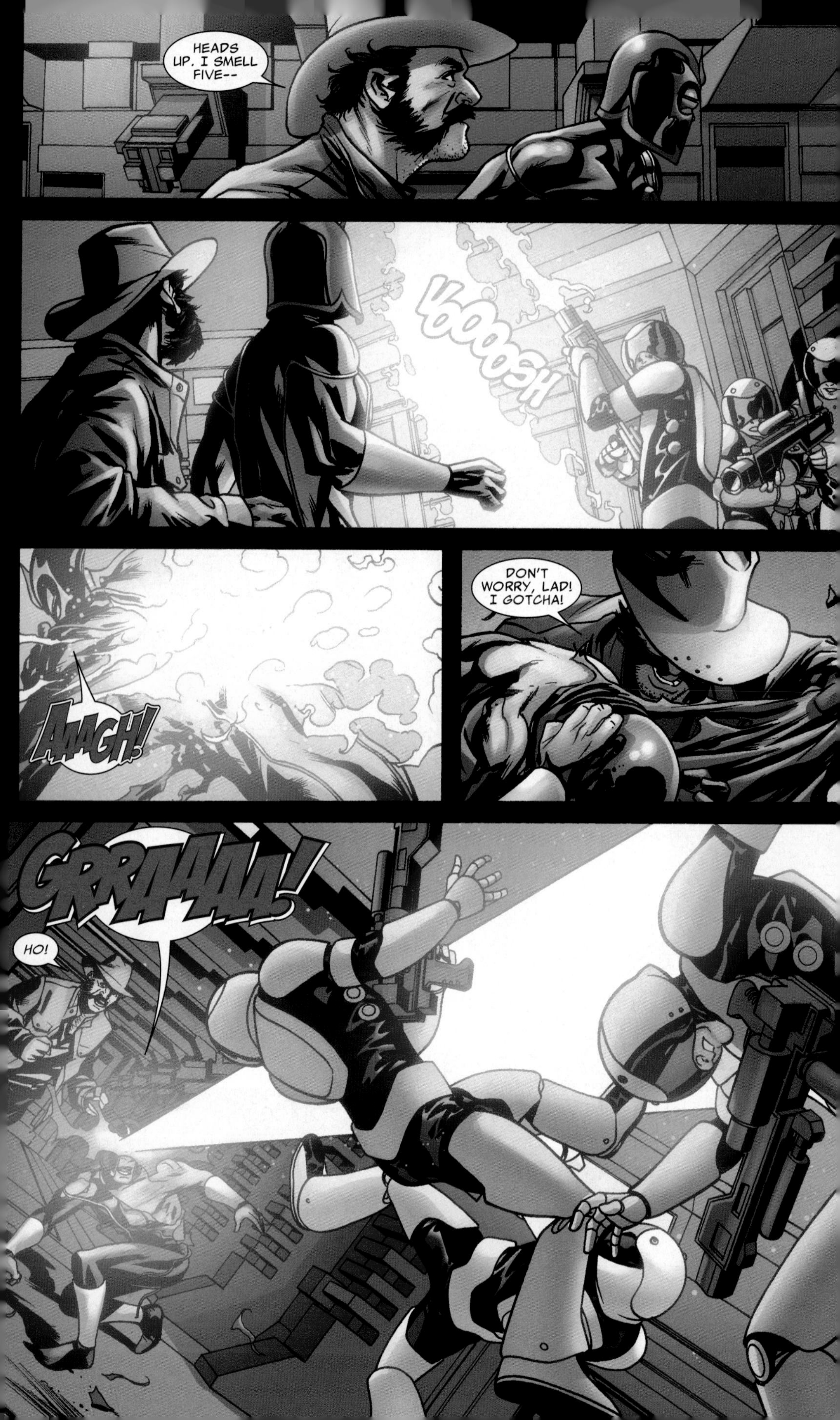
HEADS UP. I SMELL FIVE--
VOOOOSH
AAAGH!
DON'T WORRY, LAD! I GOTCHA!
GRRAAAAA!
HO!

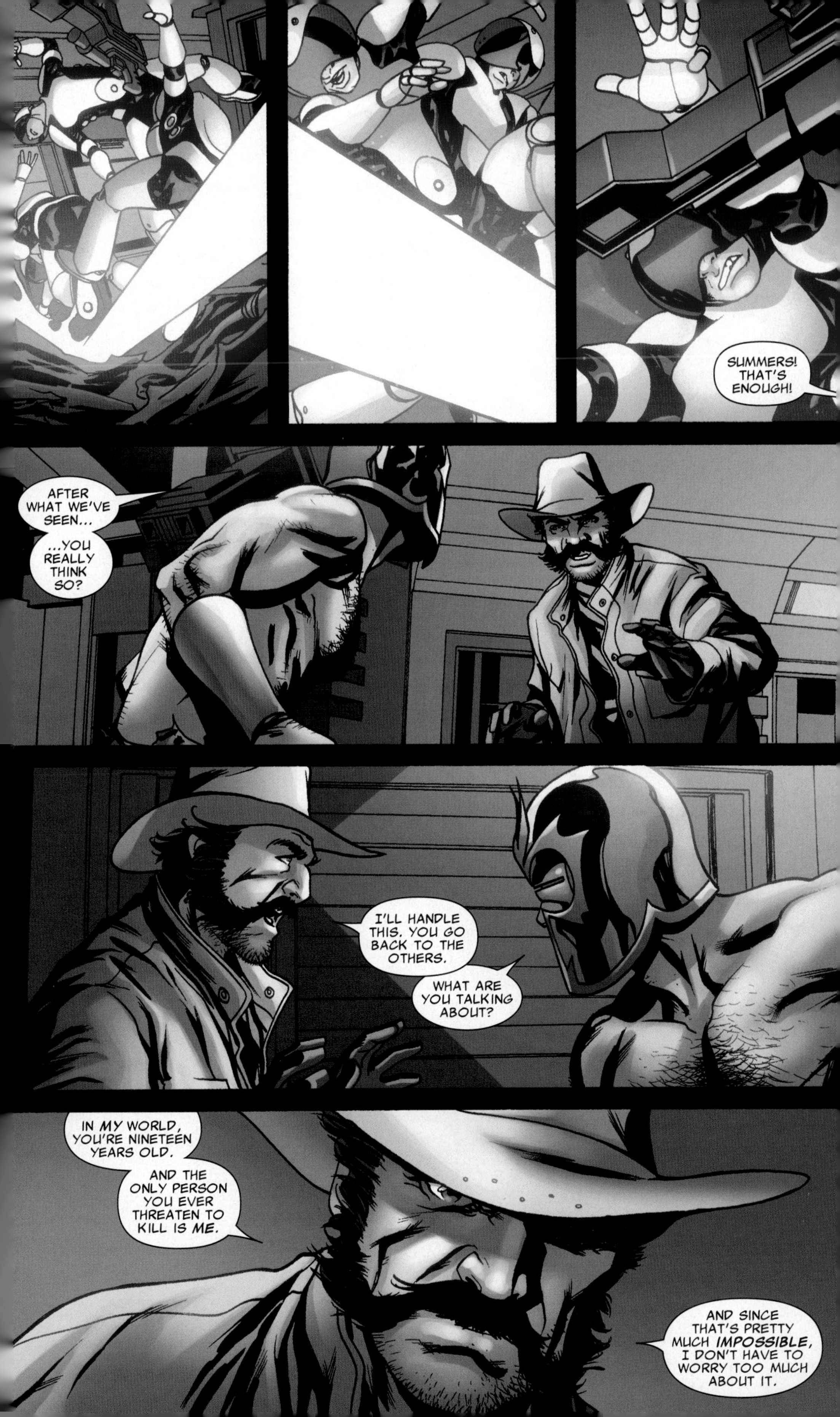
SUMMERS! THAT'S ENOUGH!
AFTER WHAT WE'VE SEEN...
...YOU REALLY THINK SO?
I'LL HANDLE THIS. YOU GO BACK TO THE OTHERS.
WHAT ARE YOU TALKING ABOUT?
IN MY WORLD, YOU'RE NINETEEN YEARS OLD.
AND THE ONLY PERSON YOU EVER THREATEN TO KILL IS ME.
AND SINCE THAT'S PRETTY MUCH IMPOSSIBLE, I DON'T HAVE TO WORRY TOO MUCH ABOUT IT.

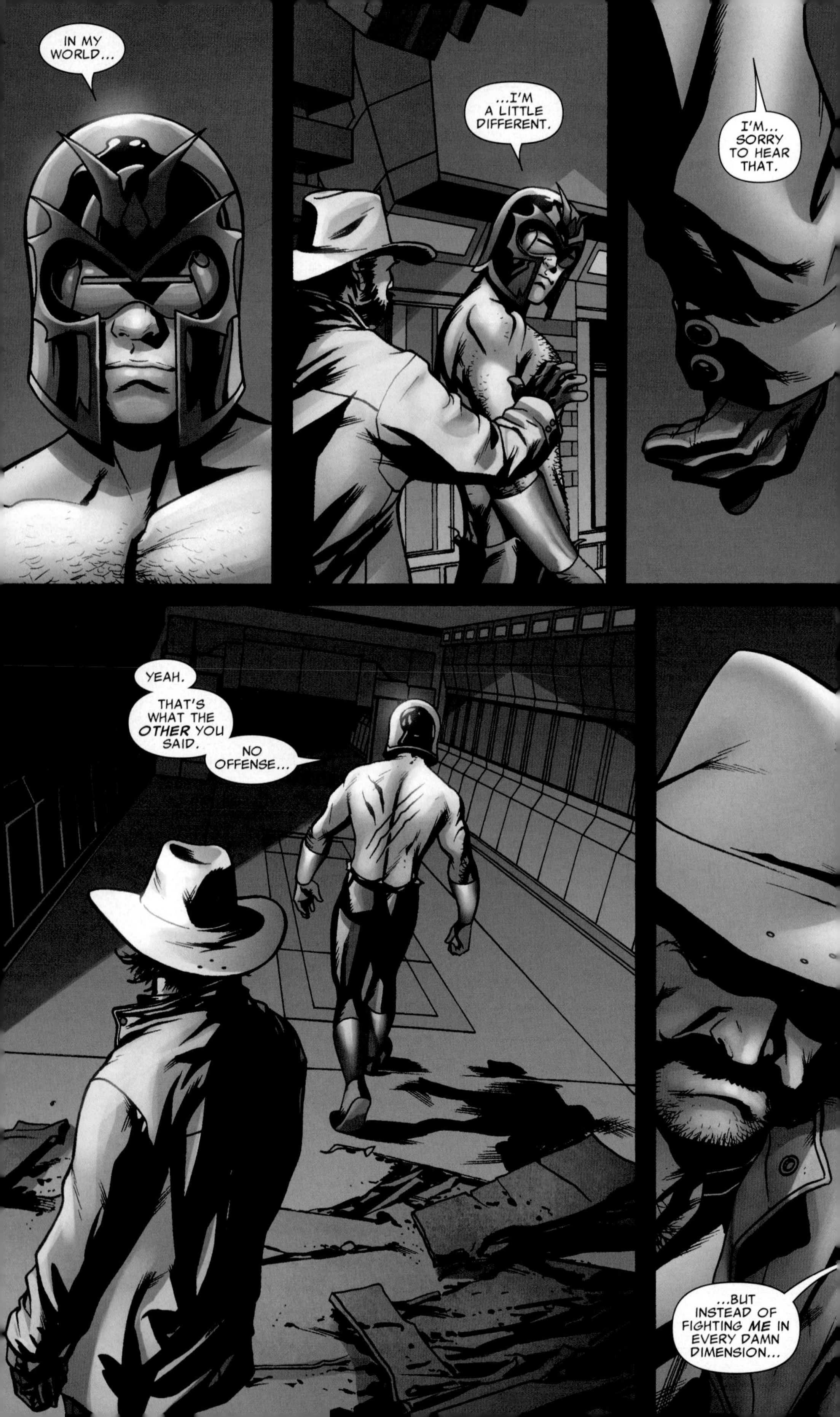
IN MY WORLD...
...I'M A LITTLE DIFFERENT.
I'M... SORRY TO HEAR THAT.
YEAH.
THAT'S WHAT THE **OTHER** YOU SAID.
NO OFFENSE...
...BUT INSTEAD OF FIGHTING **ME** IN EVERY DAMN DIMENSION...

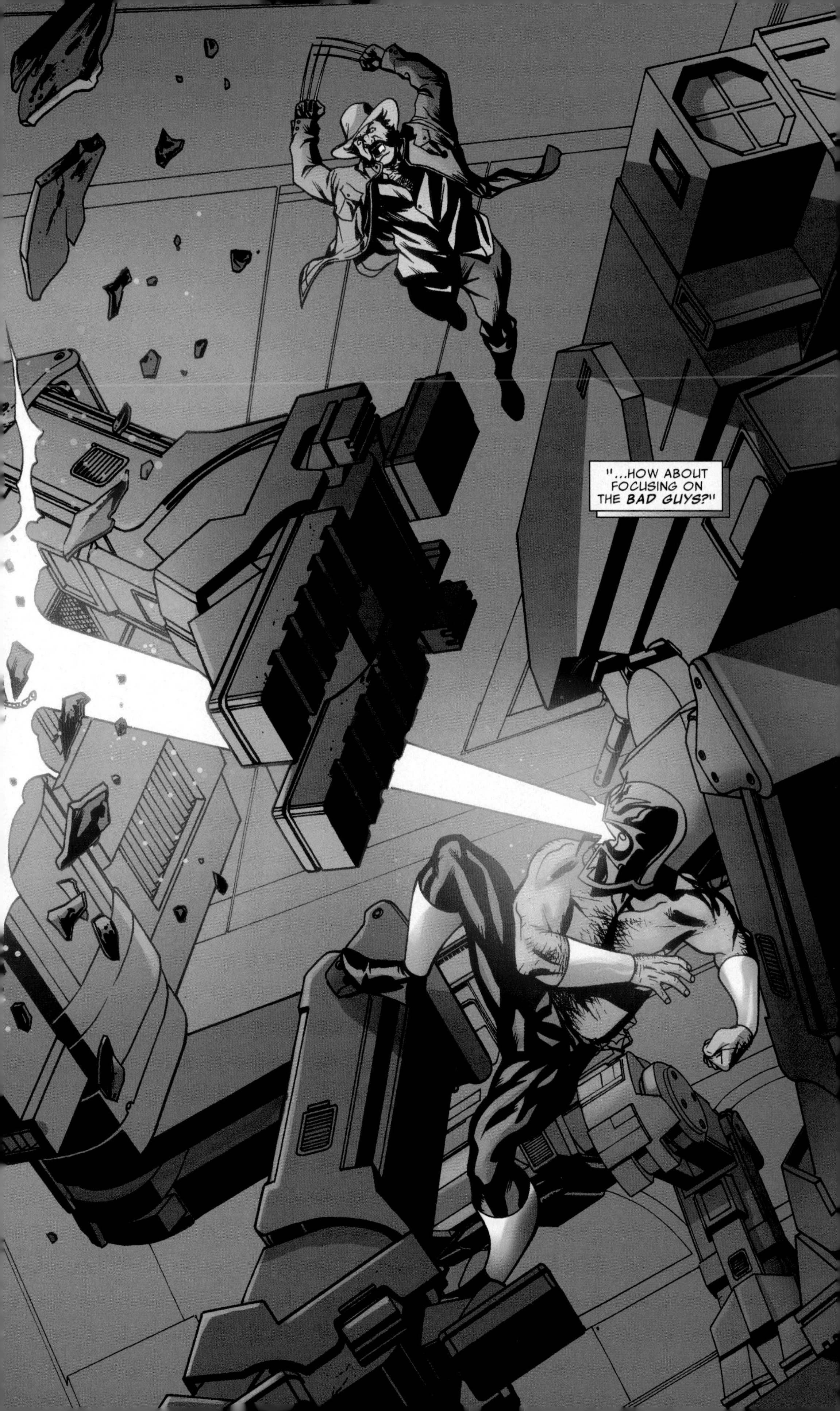
"...HOW ABOUT FOCUSING ON THE BAD GUYS?"

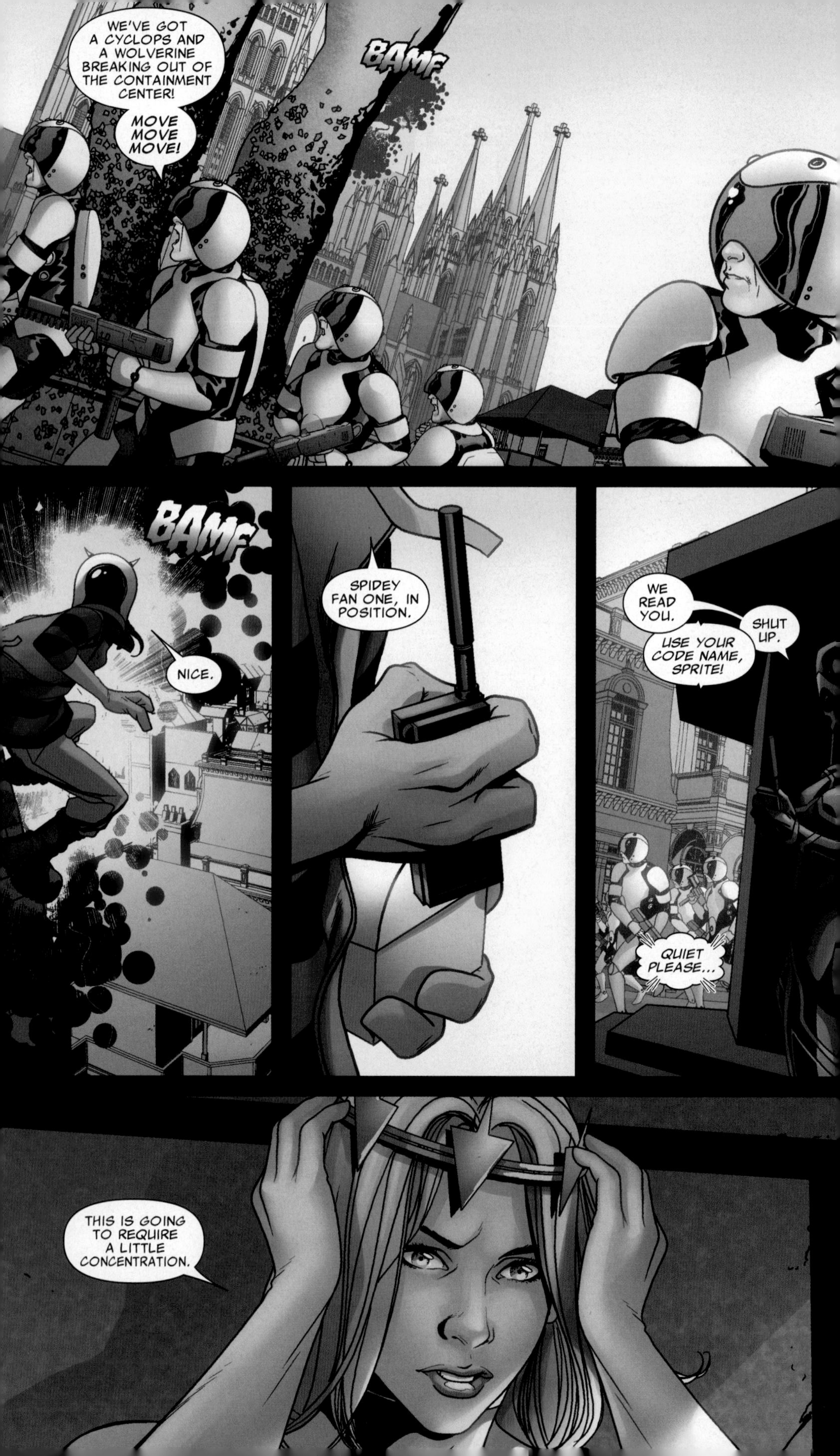
WE'VE GOT A CYCLOPS AND A WOLVERINE BREAKING OUT OF THE CONTAINMENT CENTER!
MOVE MOVE MOVE!
BAMF
BAMF
NICE.
SPIDEY FAN ONE, IN POSITION.
WE READ YOU.
USE YOUR CODE NAME, SPRITE!
SHUT UP.
QUIET PLEASE...
THIS IS GOING TO REQUIRE A LITTLE CONCENTRATION.

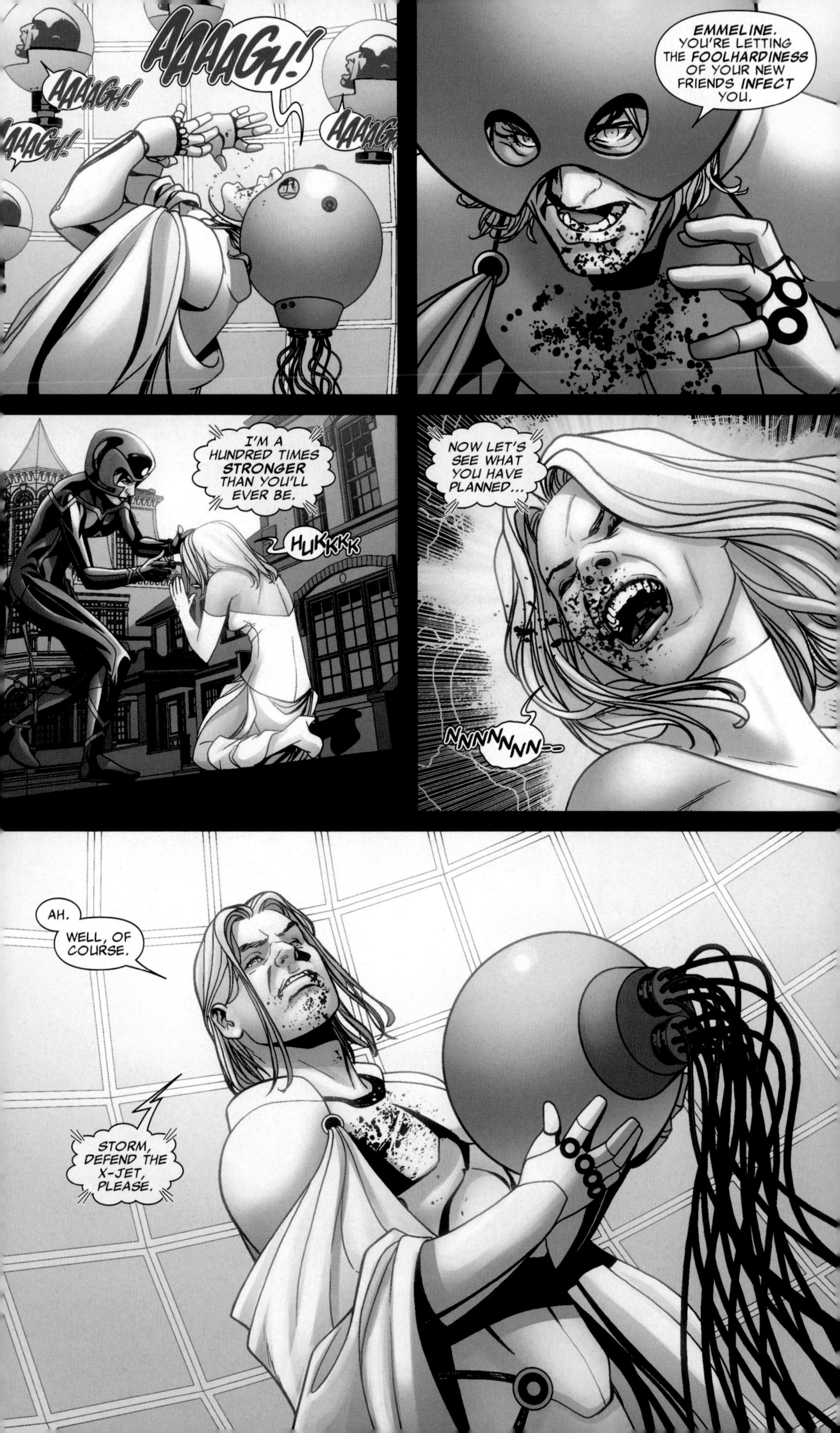
AAAAGH!
AAAAGH!
AAAGH!
AAAAGH
EMMELINE. YOU'RE LETTING THE FOOLHARDINESS OF YOUR NEW FRIENDS INFECT YOU.
I'M A HUNDRED TIMES STRONGER THAN YOU'LL EVER BE.
HUKKKK
NOW LET'S SEE WHAT YOU HAVE PLANNED...
NNNNNNN--
AH.
WELL, OF COURSE.
STORM, DEFEND THE X-JET, PLEASE.

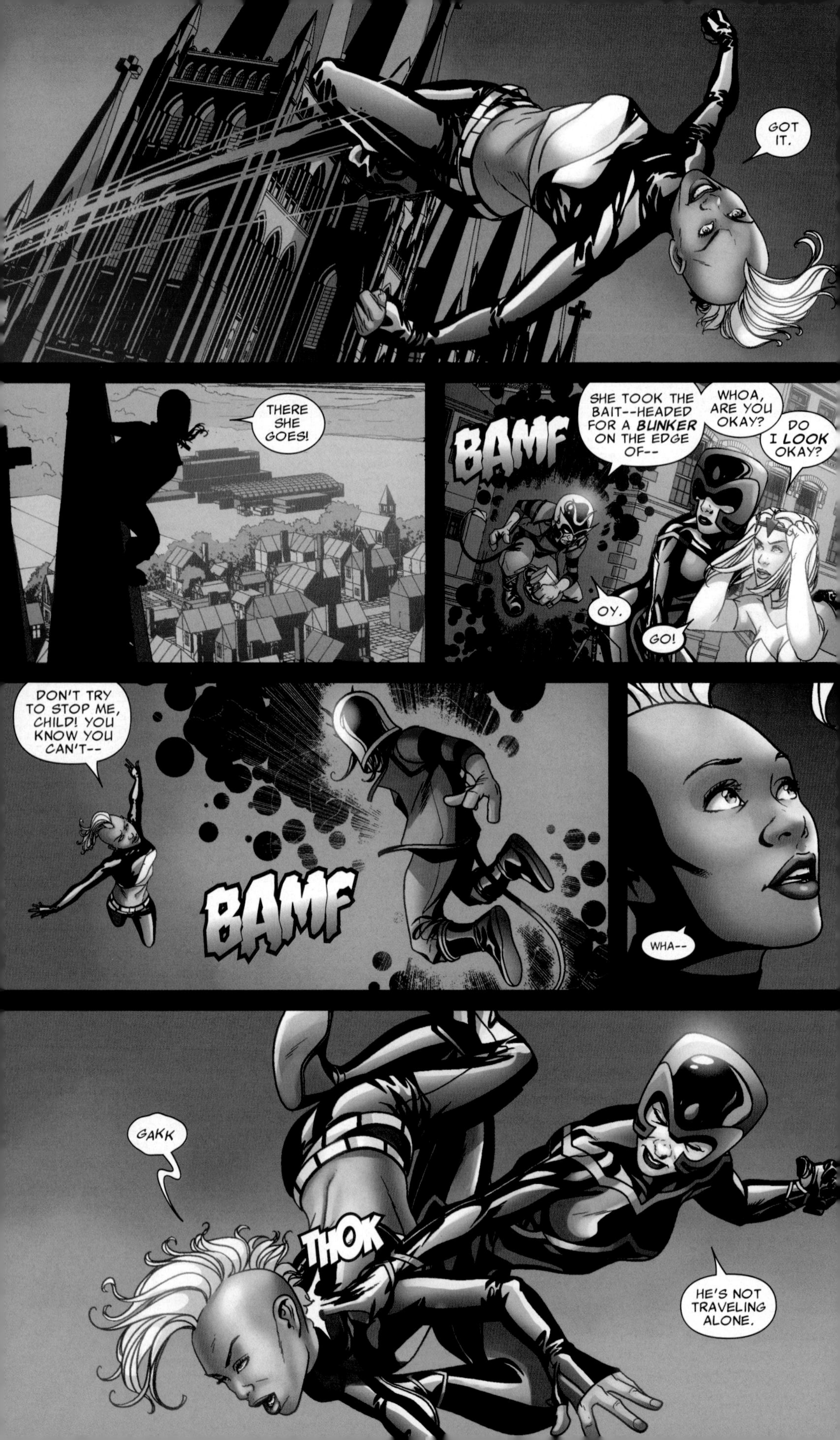
GOT IT.
THERE SHE GOES!
BAMF
SHE TOOK THE BAIT--HEADED FOR A BUNKER ON THE EDGE OF--
WHOA, ARE YOU OKAY?
DO I LOOK OKAY?
OY.
GO!
DON'T TRY TO STOP ME, CHILD! YOU KNOW YOU CAN'T--
BAMF
WHA--
GAKK
THOK
HE'S NOT TRAVELING ALONE.

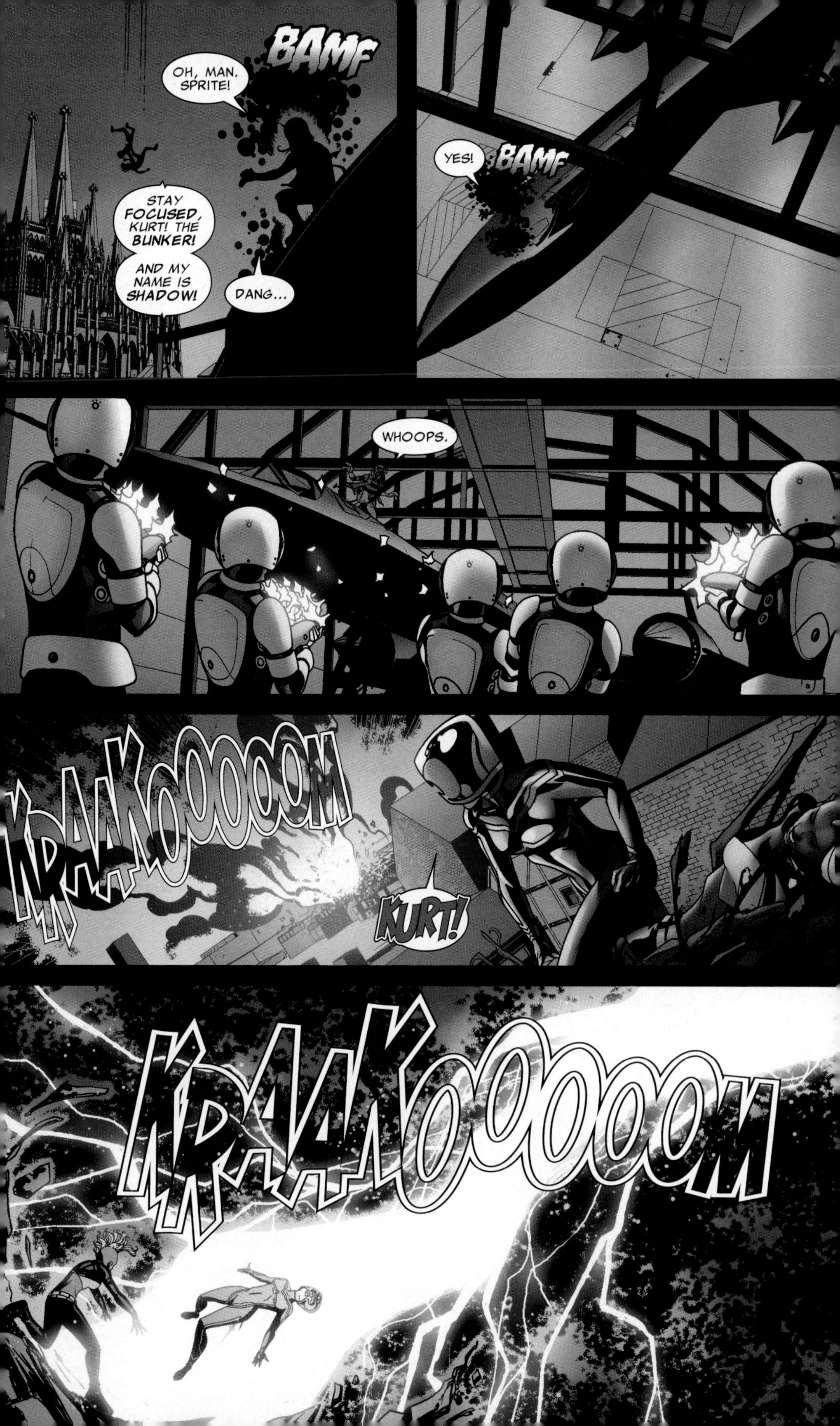
BAMF
OH, MAN. SPRITE!
STAY FOCUSED, KURT! THE BUNKER!
AND MY NAME IS SHADOW!
DANG...
YES!
BAMF
WHOOPS.
KRAAKOOOOOM
KURT!
KRAAKOOOOOOM

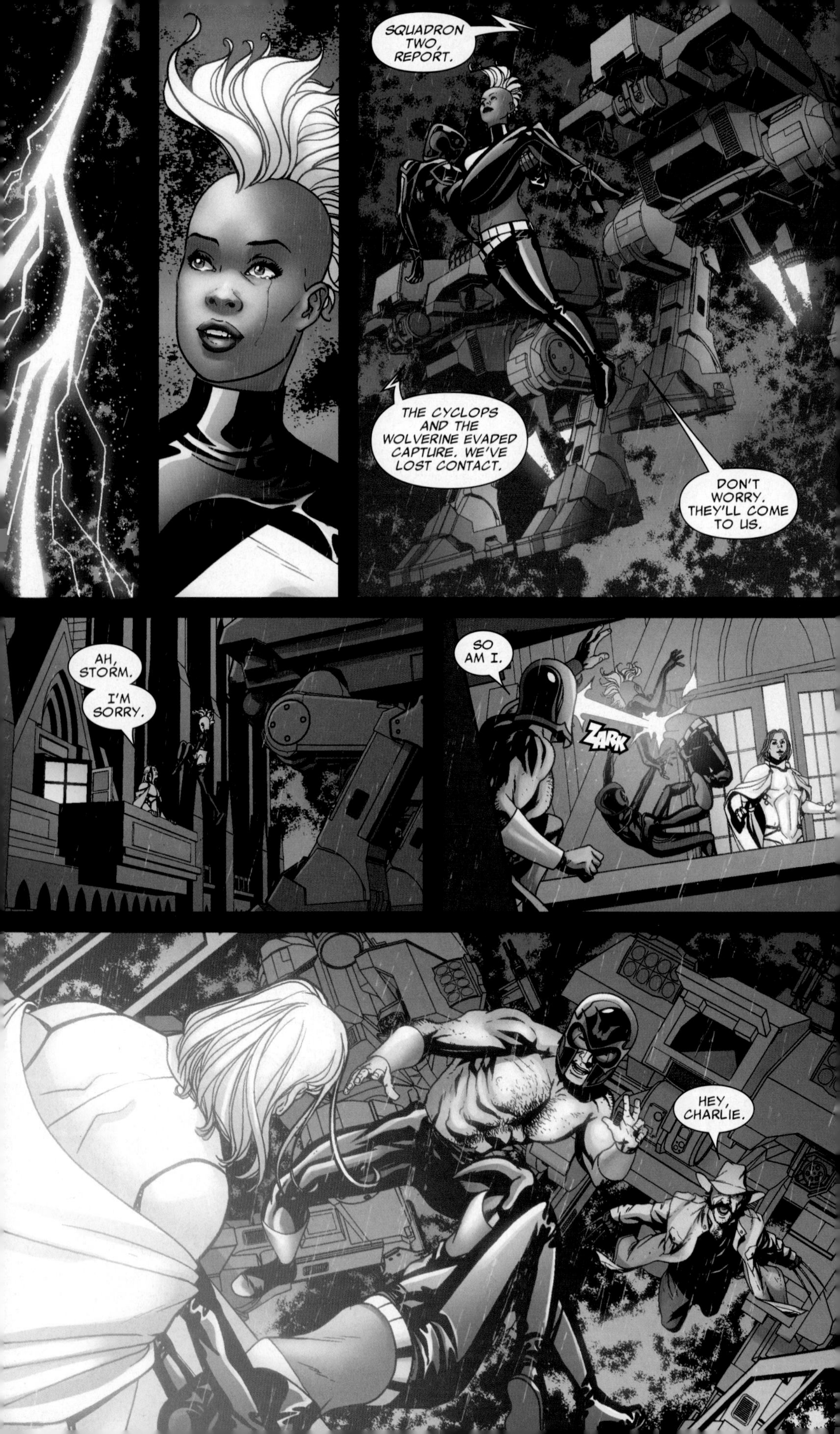
SQUADRON TWO, REPORT.
THE CYCLOPS AND THE WOLVERINE EVADED CAPTURE. WE'VE LOST CONTACT.
DON'T WORRY. THEY'LL COME TO US.
AH, STORM.
I'M SORRY.
SO AM I.
ZARK
HEY, CHARLIE.

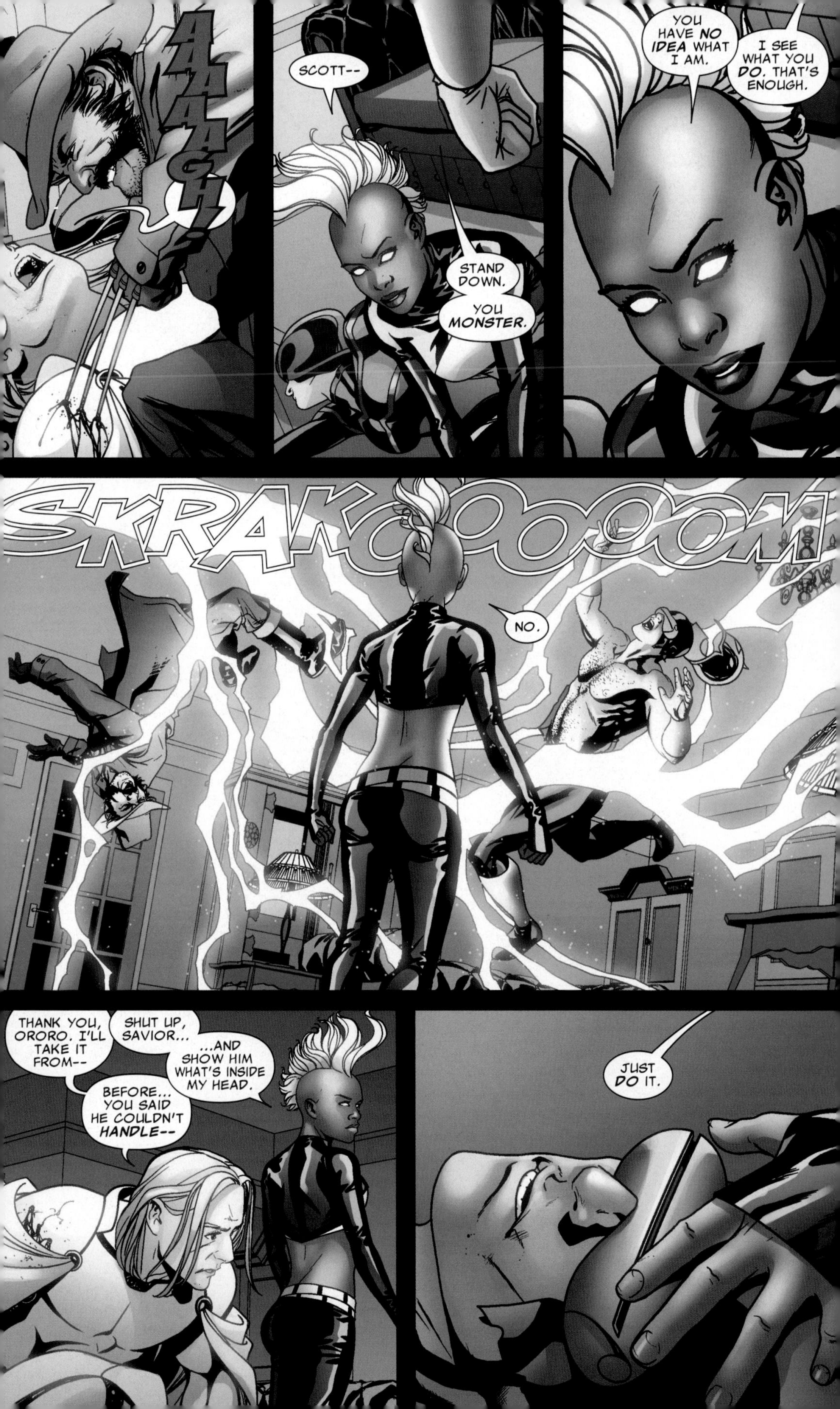
AAAAAGH!
SCOTT--
STAND DOWN.
YOU MONSTER.
YOU HAVE NO IDEA WHAT I AM.
I SEE WHAT YOU DO. THAT'S ENOUGH.
SKRAKOOOOOM
NO.
THANK YOU, ORORO. I'LL TAKE IT FROM--
SHUT UP, SAVIOR...
...AND SHOW HIM WHAT'S INSIDE MY HEAD.
BEFORE... YOU SAID HE COULDN'T HANDLE--
JUST DO IT.

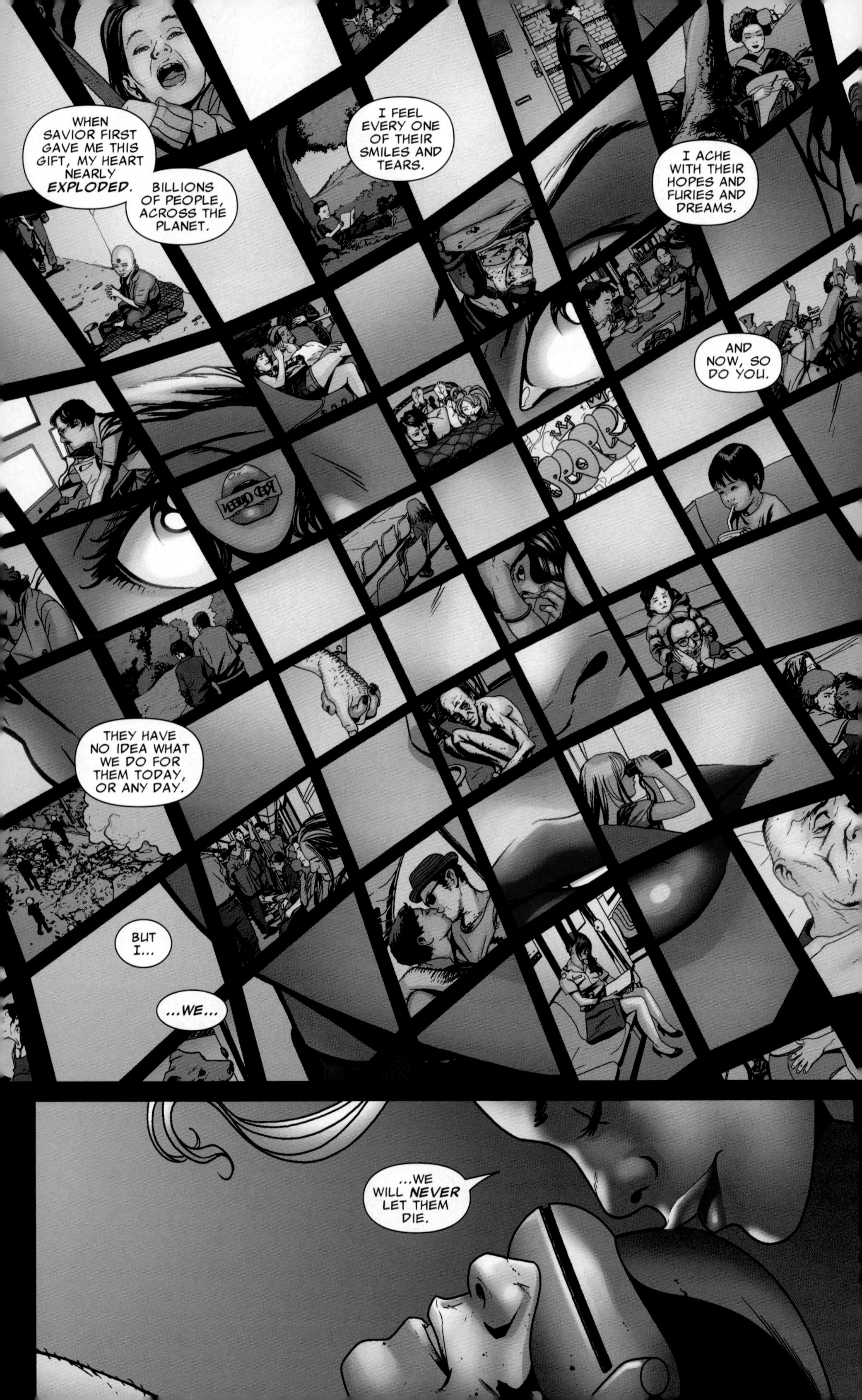
WHEN SAVIOR FIRST GAVE ME THIS GIFT, MY HEART NEARLY EXPLODED.
BILLIONS OF PEOPLE, ACROSS THE PLANET.
I FEEL EVERY ONE OF THEIR SMILES AND TEARS.
I ACHE WITH THEIR HOPES AND FURIES AND DREAMS.
AND NOW, SO DO YOU.
RED QUEEN
THEY HAVE NO IDEA WHAT WE DO FOR THEM TODAY, OR ANY DAY.
BUT I...
...WE...
...WE WILL NEVER LET THEM DIE.

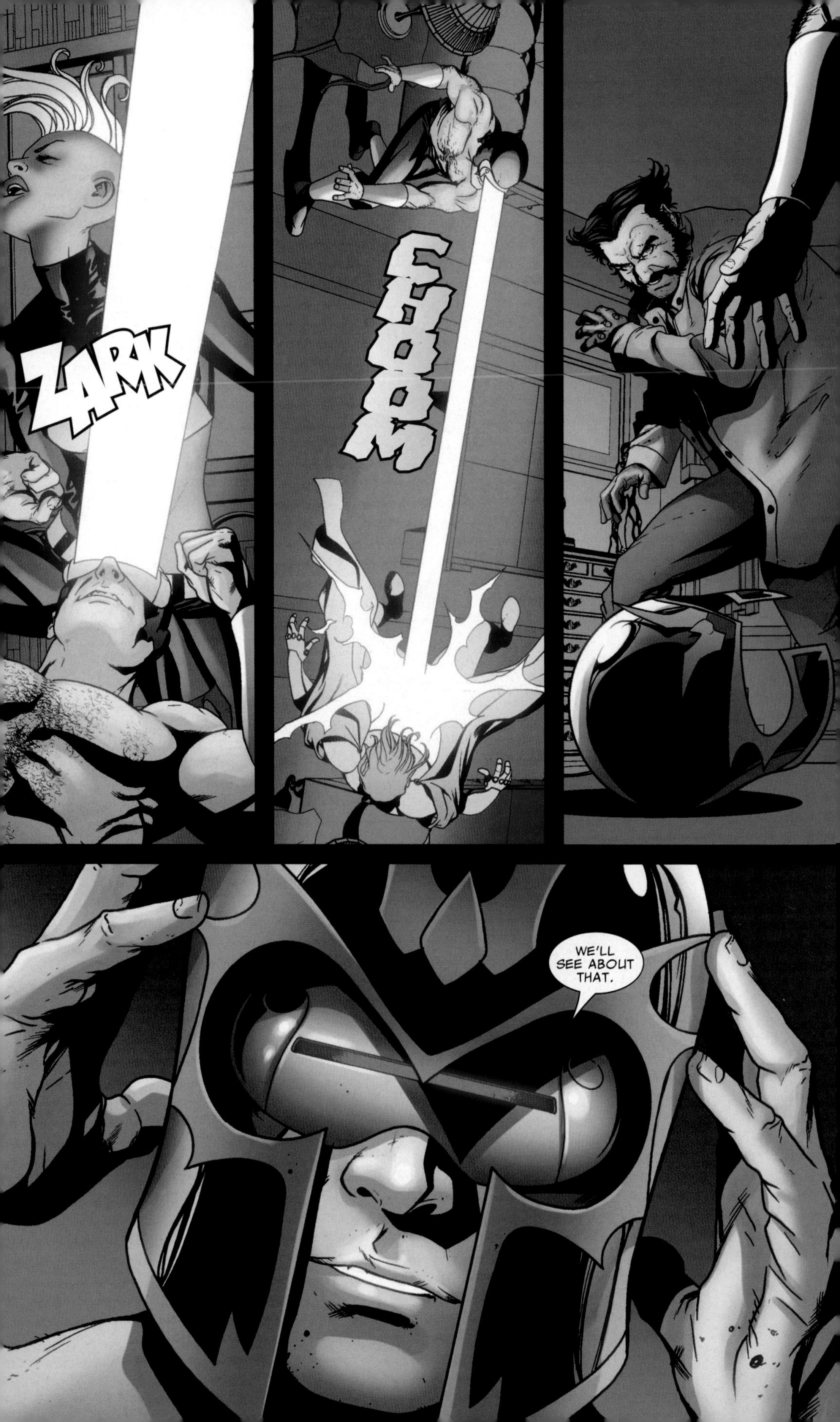
ZARK
CHOOM
WE'LL SEE ABOUT THAT.

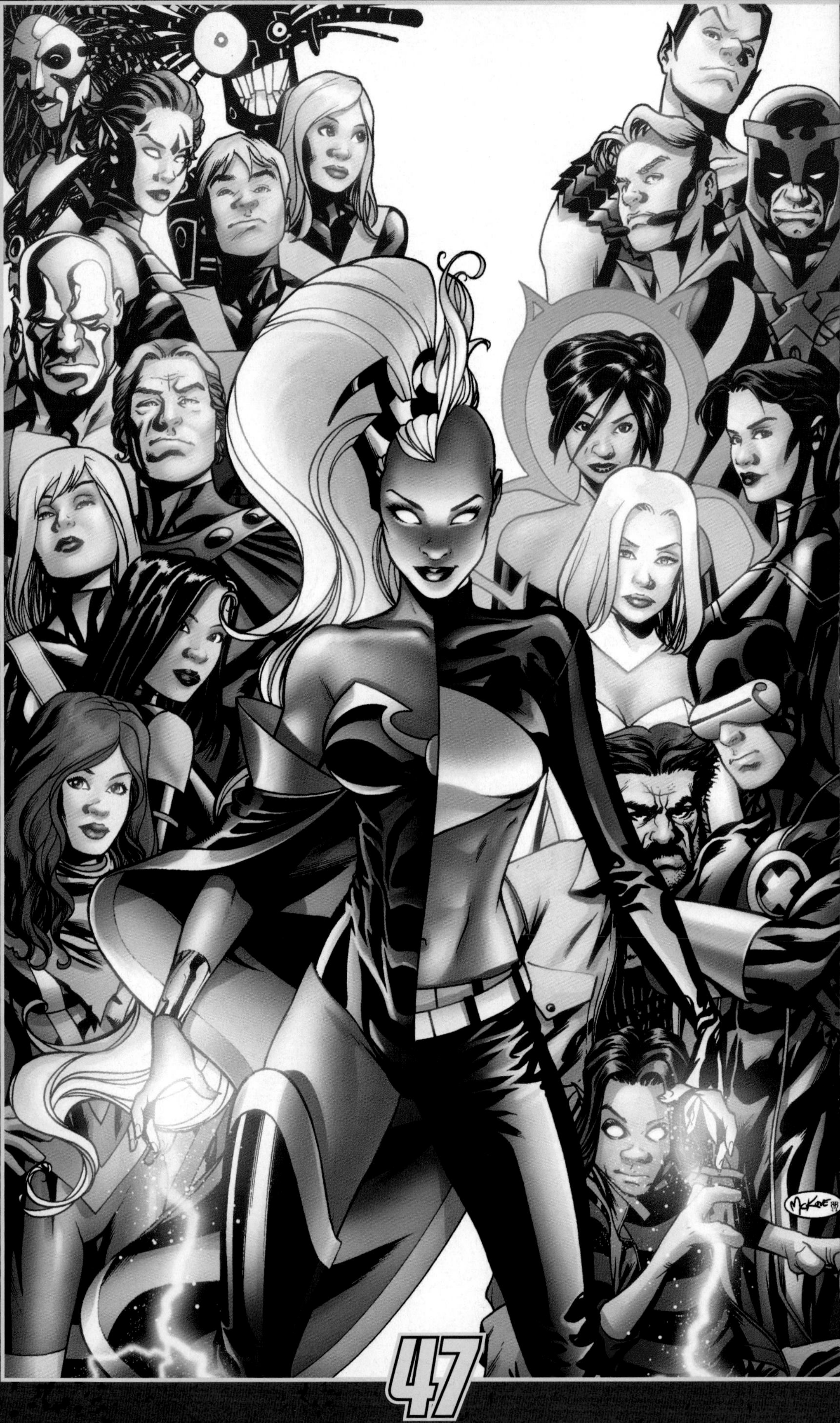
47

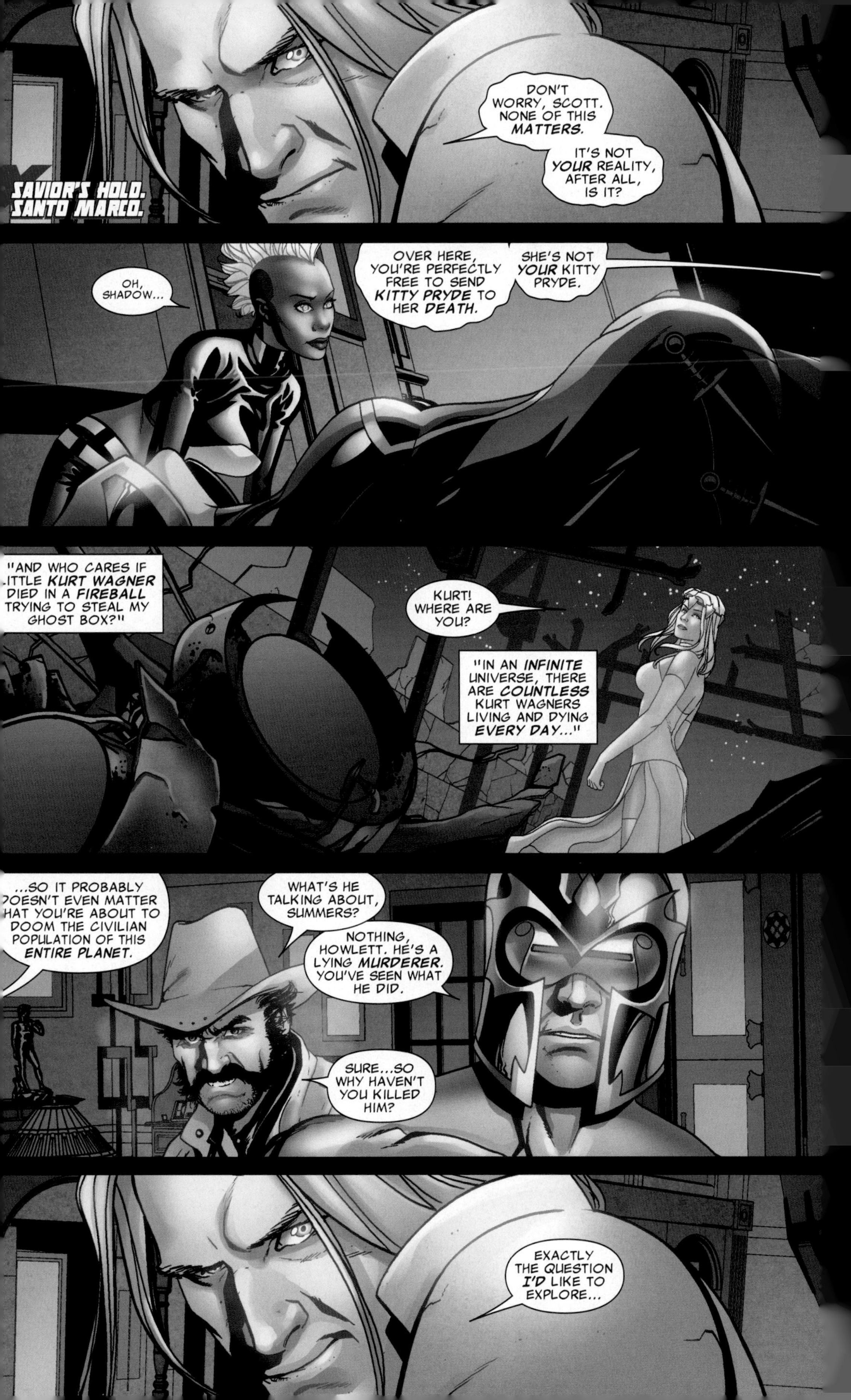
SAVIOR'S HOLD. SANTO MARCO.
DON'T WORRY, SCOTT. NONE OF THIS MATTERS.
IT'S NOT YOUR REALITY, AFTER ALL, IS IT?
OH, SHADOW...
OVER HERE, YOU'RE PERFECTLY FREE TO SEND KITTY PRYDE TO HER DEATH.
SHE'S NOT YOUR KITTY PRYDE.
"AND WHO CARES IF LITTLE KURT WAGNER DIED IN A FIREBALL TRYING TO STEAL MY GHOST BOX?"
KURT! WHERE ARE YOU?
"IN AN INFINITE UNIVERSE, THERE ARE COUNTLESS KURT WAGNERS LIVING AND DYING EVERY DAY..."
...SO IT PROBABLY DOESN'T EVEN MATTER THAT YOU'RE ABOUT TO DOOM THE CIVILIAN POPULATION OF THIS ENTIRE PLANET.
WHAT'S HE TALKING ABOUT, SUMMERS?
NOTHING, HOWLETT. HE'S A LYING MURDERER. YOU'VE SEEN WHAT HE DID.
SURE...SO WHY HAVEN'T YOU KILLED HIM?
EXACTLY THE QUESTION I'D LIKE TO EXPLORE...

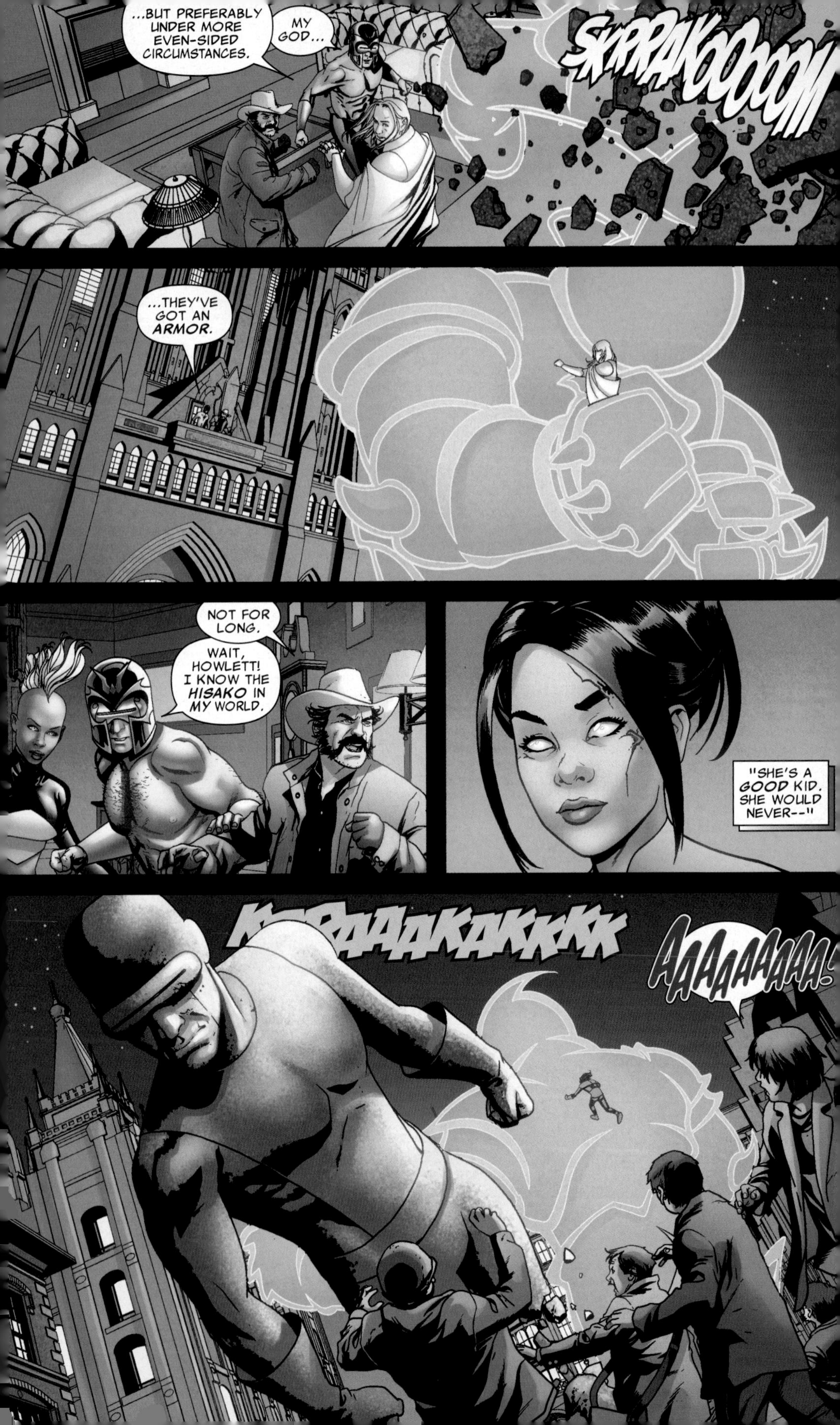
...BUT PREFERABLY UNDER MORE EVEN-SIDED CIRCUMSTANCES.
MY GOD...
SKRRAKOOOOOM
...THEY'VE GOT AN ARMOR.
NOT FOR LONG.
WAIT, HOWLETT! I KNOW THE HISAKO IN MY WORLD.
"SHE'S A GOOD KID. SHE WOULD NEVER--"
AAAAAAAAA!

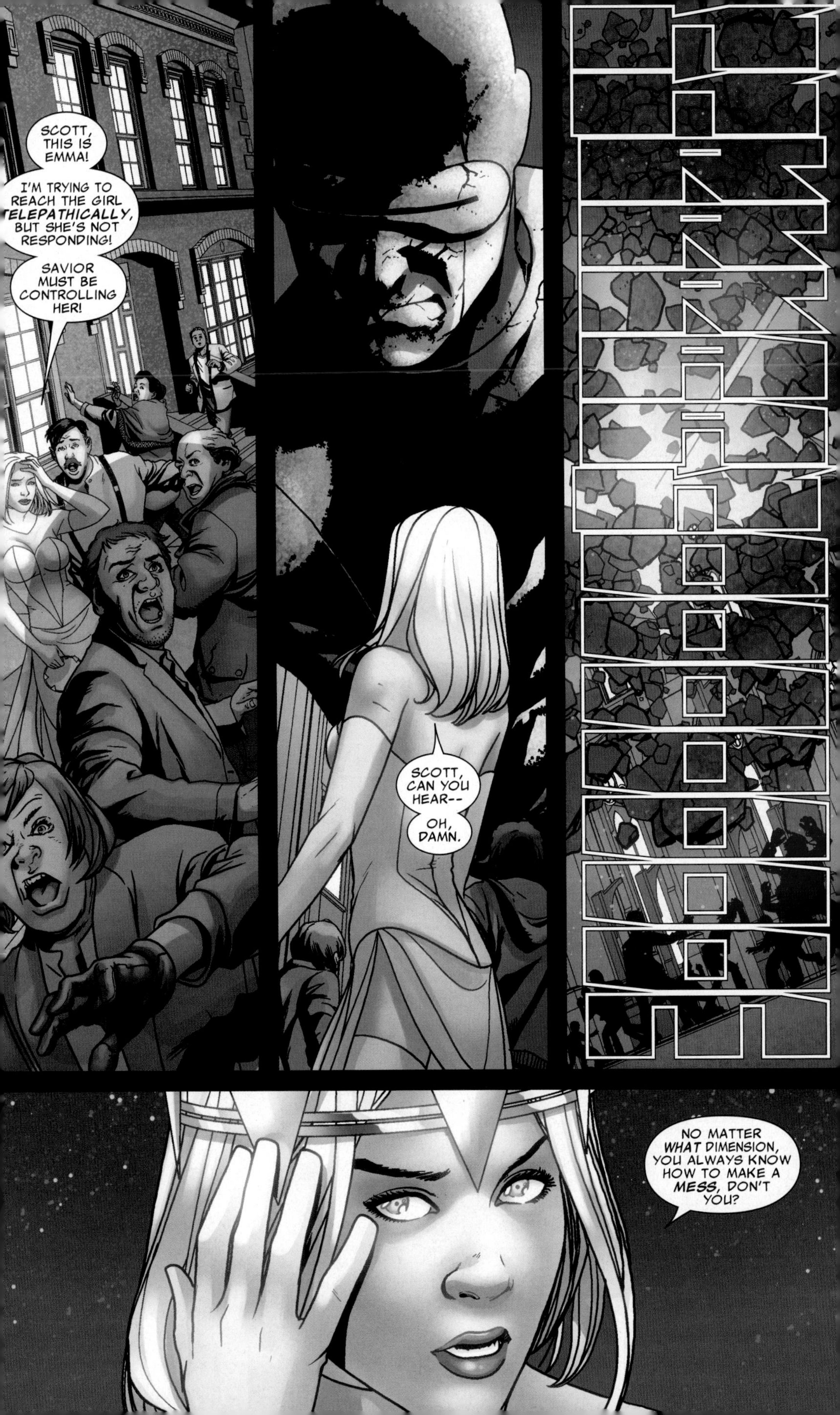
SCOTT, THIS IS EMMA!
I'M TRYING TO REACH THE GIRL *TELEPATHICALLY*, BUT SHE'S NOT RESPONDING!
SAVIOR MUST BE CONTROLLING HER!
SCOTT, CAN YOU HEAR--
OH, DAMN.
NO MATTER *WHAT* DIMENSION, YOU ALWAYS KNOW HOW TO MAKE A *MESS*, DON'T YOU?

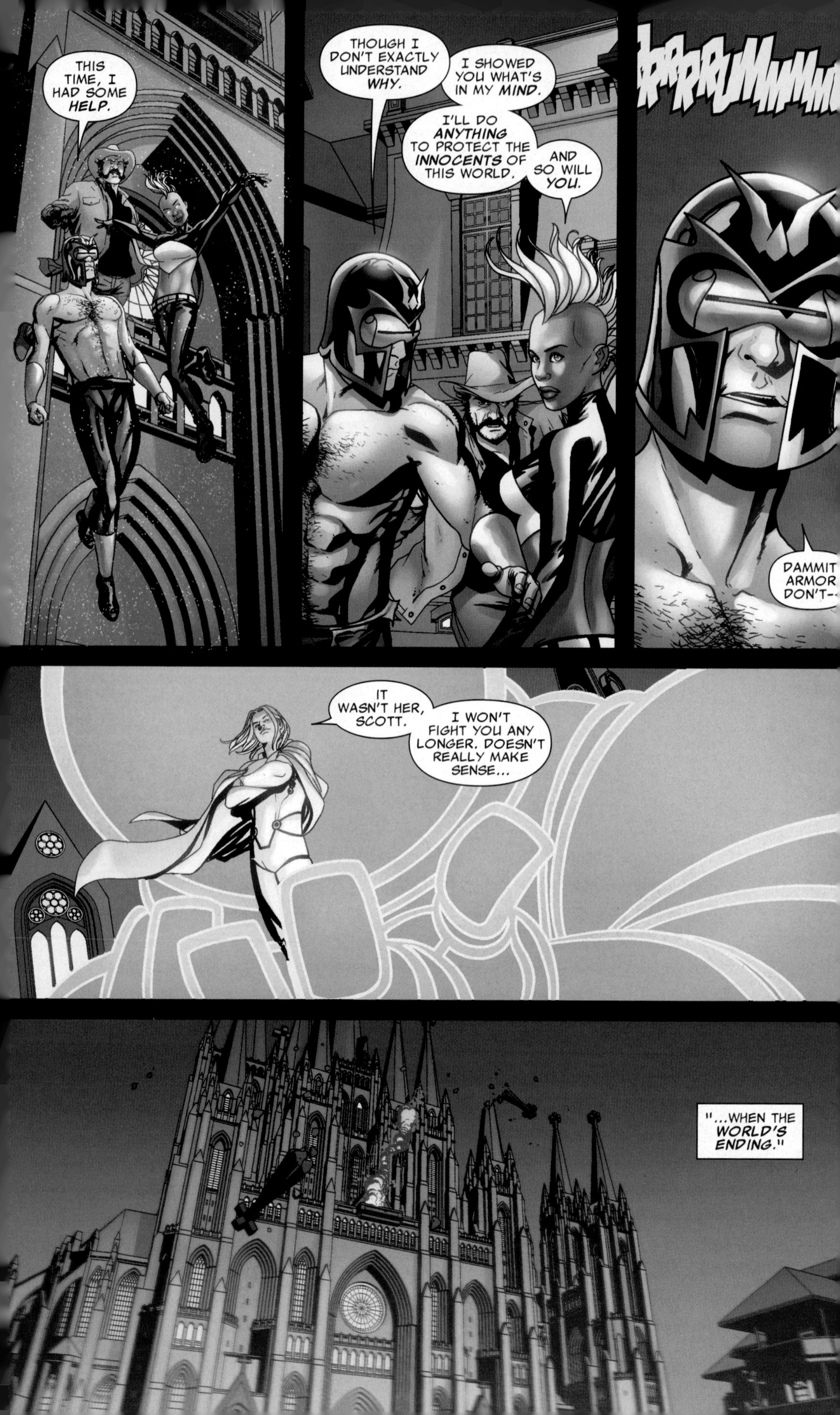
THIS TIME, I HAD SOME HELP.
THOUGH I DON'T EXACTLY UNDERSTAND WHY.
I SHOWED YOU WHAT'S IN MY MIND.
I'LL DO ANYTHING TO PROTECT THE INNOCENTS OF THIS WORLD.
AND SO WILL YOU.
DAMMIT ARMOR DON'T--
IT WASN'T HER, SCOTT.
I WON'T FIGHT YOU ANY LONGER. DOESN'T REALLY MAKE SENSE...
"...WHEN THE WORLD'S ENDING."

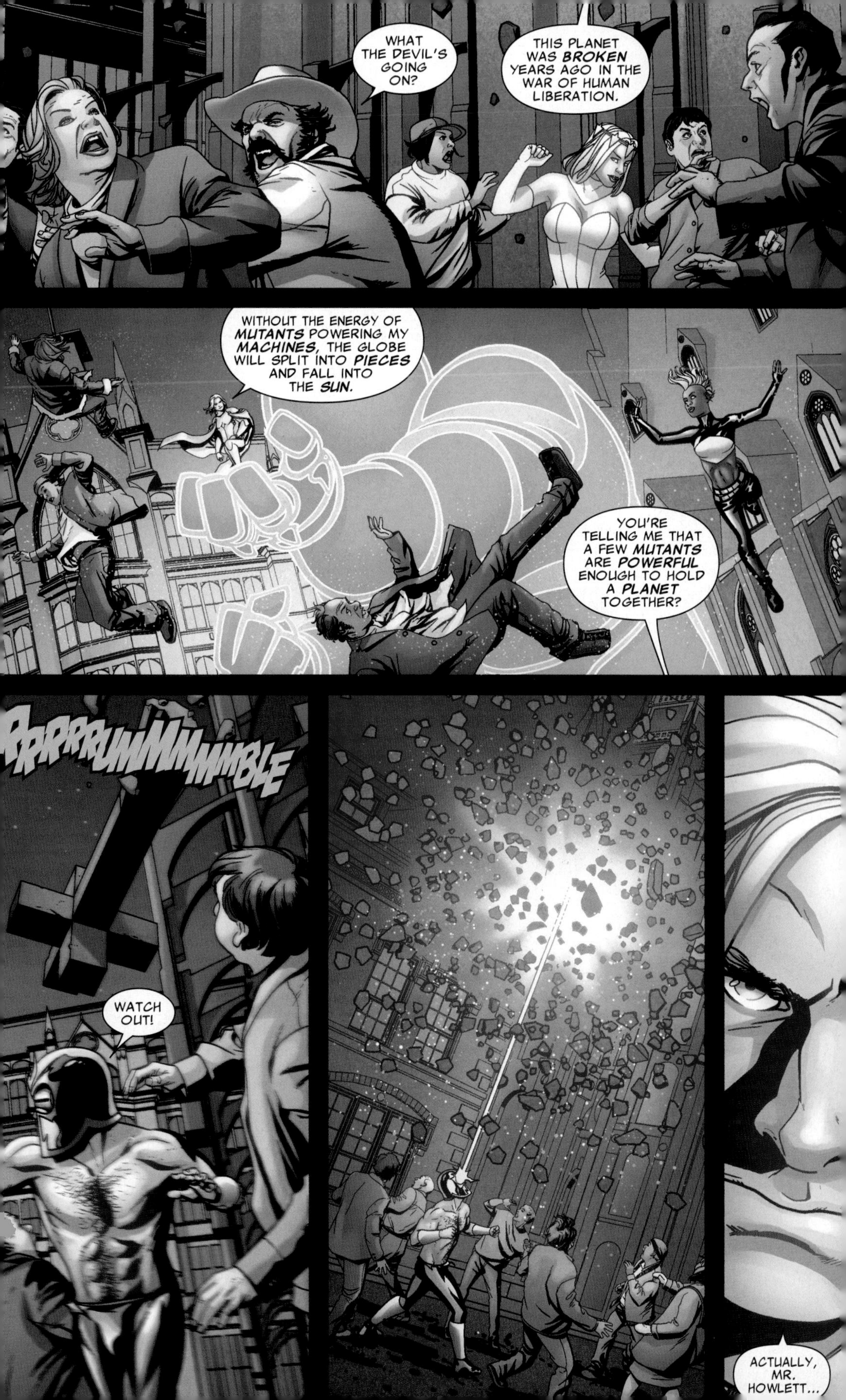

WHAT THE DEVIL'S GOING ON?
THIS PLANET WAS **BROKEN** YEARS AGO IN THE WAR OF HUMAN LIBERATION.
WITHOUT THE ENERGY OF ***MUTANTS*** POWERING MY ***MACHINES***, THE GLOBE WILL SPLIT INTO ***PIECES*** AND FALL INTO THE ***SUN.***
YOU'RE TELLING ME THAT A FEW ***MUTANTS*** ARE ***POWERFUL*** ENOUGH TO HOLD A ***PLANET*** TOGETHER?
RRRRRUMMMMMMBLE
WATCH OUT!
ACTUALLY, MR. HOWLETT...

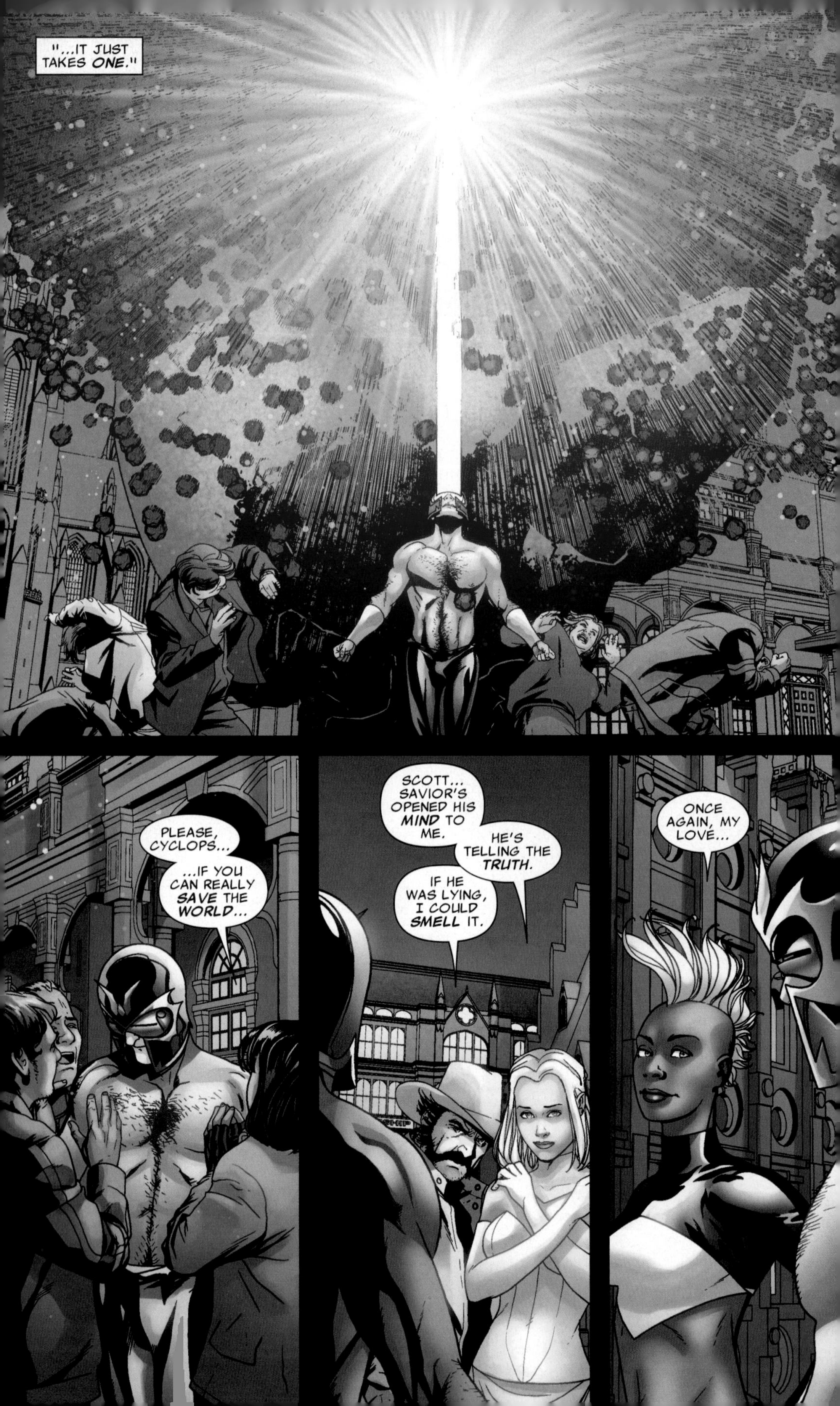
"...IT JUST TAKES ONE."
PLEASE, CYCLOPS...
...IF YOU CAN REALLY SAVE THE WORLD...
SCOTT... SAVIOR'S OPENED HIS MIND TO ME.
HE'S TELLING THE TRUTH.
IF HE WAS LYING, I COULD SMELL IT.
ONCE AGAIN, MY LOVE...

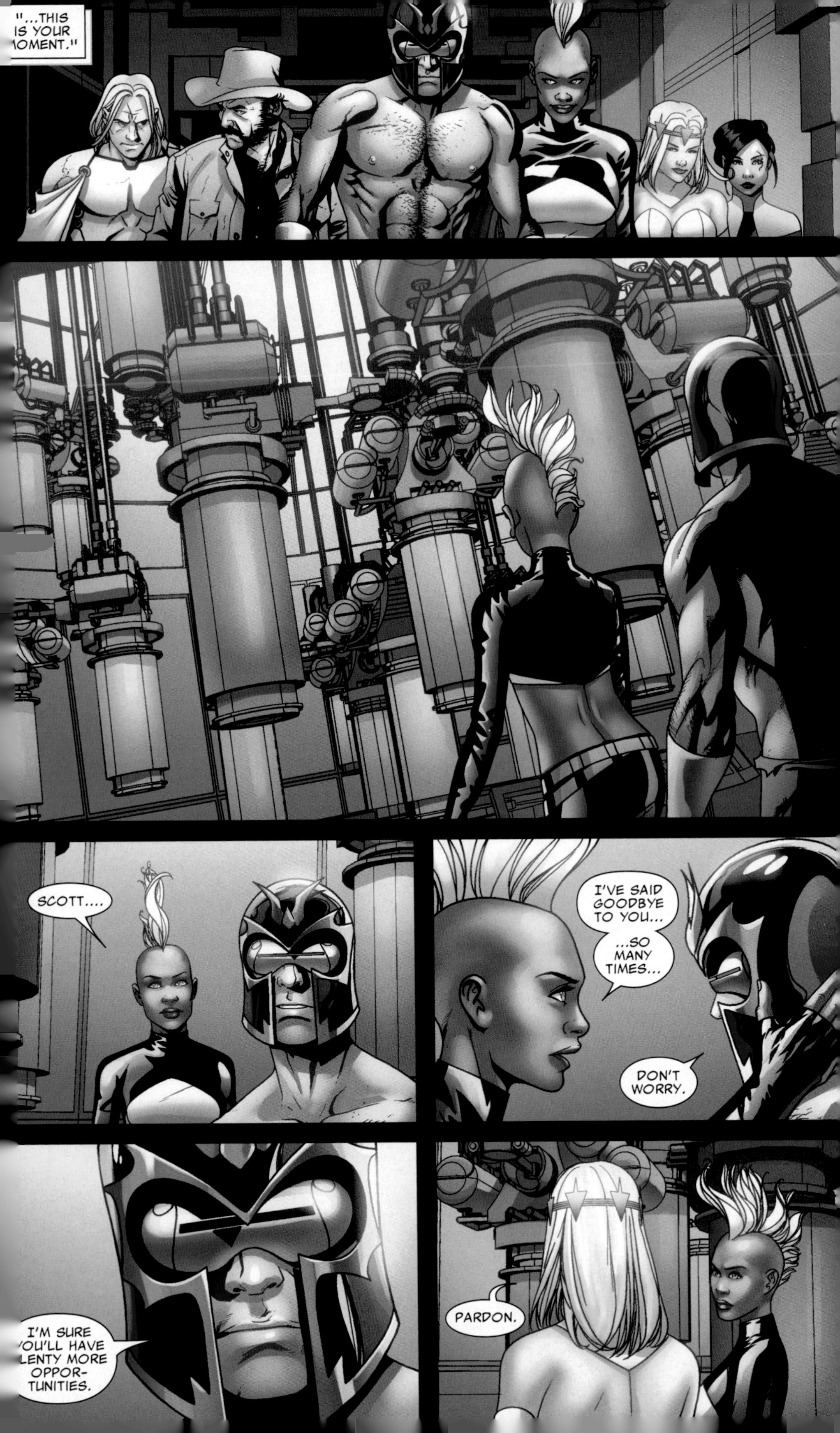
"...THIS
IS YOUR
MOMENT."
SCOTT....
I'VE SAID GOODBYE TO YOU...
...SO MANY TIMES...
DON'T WORRY.
I'M SURE YOU'LL HAVE PLENTY MORE OPPOR-TUNITIES.
PARDON.

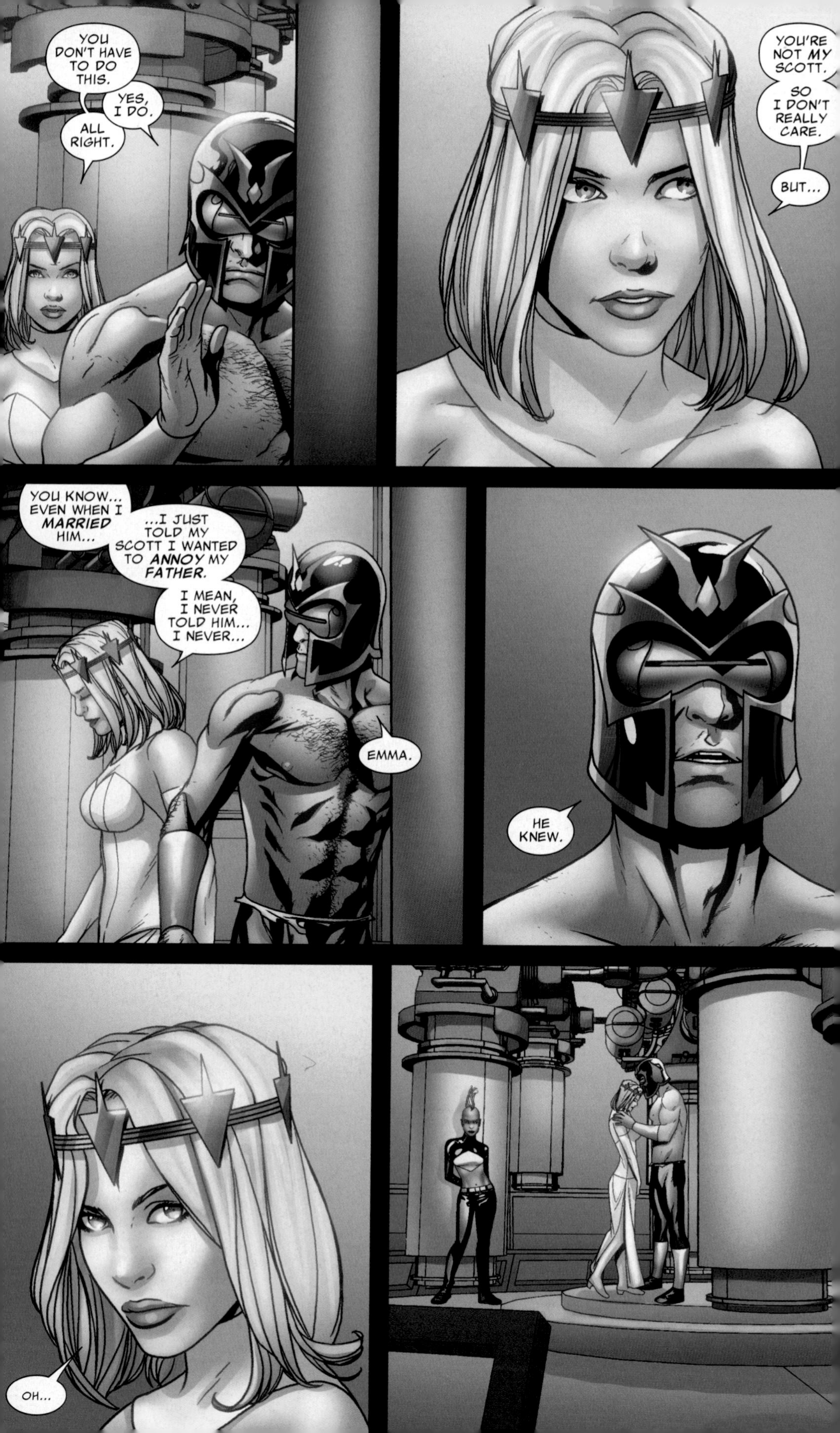
YOU DON'T HAVE TO DO THIS.
YES, I DO.
ALL RIGHT.
YOU'RE NOT MY SCOTT.
SO I DON'T REALLY CARE.
BUT...
YOU KNOW... EVEN WHEN I MARRIED HIM...
...I JUST TOLD MY SCOTT I WANTED TO ANNOY MY FATHER.
I MEAN, I NEVER TOLD HIM... I NEVER...
EMMA.
HE KNEW.
OH...

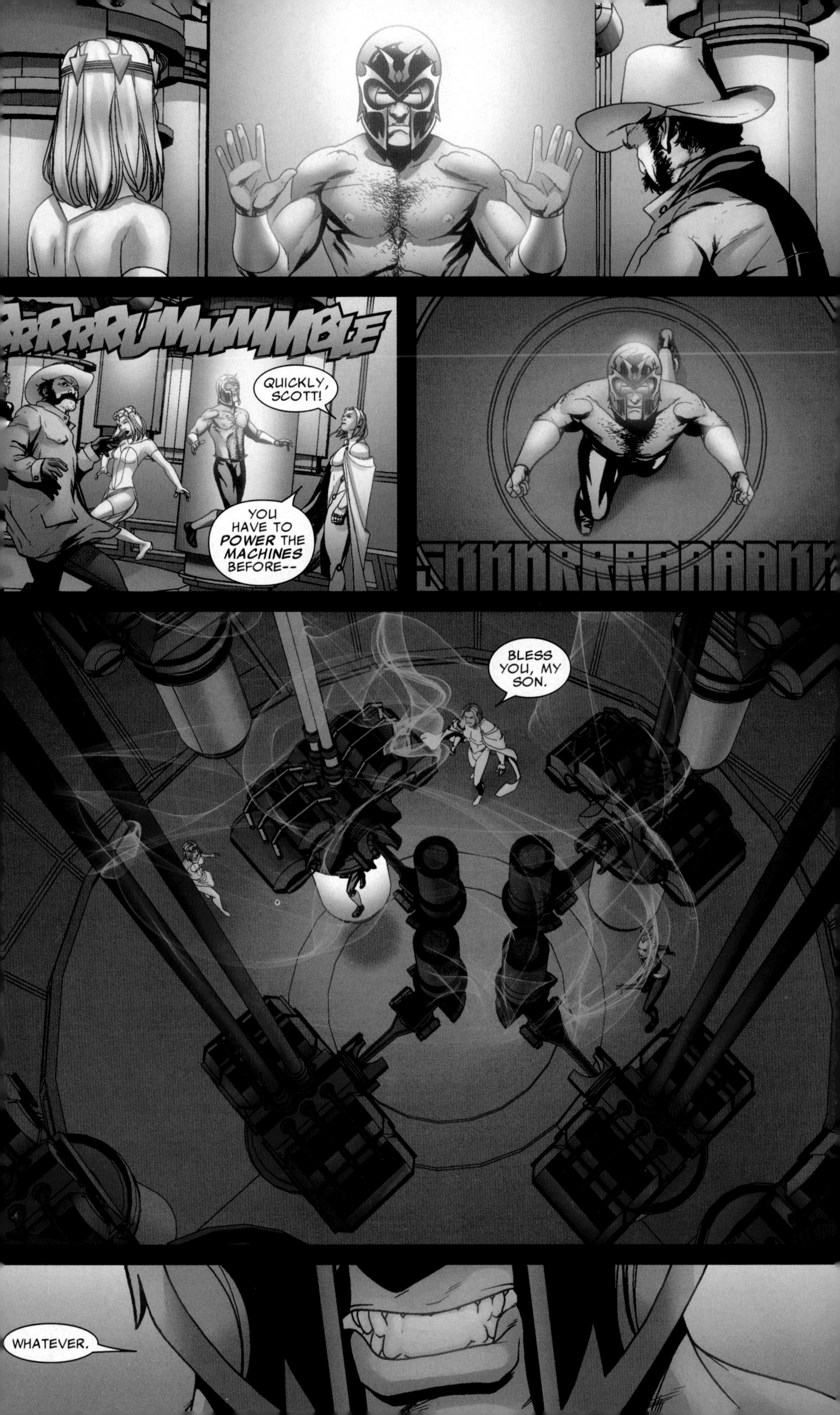
RRRRRUMMMMMBLE
QUICKLY, SCOTT!
YOU HAVE TO POWER THE MACHINES BEFORE--
KKKRRRRAAAKK
BLESS YOU, MY SON.
WHATEVER.

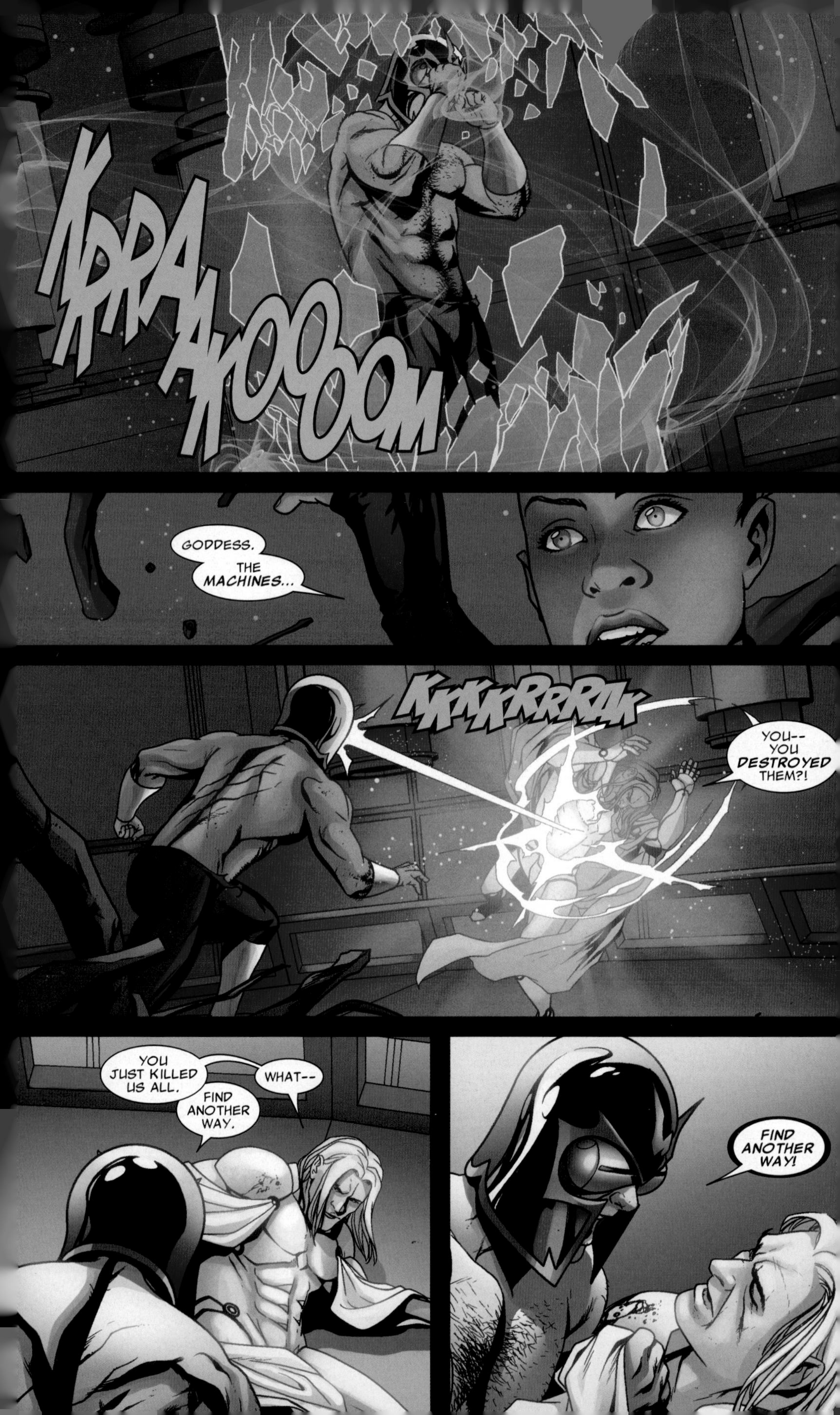
KRRAKOOOOOM
GODDESS. THE MACHINES...
KKKKRRRRAK
YOU-- YOU DESTROYED THEM?!
YOU JUST KILLED US ALL.
WHAT--
FIND ANOTHER WAY.
FIND ANOTHER WAY!

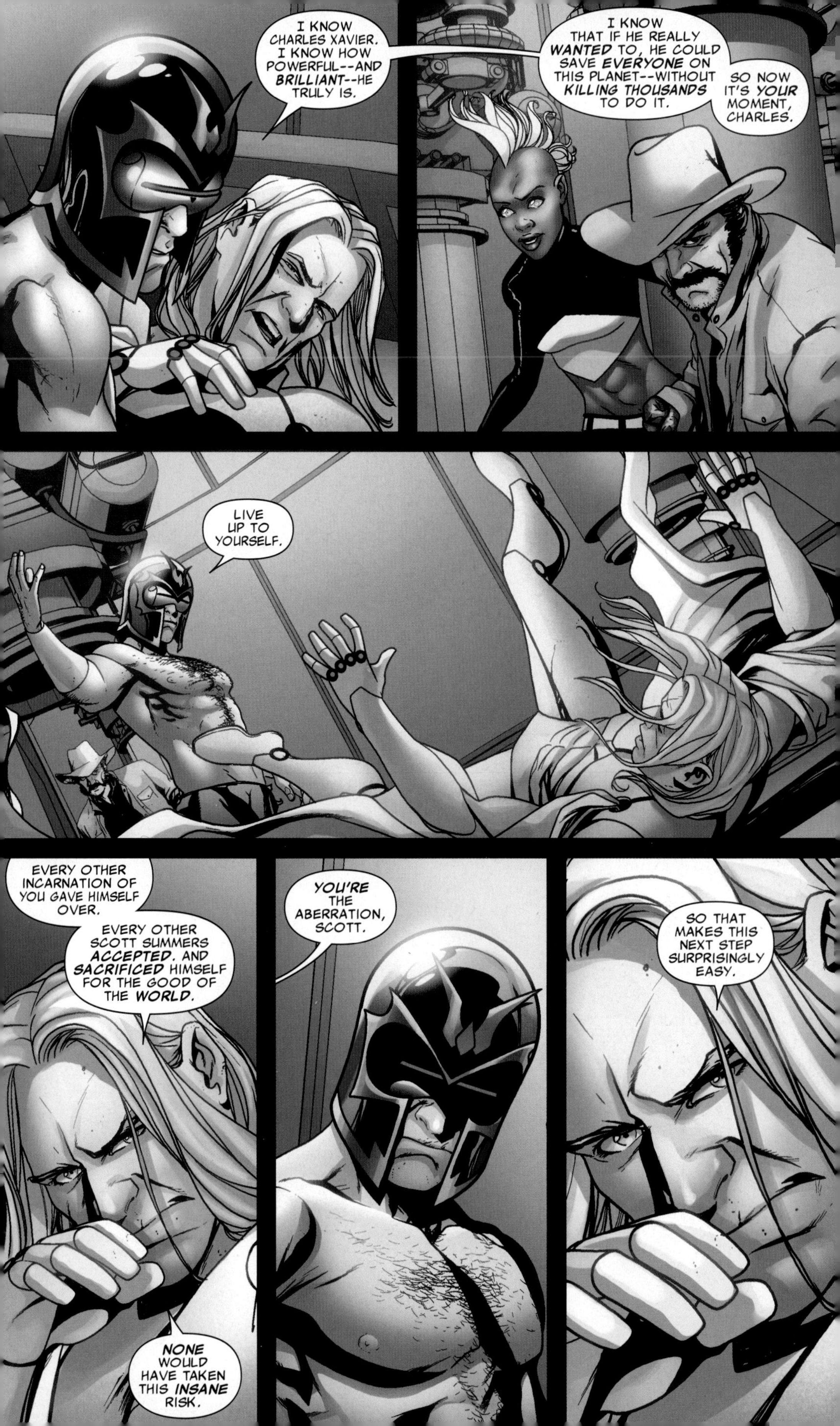
I KNOW CHARLES XAVIER. I KNOW HOW POWERFUL--AND **BRILLIANT**--HE TRULY IS.
I KNOW THAT IF HE REALLY **WANTED** TO, HE COULD SAVE **EVERYONE** ON THIS PLANET--WITHOUT **KILLING THOUSANDS** TO DO IT.
SO NOW IT'S **YOUR** MOMENT, CHARLES.
LIVE UP TO YOURSELF.
EVERY OTHER INCARNATION OF YOU GAVE HIMSELF OVER.
EVERY OTHER SCOTT SUMMERS **ACCEPTED**. AND **SACRIFICED** HIMSELF FOR THE GOOD OF THE **WORLD**.
NONE WOULD HAVE TAKEN THIS **INSANE** RISK.
YOU'RE THE ABERRATION, SCOTT.
SO THAT MAKES THIS NEXT STEP SURPRISINGLY EASY.

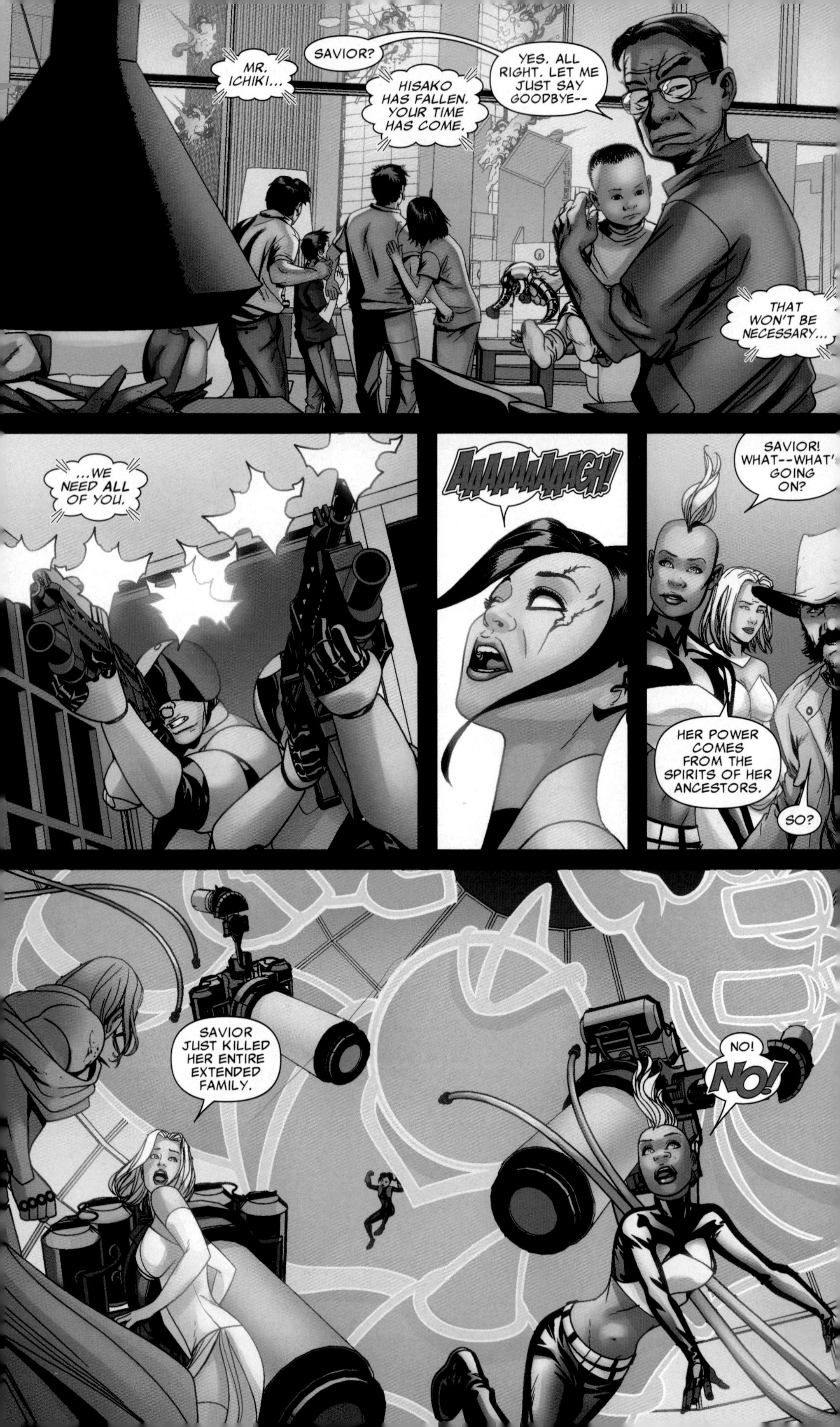
MR. ICHIKI...
SAVIOR?
HISAKO HAS FALLEN. YOUR TIME HAS COME.
YES. ALL RIGHT. LET ME JUST SAY GOODBYE--
THAT WON'T BE NECESSARY...
...WE NEED ALL OF YOU.
AAAAAAAAAGH!
SAVIOR! WHAT--WHAT'S GOING ON?
HER POWER COMES FROM THE SPIRITS OF HER ANCESTORS.
SO?
SAVIOR JUST KILLED HER ENTIRE EXTENDED FAMILY.
NO!
NO!

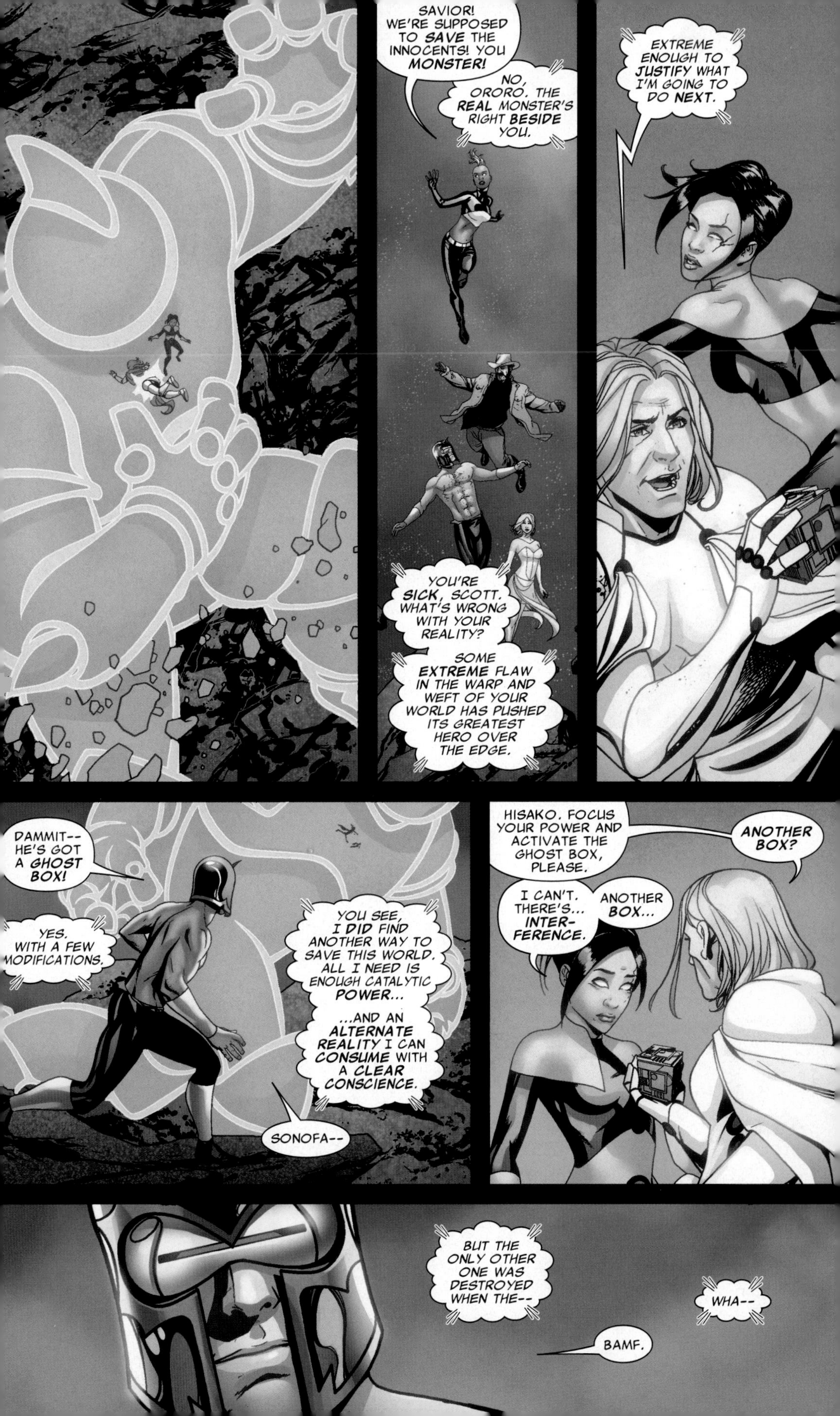
SAVIOR! WE'RE SUPPOSED TO SAVE THE INNOCENTS! YOU MONSTER!
NO, ORORO. THE REAL MONSTER'S RIGHT BESIDE YOU.
YOU'RE SICK, SCOTT. WHAT'S WRONG WITH YOUR REALITY?
SOME EXTREME FLAW IN THE WARP AND WEFT OF YOUR WORLD HAS PUSHED ITS GREATEST HERO OVER THE EDGE.
EXTREME ENOUGH TO JUSTIFY WHAT I'M GOING TO DO NEXT.
DAMMIT-- HE'S GOT A GHOST BOX!
YES. WITH A FEW MODIFICATIONS.
YOU SEE, I DID FIND ANOTHER WAY TO SAVE THIS WORLD. ALL I NEED IS ENOUGH CATALYTIC POWER...
...AND AN ALTERNATE REALITY I CAN CONSUME WITH A CLEAR CONSCIENCE.
SONOFA--
HISAKO. FOCUS YOUR POWER AND ACTIVATE THE GHOST BOX, PLEASE.
ANOTHER BOX?
I CAN'T. THERE'S... INTER-FERENCE.
ANOTHER BOX...
BUT THE ONLY OTHER ONE WAS DESTROYED WHEN THE--
WHA--
BAMF.

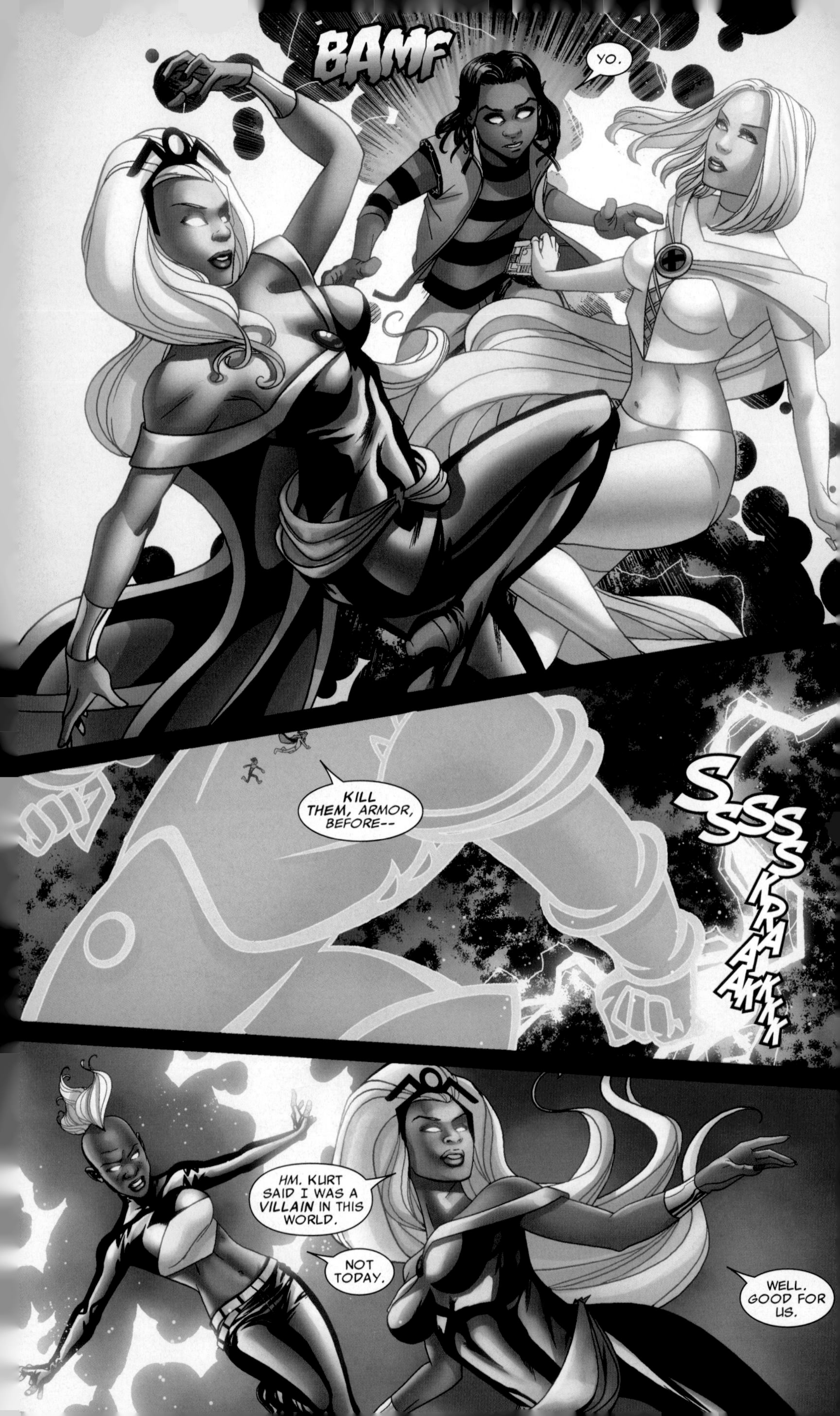
BAMF
YO.
KILL THEM, ARMOR, BEFORE--
SSSSSKRAAKKKK
HM. KURT SAID I WAS A VILLAIN IN THIS WORLD.
NOT TODAY.
WELL. GOOD FOR US.

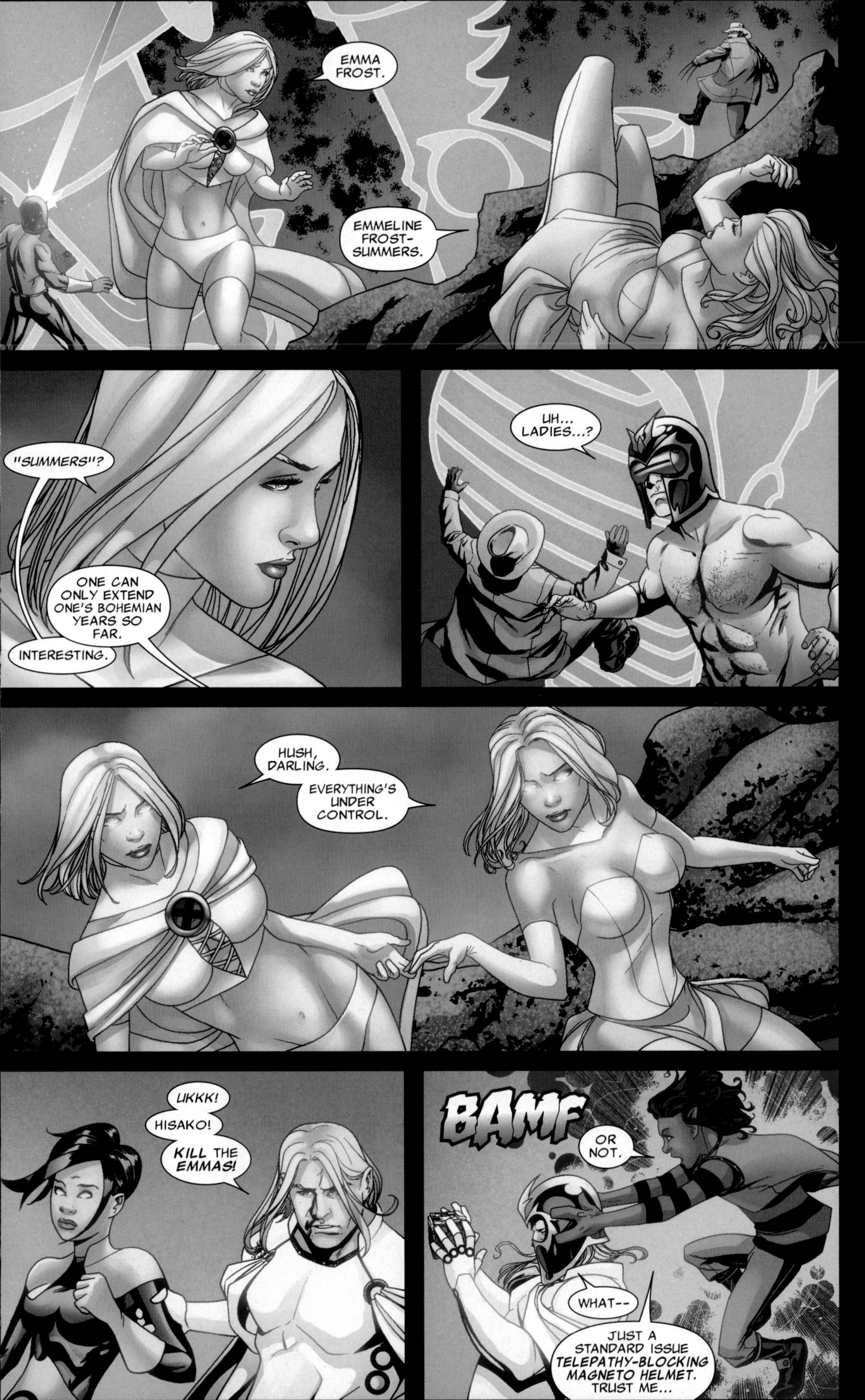
EMMA FROST.
EMMELINE FROST-SUMMERS.
"SUMMERS"?
INTERESTING.
ONE CAN ONLY EXTEND ONE'S BOHEMIAN YEARS SO FAR.
UH... LADIES...?
HUSH, DARLING.
EVERYTHING'S UNDER CONTROL.
UKKK!
HISAKO!
KILL THE EMMAS!
BAMF
OR NOT.
WHAT--
JUST A STANDARD ISSUE TELEPATHY-BLOCKING MAGNETO HELMET. TRUST ME...

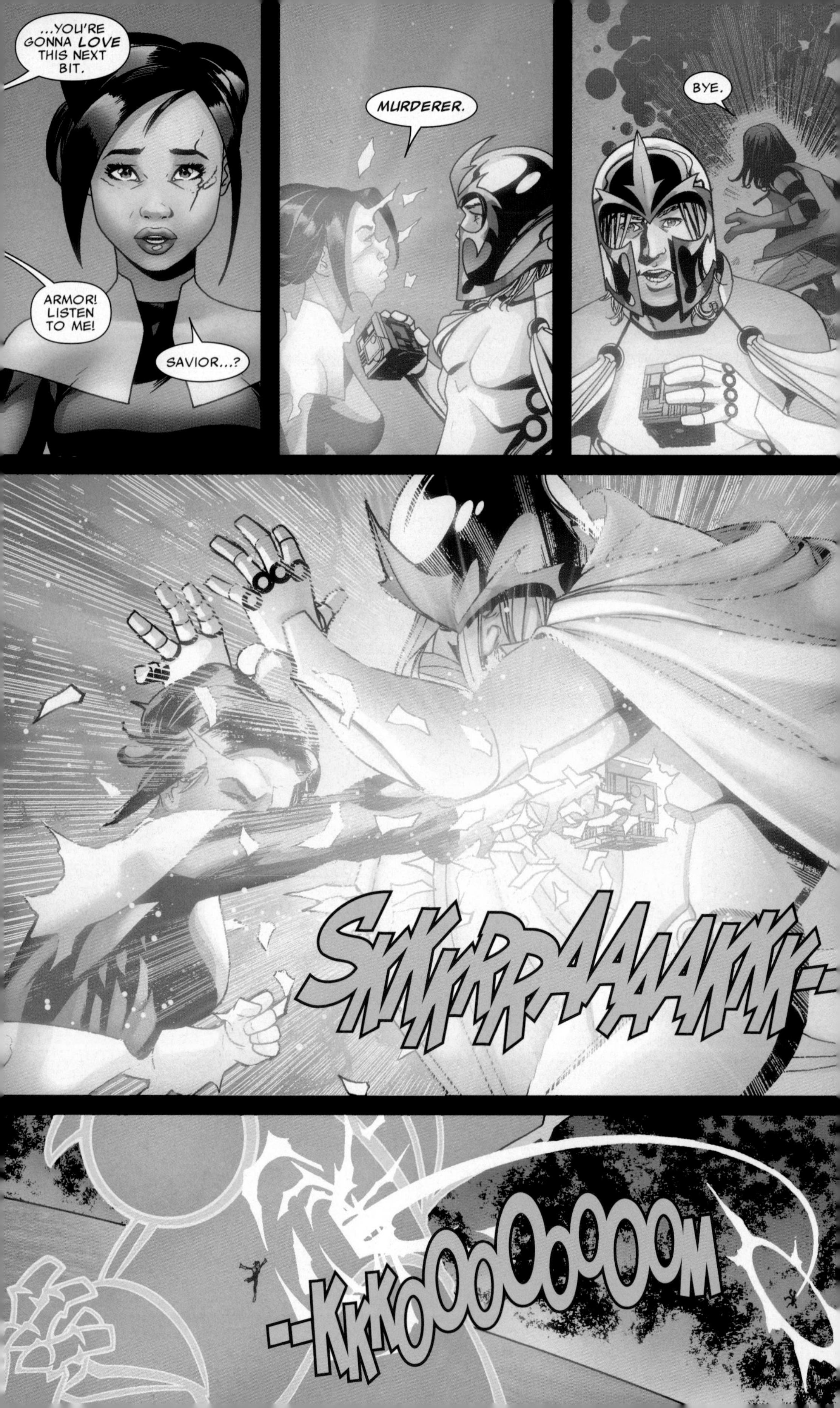

...YOU'RE GONNA LOVE THIS NEXT BIT.
ARMOR! LISTEN TO ME!
SAVIOR...?
MURDERER.
BYE.
SKKKRRAAAAKKK-
--KKKOOOOOOOOOM

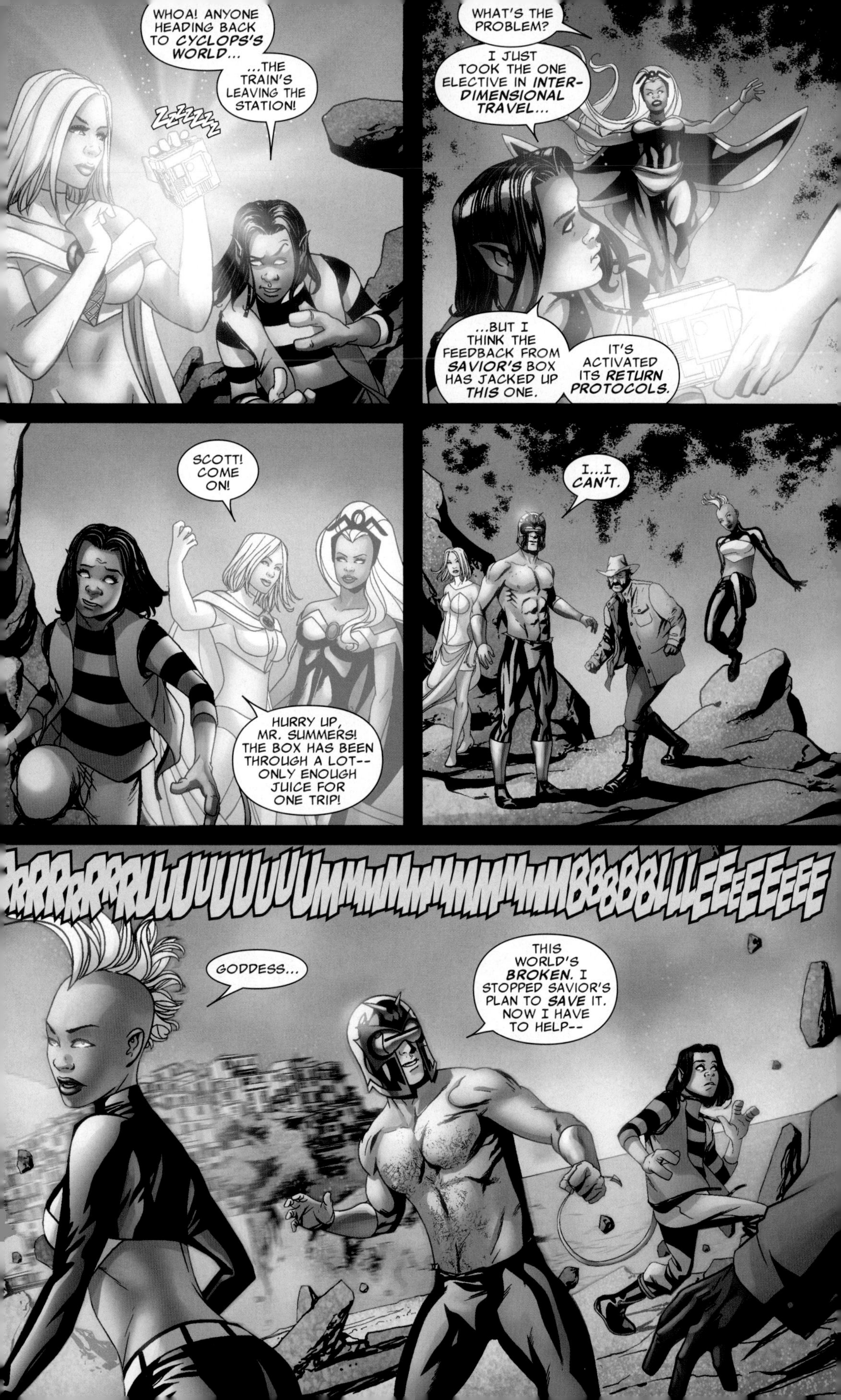

WHOA! ANYONE HEADING BACK TO *CYCLOPS'S WORLD*...
...THE TRAIN'S LEAVING THE STATION!
ZZZZZZZ
WHAT'S THE PROBLEM?
I JUST TOOK THE ONE ELECTIVE IN *INTER-DIMENSIONAL TRAVEL*...
...BUT I THINK THE FEEDBACK FROM *SAVIOR'S* BOX HAS JACKED UP *THIS* ONE.
IT'S ACTIVATED ITS *RETURN PROTOCOLS*.
SCOTT! COME ON!
HURRY UP, MR. SUMMERS! THE BOX HAS BEEN THROUGH A LOT-- ONLY ENOUGH JUICE FOR ONE TRIP!
I...I *CAN'T*.
RRRRRRRUUUUUUUUMMMMMMMMMMMMMMBBBBBLLEEEEEEEE
GODDESS...
THIS WORLD'S *BROKEN*. I STOPPED SAVIOR'S PLAN TO *SAVE* IT. NOW I HAVE TO HELP--

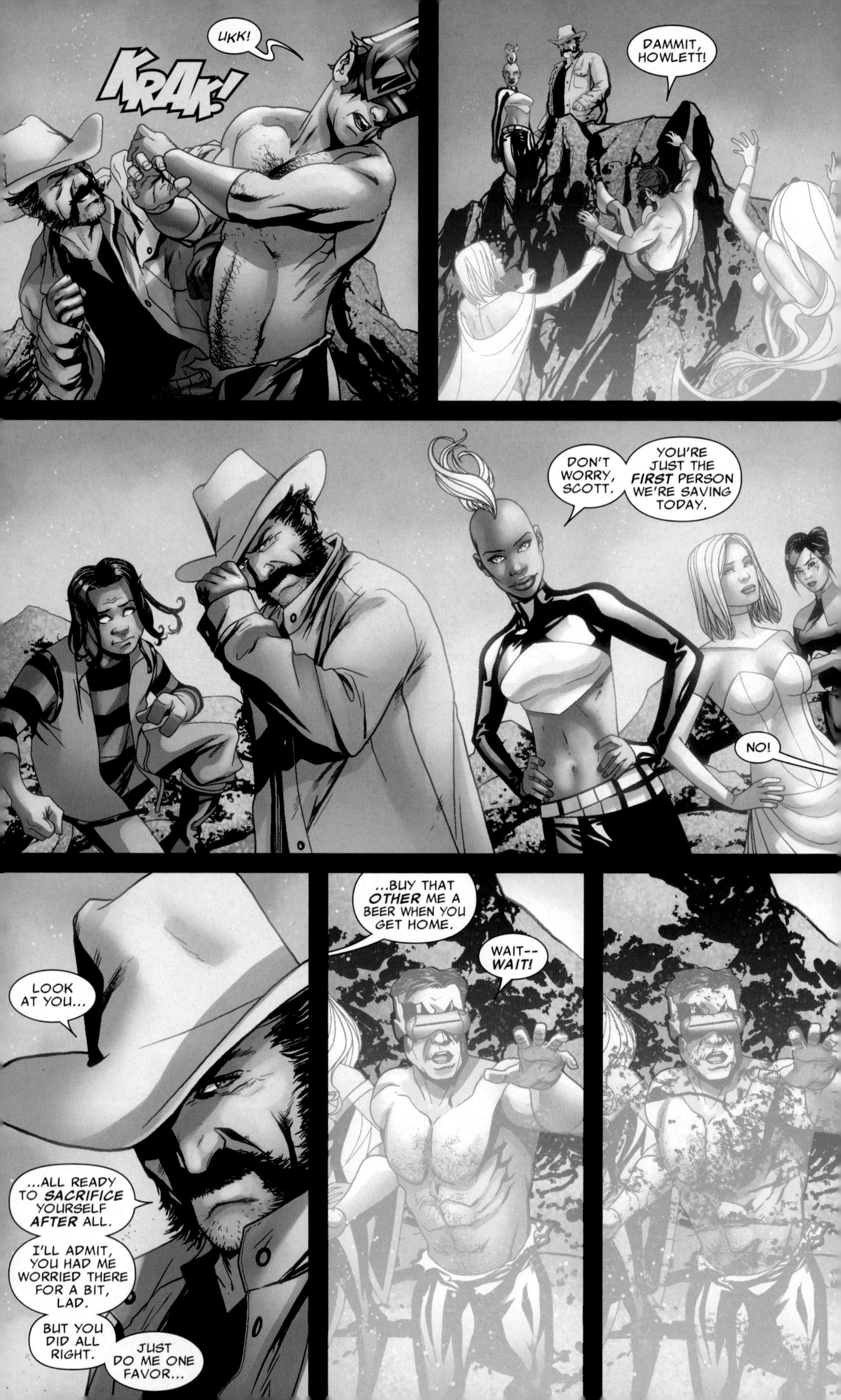
KRAK!
UKK!
DAMMIT, HOWLETT!
DON'T WORRY, SCOTT.
YOU'RE JUST THE FIRST PERSON WE'RE SAVING TODAY.
NO!
LOOK AT YOU...
...ALL READY TO SACRIFICE YOURSELF AFTER ALL.
I'LL ADMIT, YOU HAD ME WORRIED THERE FOR A BIT, LAD.
BUT YOU DID ALL RIGHT.
JUST DO ME ONE FAVOR...
...BUY THAT OTHER ME A BEER WHEN YOU GET HOME.
WAIT-- WAIT!

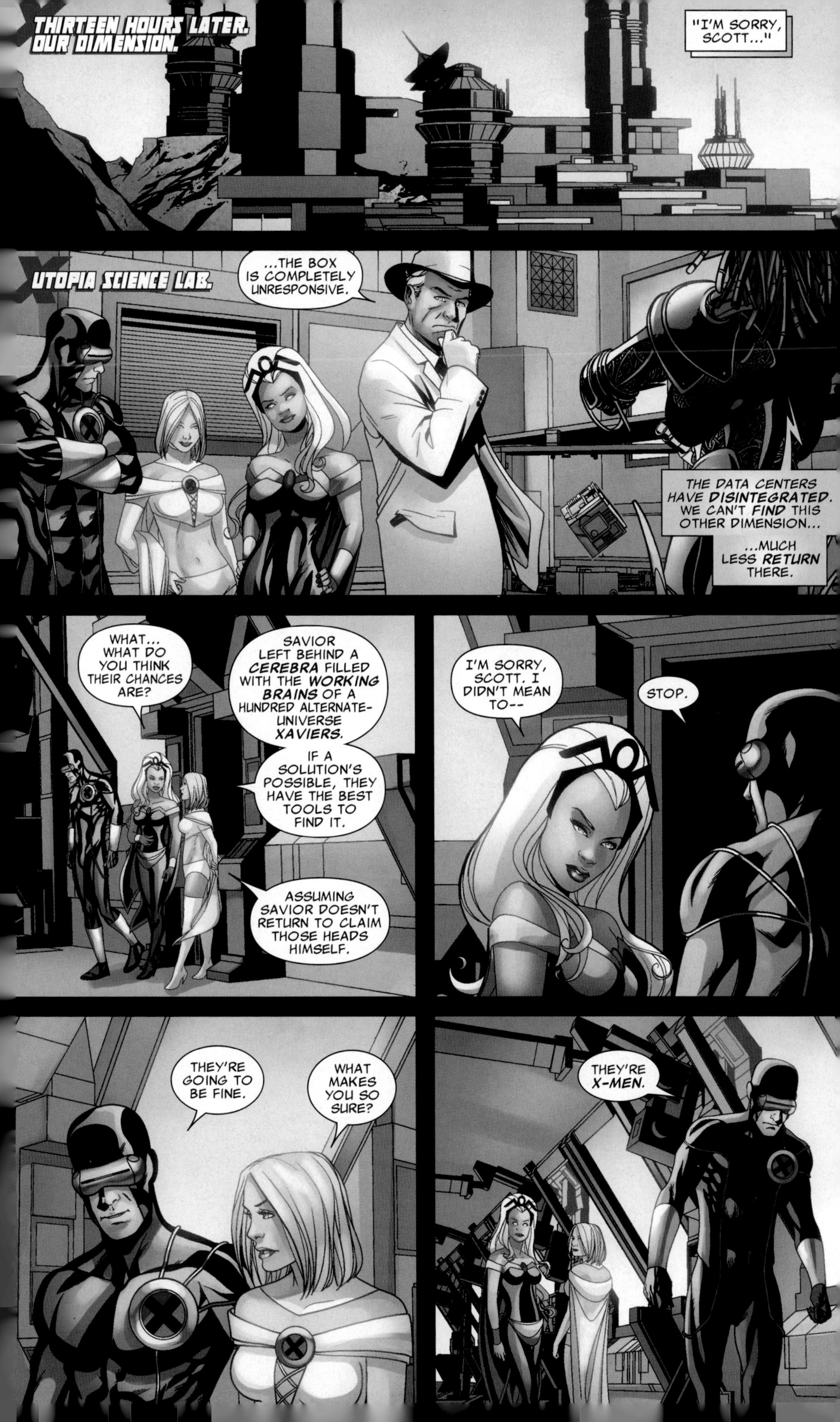
THIRTEEN HOURS LATER. OUR DIMENSION.
"I'M SORRY, SCOTT..."
UTOPIA SCIENCE LAB.
...THE BOX IS COMPLETELY UNRESPONSIVE.
THE DATA CENTERS HAVE DISINTEGRATED. WE CAN'T FIND THIS OTHER DIMENSION...
...MUCH LESS RETURN THERE.
WHAT... WHAT DO YOU THINK THEIR CHANCES ARE?
SAVIOR LEFT BEHIND A CEREBRA FILLED WITH THE WORKING BRAINS OF A HUNDRED ALTERNATE-UNIVERSE XAVIERS.
IF A SOLUTION'S POSSIBLE, THEY HAVE THE BEST TOOLS TO FIND IT.
ASSUMING SAVIOR DOESN'T RETURN TO CLAIM THOSE HEADS HIMSELF.
I'M SORRY, SCOTT. I DIDN'T MEAN TO--
STOP.
THEY'RE GOING TO BE FINE.
WHAT MAKES YOU SO SURE?
THEY'RE X-MEN.

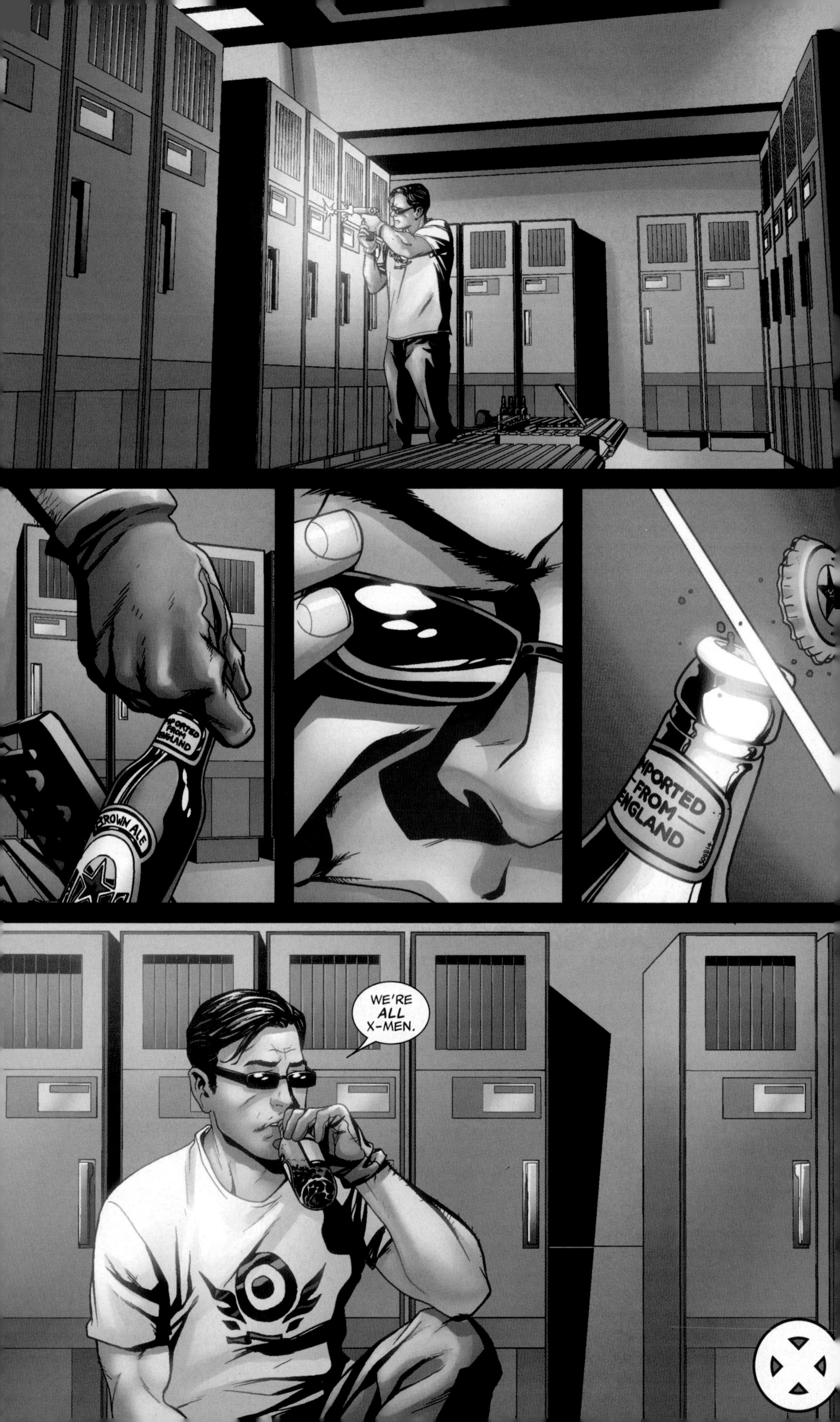
IMPORTED FROM ENGLAND
BROWN ALE
IMPORTED FROM ENGLAND
WE'RE ALL X-MEN.

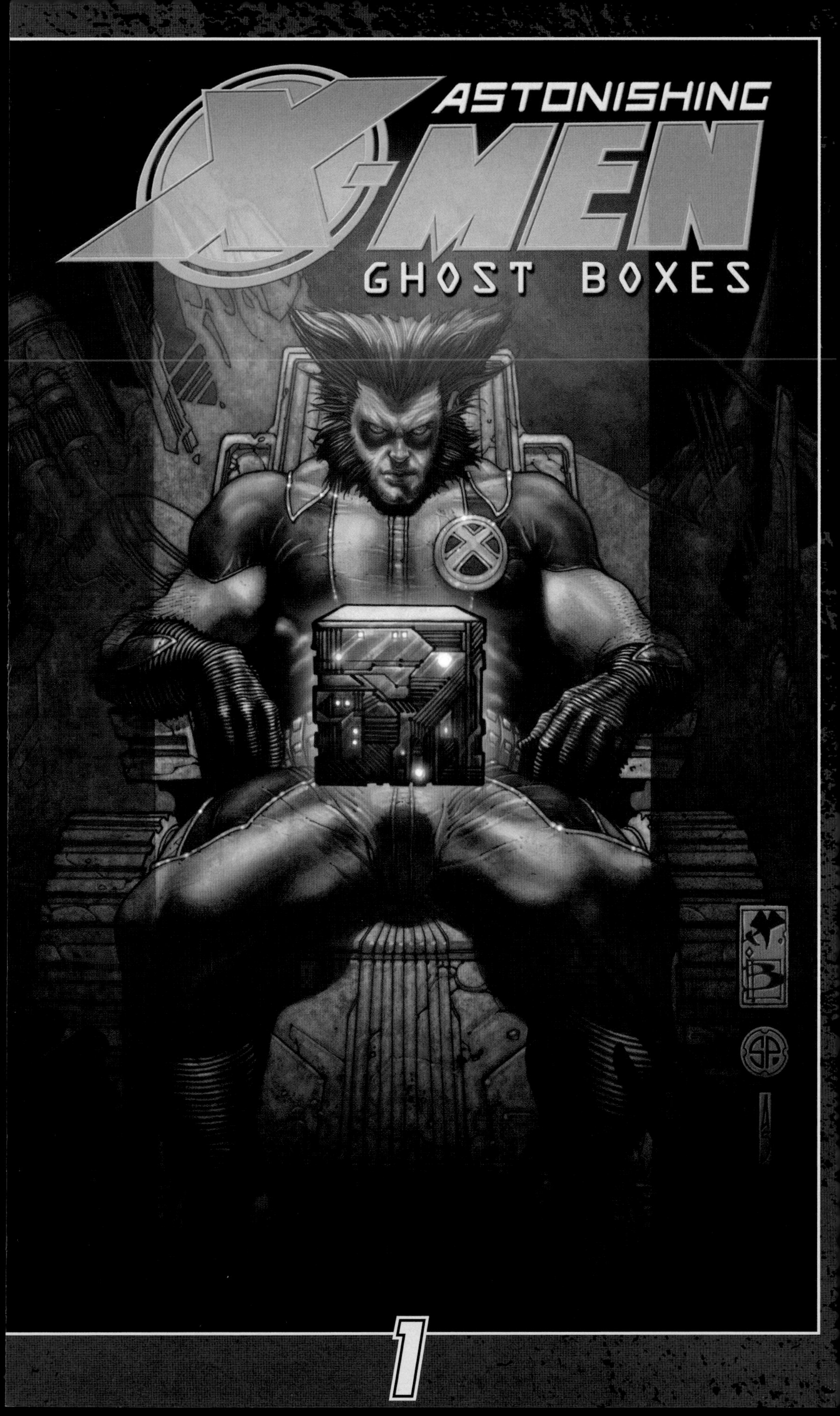
ASTONISHING
X-MEN
GHOST BOXES
1

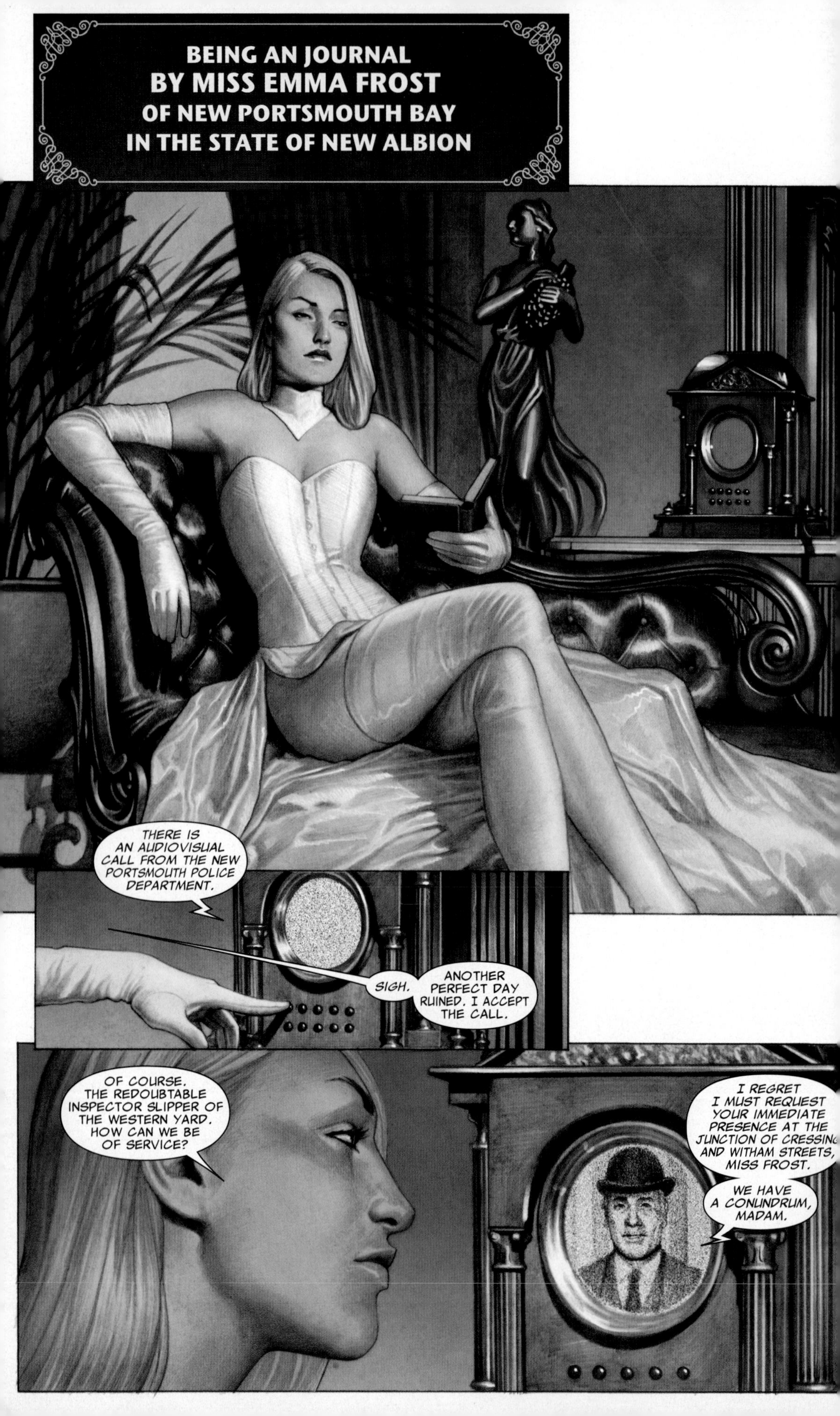
BEING AN JOURNAL
BY MISS EMMA FROST
OF NEW PORTSMOUTH BAY
IN THE STATE OF NEW ALBION
THERE IS AN AUDIOVISUAL CALL FROM THE NEW PORTSMOUTH POLICE DEPARTMENT.
SIGH.
ANOTHER PERFECT DAY RUINED. I ACCEPT THE CALL.
OF COURSE. THE REDOUBTABLE INSPECTOR SLIPPER OF THE WESTERN YARD. HOW CAN WE BE OF SERVICE?
I REGRET I MUST REQUEST YOUR IMMEDIATE PRESENCE AT THE JUNCTION OF CRESSING AND WITHAM STREETS, MISS FROST.
WE HAVE A CONUNDRUM, MADAM.

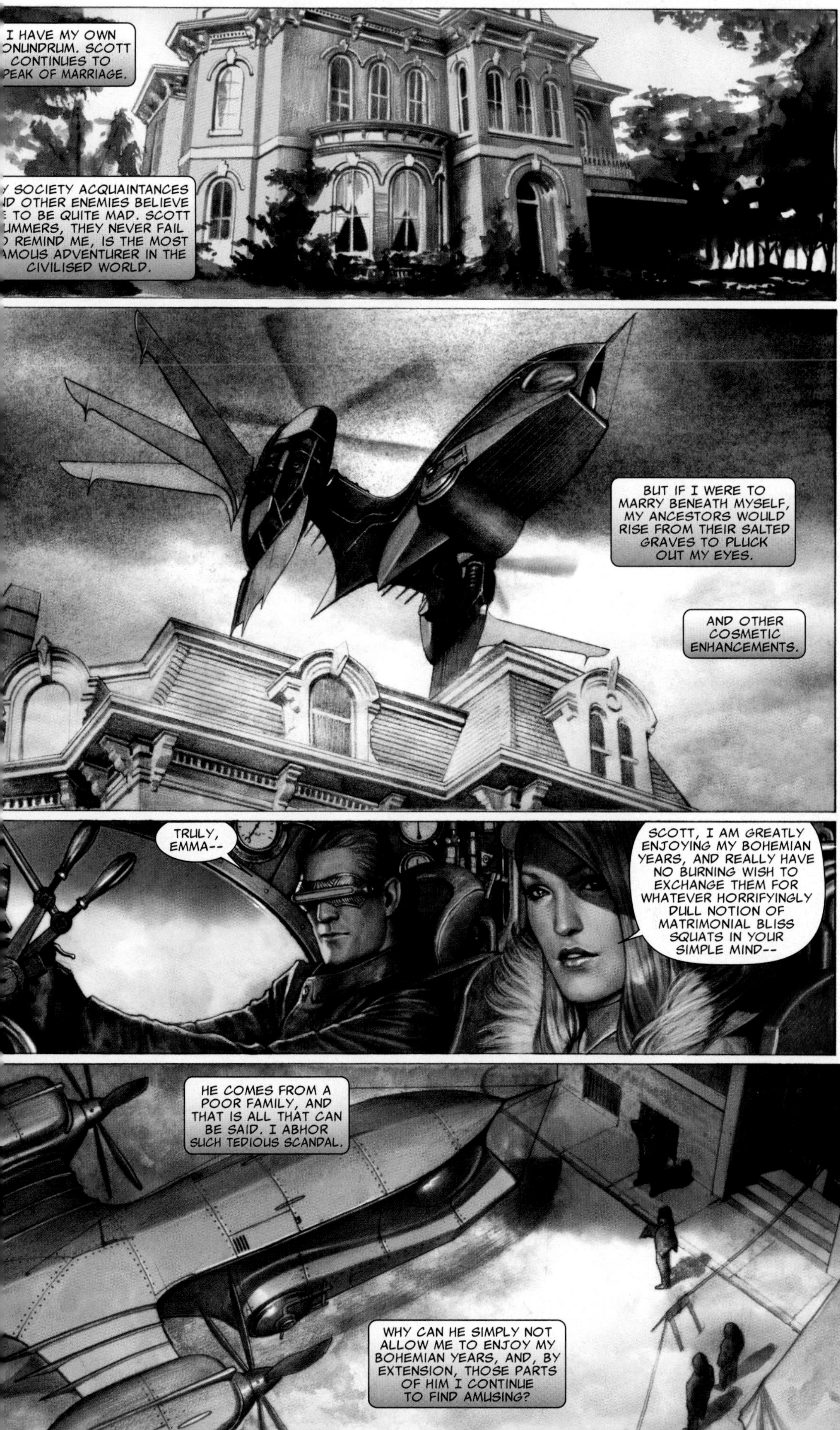
I HAVE MY OWN ONUNDRUM. SCOTT CONTINUES TO PEAK OF MARRIAGE.
Y SOCIETY ACQUAINTANCES ND OTHER ENEMIES BELIEVE E TO BE QUITE MAD. SCOTT UMMERS, THEY NEVER FAIL O REMIND ME, IS THE MOST AMOUS ADVENTURER IN THE CIVILISED WORLD.
BUT IF I WERE TO MARRY BENEATH MYSELF, MY ANCESTORS WOULD RISE FROM THEIR SALTED GRAVES TO PLUCK OUT MY EYES.
AND OTHER COSMETIC ENHANCEMENTS.
TRULY, EMMA--
SCOTT, I AM GREATLY ENJOYING MY BOHEMIAN YEARS, AND REALLY HAVE NO BURNING WISH TO EXCHANGE THEM FOR WHATEVER HORRIFYINGLY DULL NOTION OF MATRIMONIAL BLISS SQUATS IN YOUR SIMPLE MIND--
HE COMES FROM A POOR FAMILY, AND THAT IS ALL THAT CAN BE SAID. I ABHOR SUCH TEDIOUS SCANDAL.
WHY CAN HE SIMPLY NOT ALLOW ME TO ENJOY MY BOHEMIAN YEARS, AND, BY EXTENSION, THOSE PARTS OF HIM I CONTINUE TO FIND AMUSING?

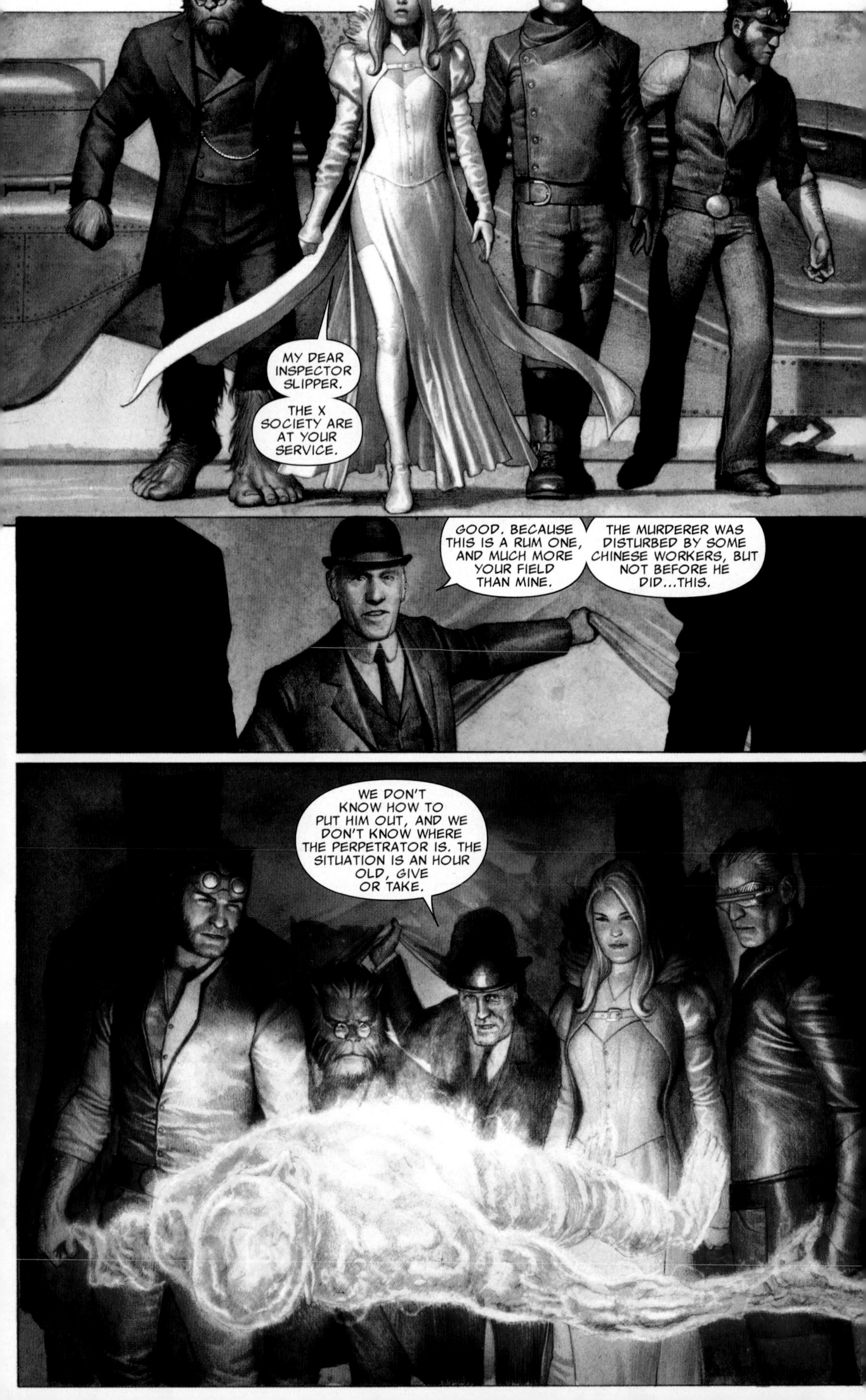
MY DEAR INSPECTOR SLIPPER.
THE X SOCIETY ARE AT YOUR SERVICE.
GOOD. BECAUSE THIS IS A RUM ONE, AND MUCH MORE YOUR FIELD THAN MINE.
THE MURDERER WAS DISTURBED BY SOME CHINESE WORKERS, BUT NOT BEFORE HE DID...THIS.
WE DON'T KNOW HOW TO PUT HIM OUT, AND WE DON'T KNOW WHERE THE PERPETRATOR IS. THE SITUATION IS AN HOUR OLD, GIVE OR TAKE.

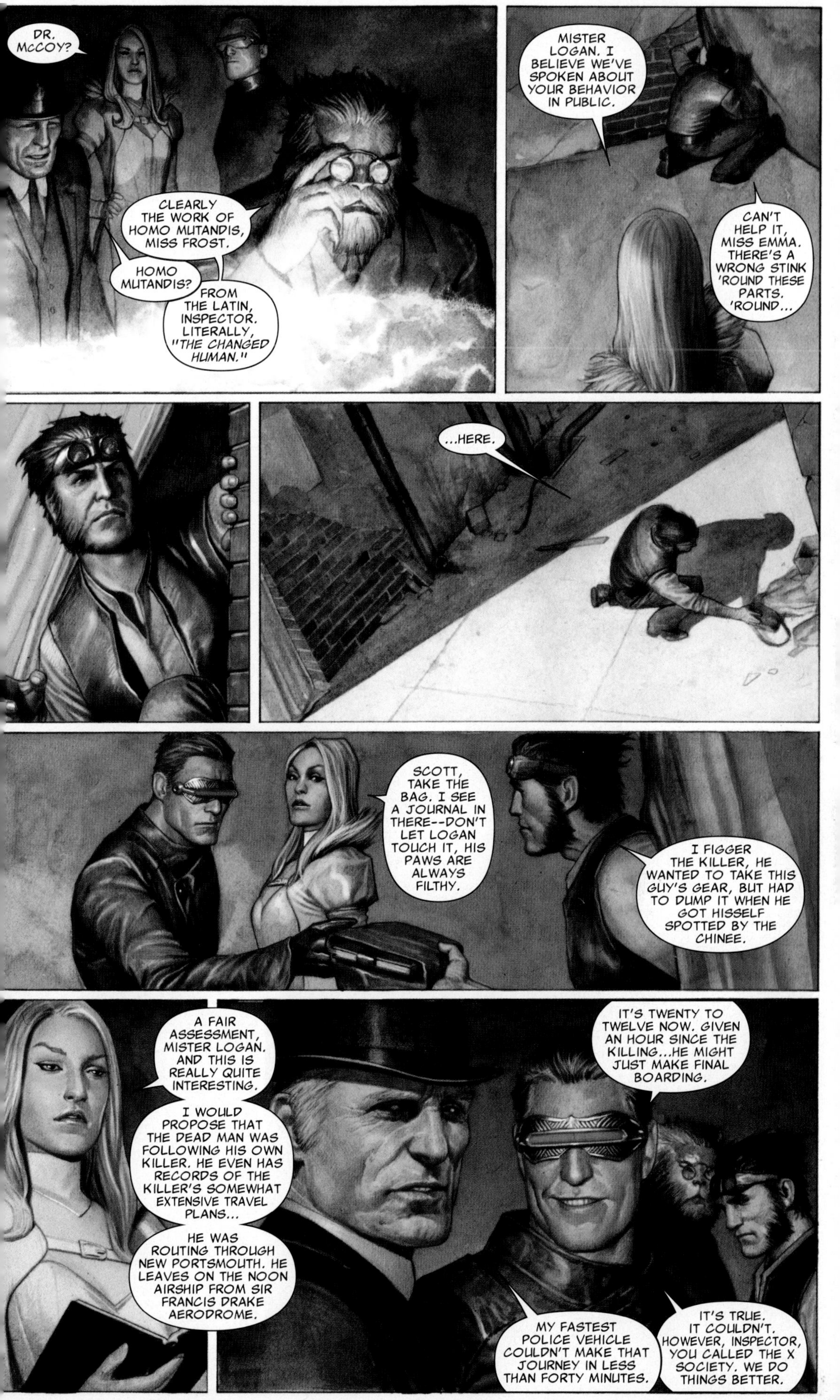
DR. McCOY?
CLEARLY THE WORK OF HOMO MUTANDIS, MISS FROST.
HOMO MUTANDIS?
FROM THE LATIN, INSPECTOR. LITERALLY, "THE CHANGED HUMAN."
MISTER LOGAN. I BELIEVE WE'VE SPOKEN ABOUT YOUR BEHAVIOR IN PUBLIC.
CAN'T HELP IT, MISS EMMA. THERE'S A WRONG STINK 'ROUND THESE PARTS. 'ROUND...
...HERE.
SCOTT, TAKE THE BAG. I SEE A JOURNAL IN THERE--DON'T LET LOGAN TOUCH IT, HIS PAWS ARE ALWAYS FILTHY.
I FIGGER THE KILLER, HE WANTED TO TAKE THIS GUY'S GEAR, BUT HAD TO DUMP IT WHEN HE GOT HISSELF SPOTTED BY THE CHINEE.
A FAIR ASSESSMENT, MISTER LOGAN. AND THIS IS REALLY QUITE INTERESTING.
I WOULD PROPOSE THAT THE DEAD MAN WAS FOLLOWING HIS OWN KILLER. HE EVEN HAS RECORDS OF THE KILLER'S SOMEWHAT EXTENSIVE TRAVEL PLANS...
HE WAS ROUTING THROUGH NEW PORTSMOUTH. HE LEAVES ON THE NOON AIRSHIP FROM SIR FRANCIS DRAKE AERODROME.
IT'S TWENTY TO TWELVE NOW. GIVEN AN HOUR SINCE THE KILLING...HE MIGHT JUST MAKE FINAL BOARDING.
MY FASTEST POLICE VEHICLE COULDN'T MAKE THAT JOURNEY IN LESS THAN FORTY MINUTES.
IT'S TRUE. IT COULDN'T. HOWEVER, INSPECTOR, YOU CALLED THE X SOCIETY. WE DO THINGS BETTER.

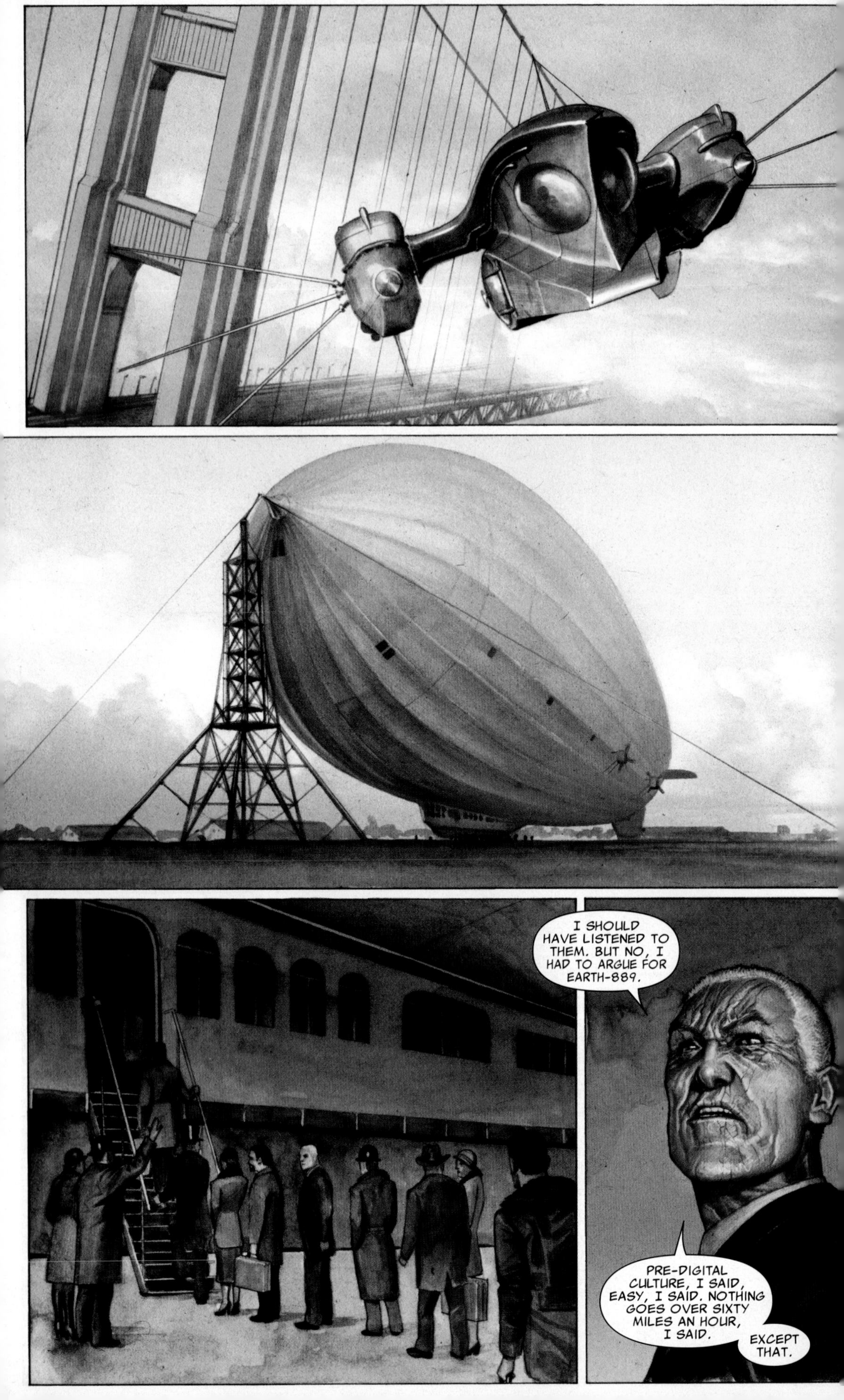
I SHOULD HAVE LISTENED TO THEM. BUT NO, I HAD TO ARGUE FOR EARTH-889.
PRE-DIGITAL CULTURE, I SAID, EASY, I SAID. NOTHING GOES OVER SIXTY MILES AN HOUR, I SAID.
EXCEPT THAT.

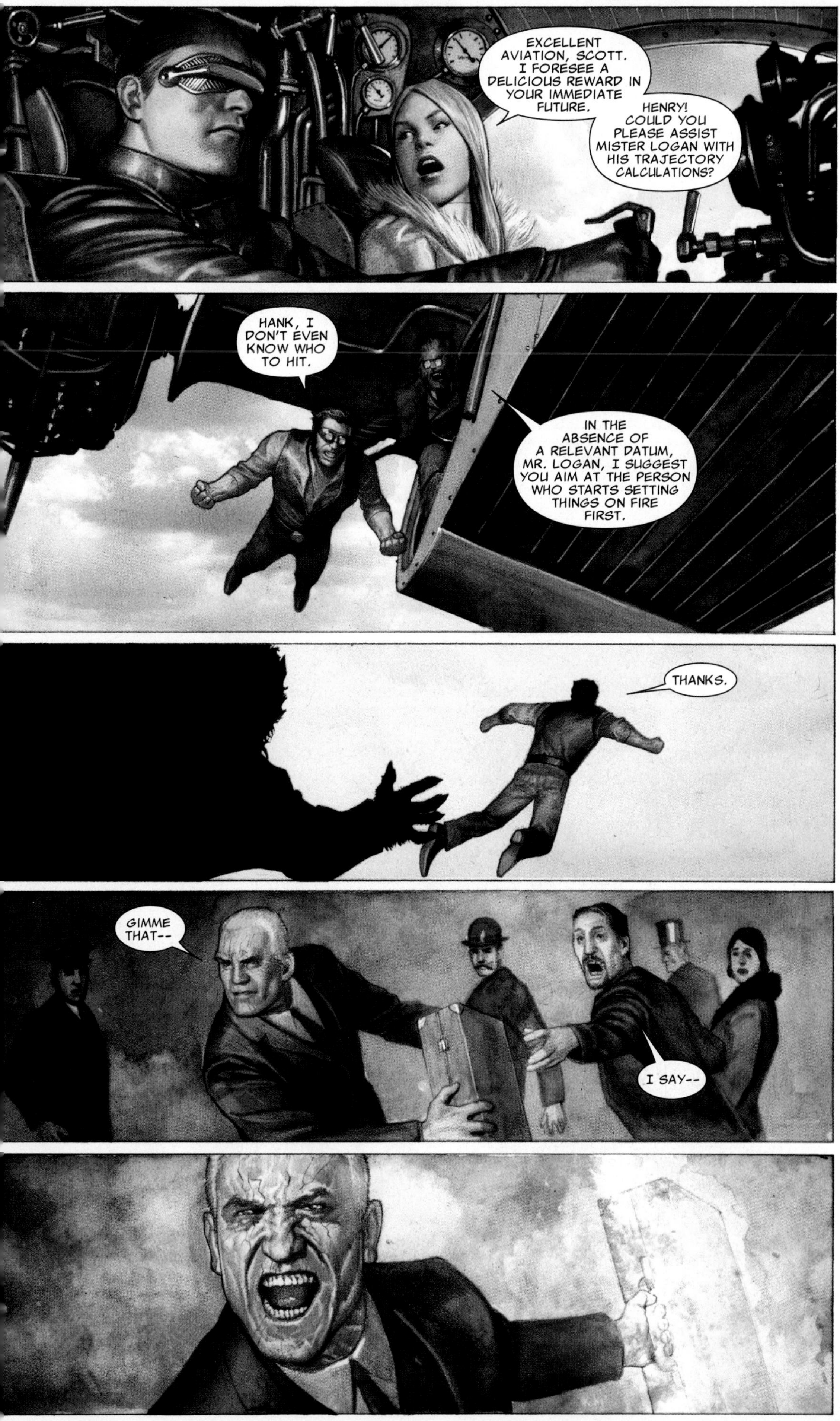
EXCELLENT AVIATION, SCOTT. I FORESEE A DELICIOUS REWARD IN YOUR IMMEDIATE FUTURE.
HENRY! COULD YOU PLEASE ASSIST MISTER LOGAN WITH HIS TRAJECTORY CALCULATIONS?
HANK, I DON'T EVEN KNOW WHO TO HIT.
IN THE ABSENCE OF A RELEVANT DATUM, MR. LOGAN, I SUGGEST YOU AIM AT THE PERSON WHO STARTS SETTING THINGS ON FIRE FIRST.
THANKS.
GIMME THAT--
I SAY--

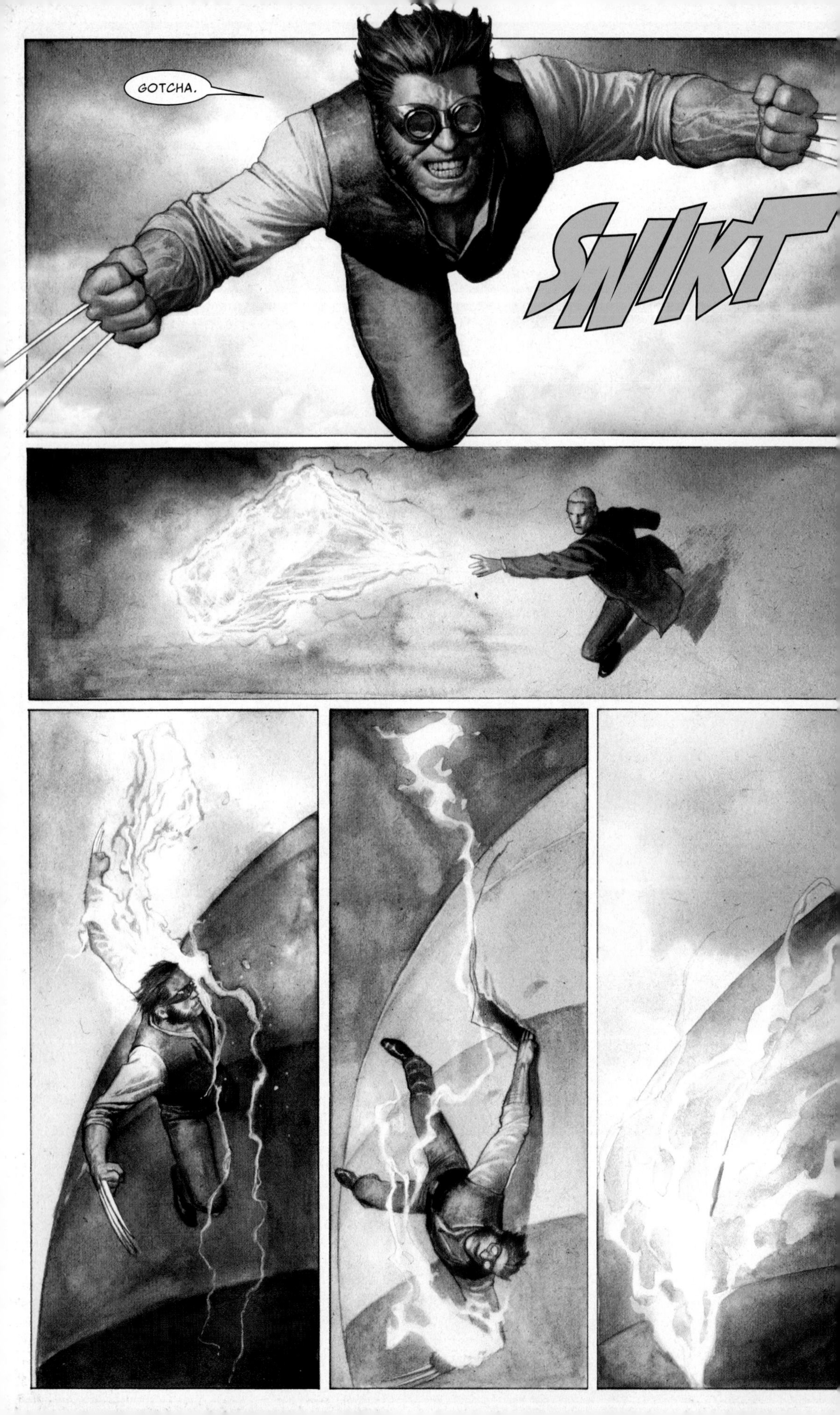
GOTCHA.
SNIKT

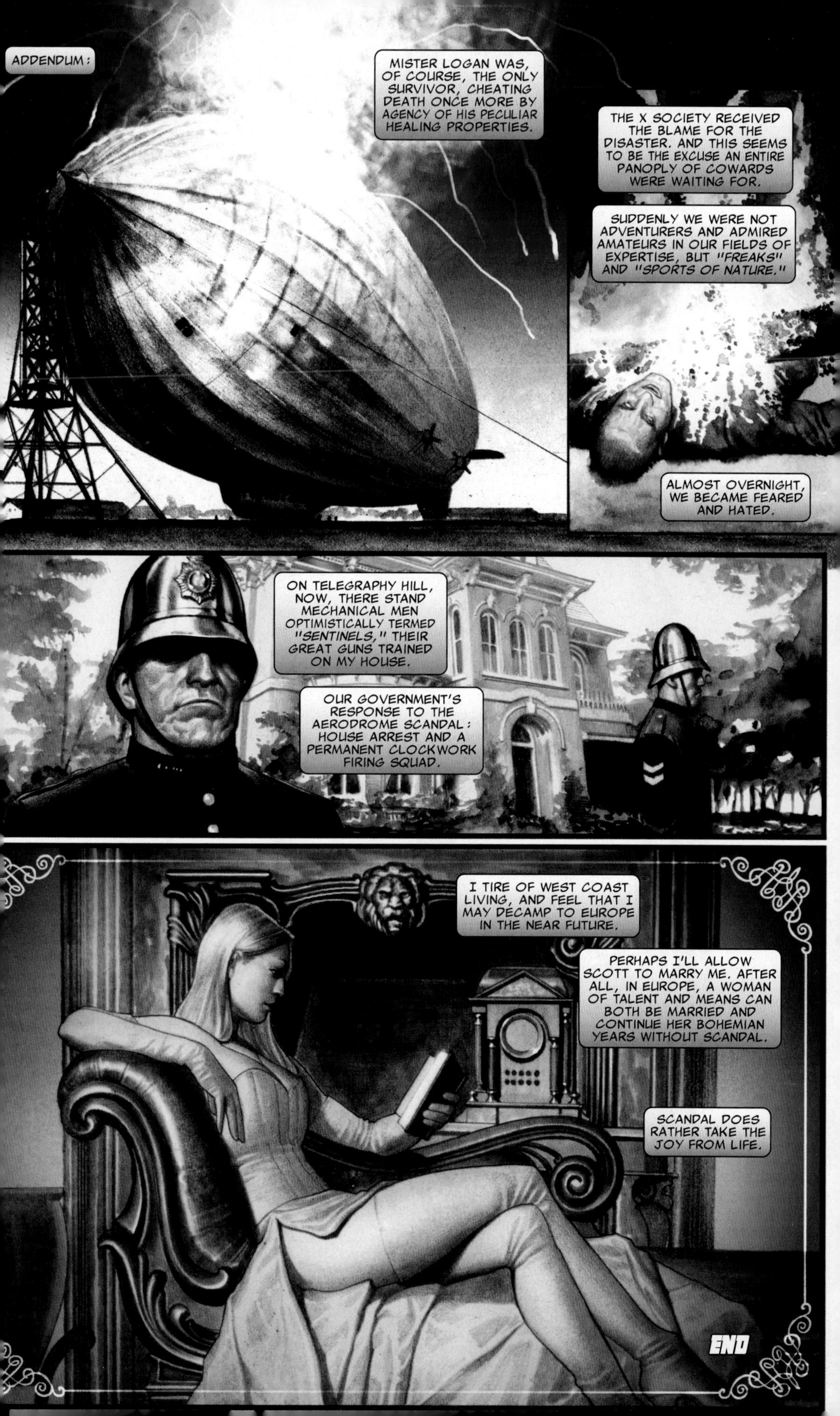
ADDENDUM:
MISTER LOGAN WAS, OF COURSE, THE ONLY SURVIVOR, CHEATING DEATH ONCE MORE BY AGENCY OF HIS PECULIAR HEALING PROPERTIES.
THE X SOCIETY RECEIVED THE BLAME FOR THE DISASTER. AND THIS SEEMS TO BE THE EXCUSE AN ENTIRE PANOPLY OF COWARDS WERE WAITING FOR.
SUDDENLY WE WERE NOT ADVENTURERS AND ADMIRED AMATEURS IN OUR FIELDS OF EXPERTISE, BUT "FREAKS" AND "SPORTS OF NATURE."
ALMOST OVERNIGHT, WE BECAME FEARED AND HATED.
ON TELEGRAPHY HILL, NOW, THERE STAND MECHANICAL MEN OPTIMISTICALLY TERMED "SENTINELS," THEIR GREAT GUNS TRAINED ON MY HOUSE.
OUR GOVERNMENT'S RESPONSE TO THE AERODROME SCANDAL: HOUSE ARREST AND A PERMANENT CLOCKWORK FIRING SQUAD.
I TIRE OF WEST COAST LIVING, AND FEEL THAT I MAY DECAMP TO EUROPE IN THE NEAR FUTURE.
PERHAPS I'LL ALLOW SCOTT TO MARRY ME. AFTER ALL, IN EUROPE, A WOMAN OF TALENT AND MEANS CAN BOTH BE MARRIED AND CONTINUE HER BOHEMIAN YEARS WITHOUT SCANDAL.
SCANDAL DOES RATHER TAKE THE JOY FROM LIFE.
END

CHARACTER DESIGNS
by **Mike McKone**

ARMOR

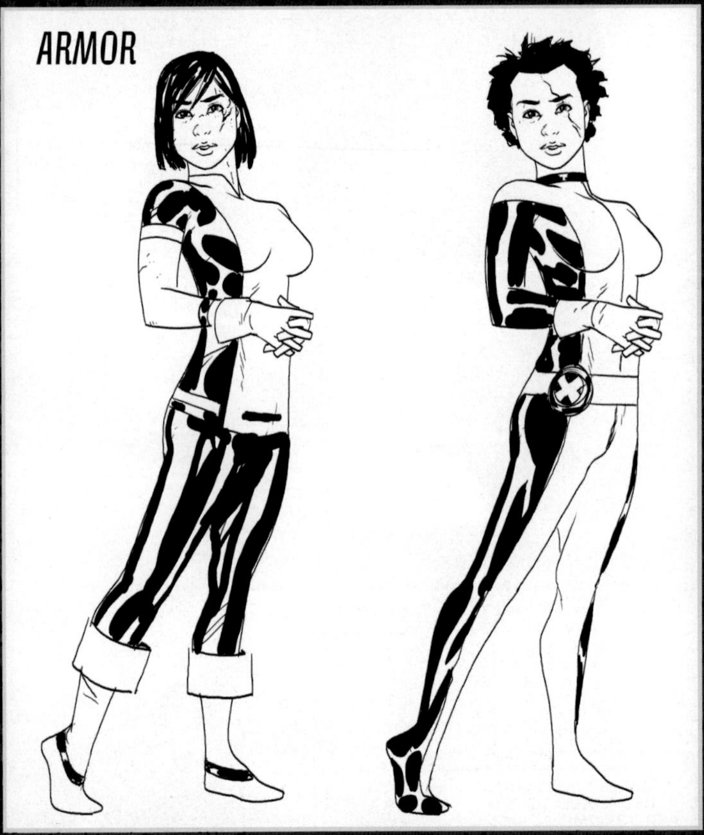

KURT

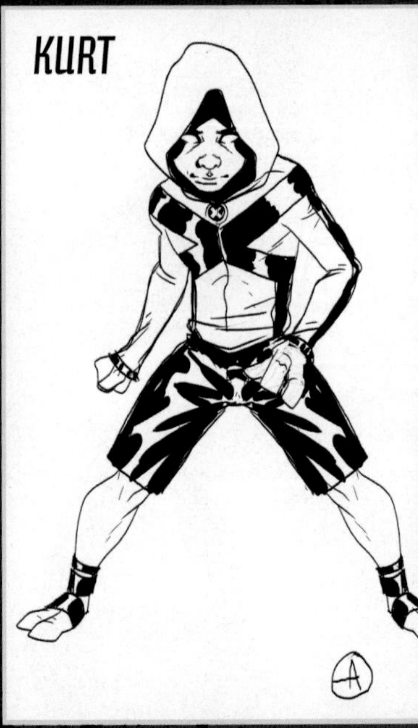
A

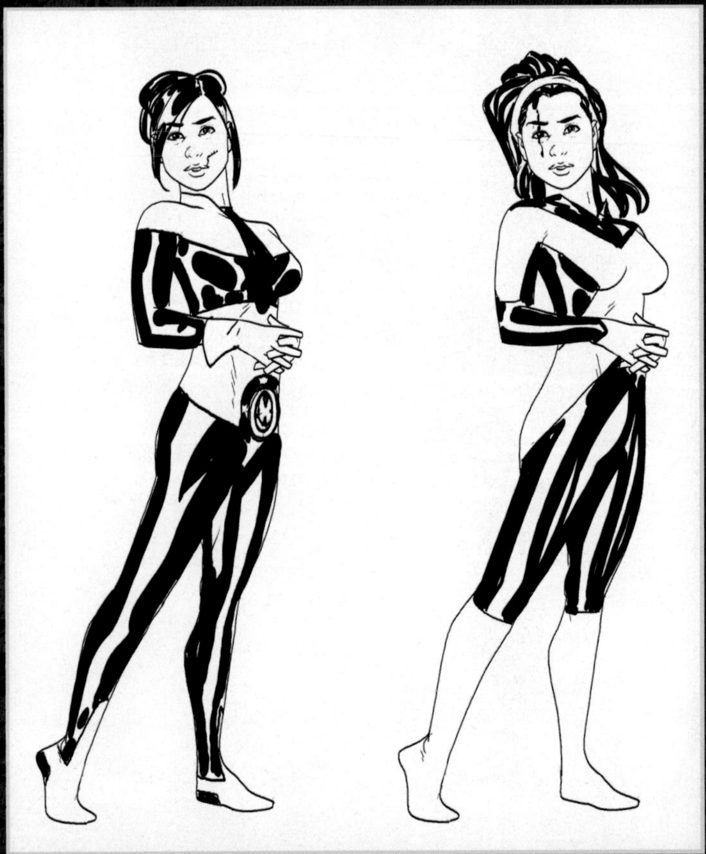

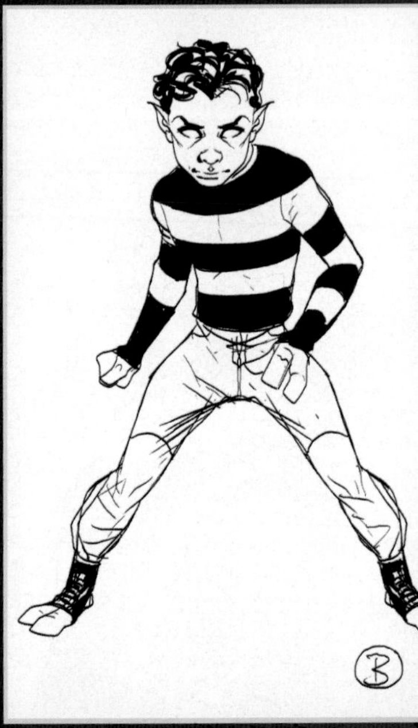
B

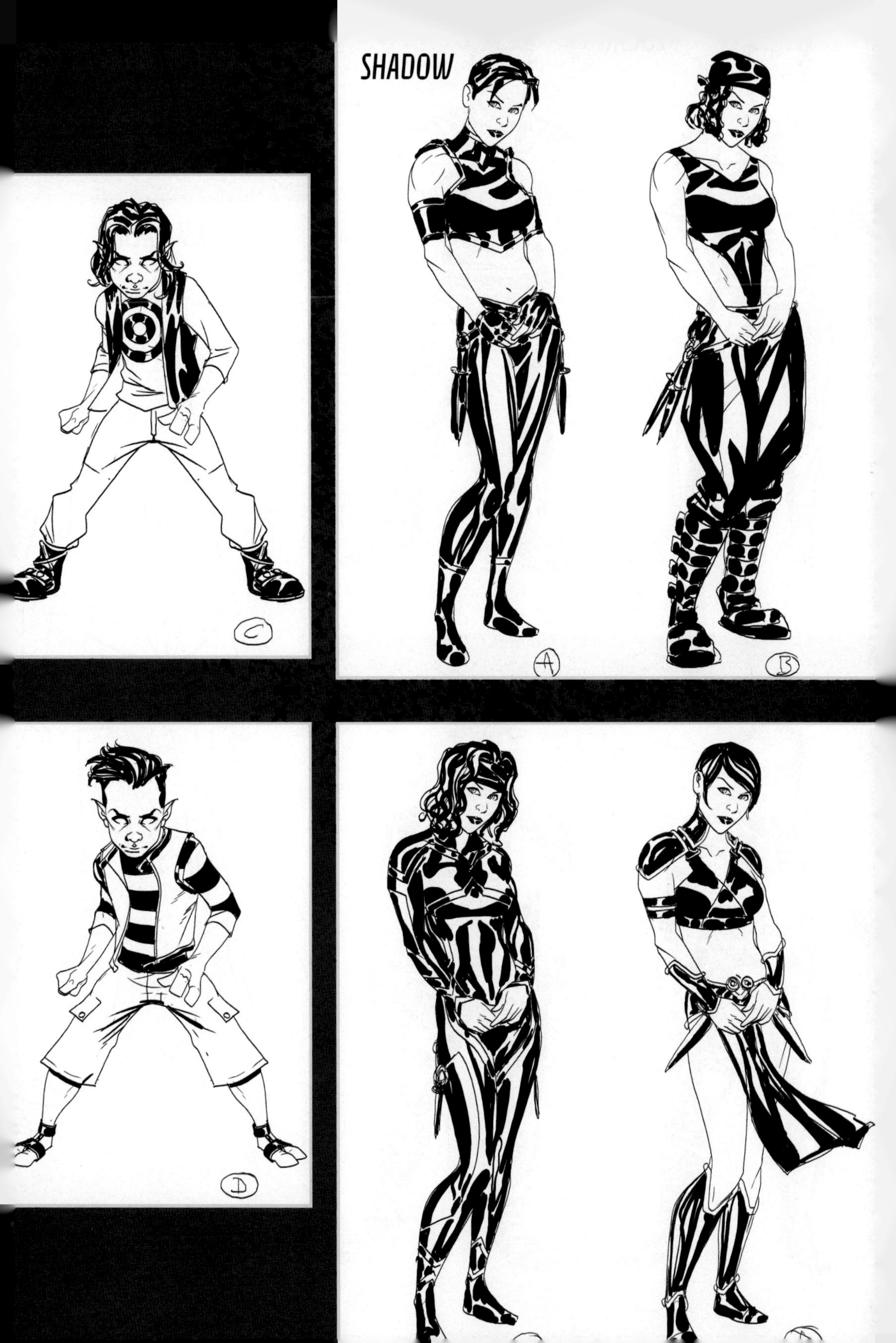
SHADOW
A
B
C
D

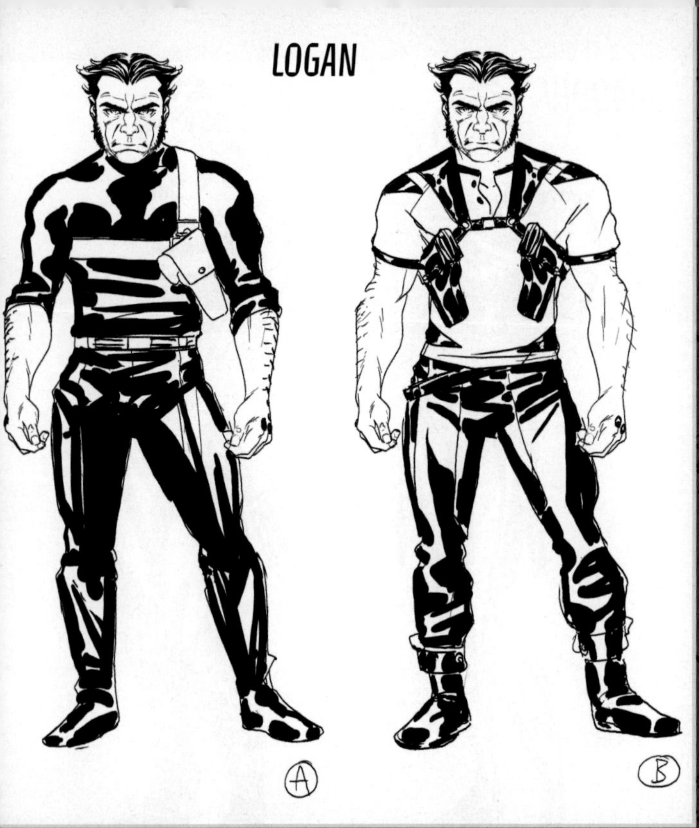
LOGAN
A
B

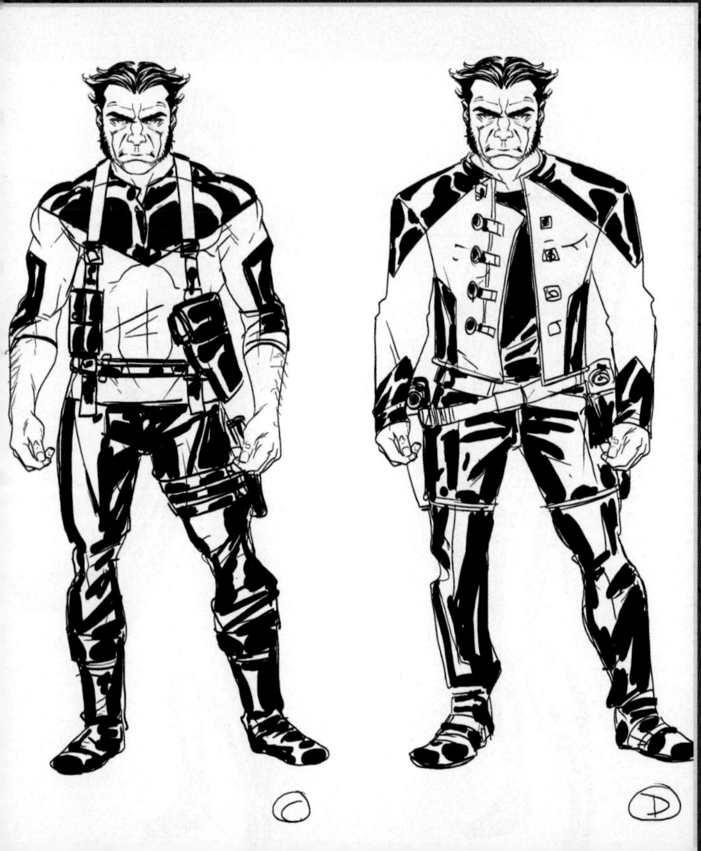
C
D

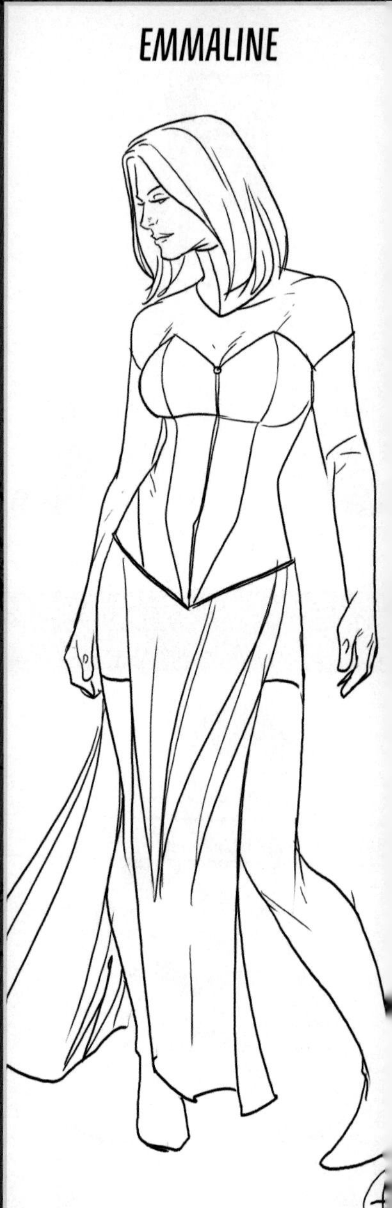
EMMALINE

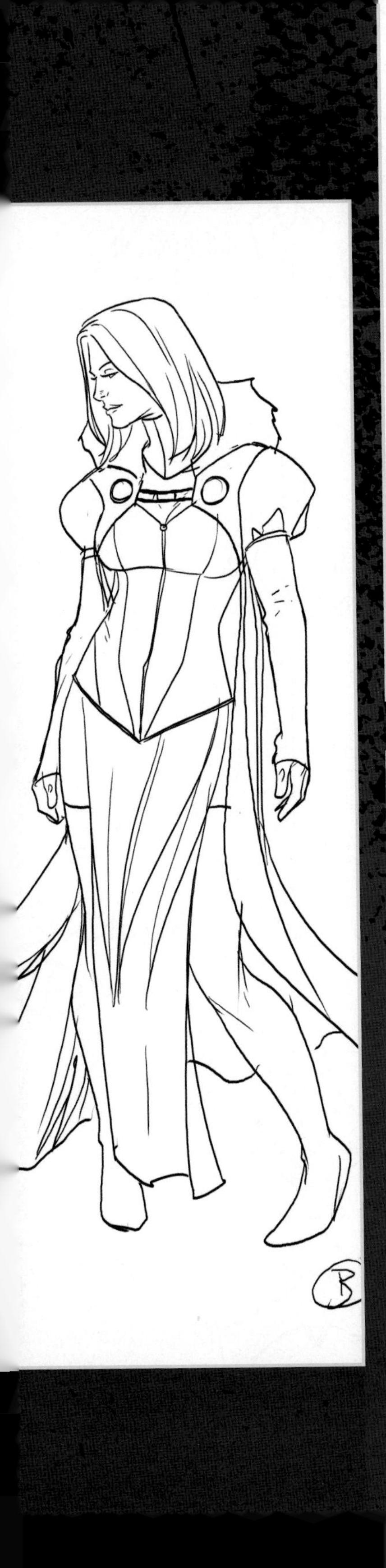

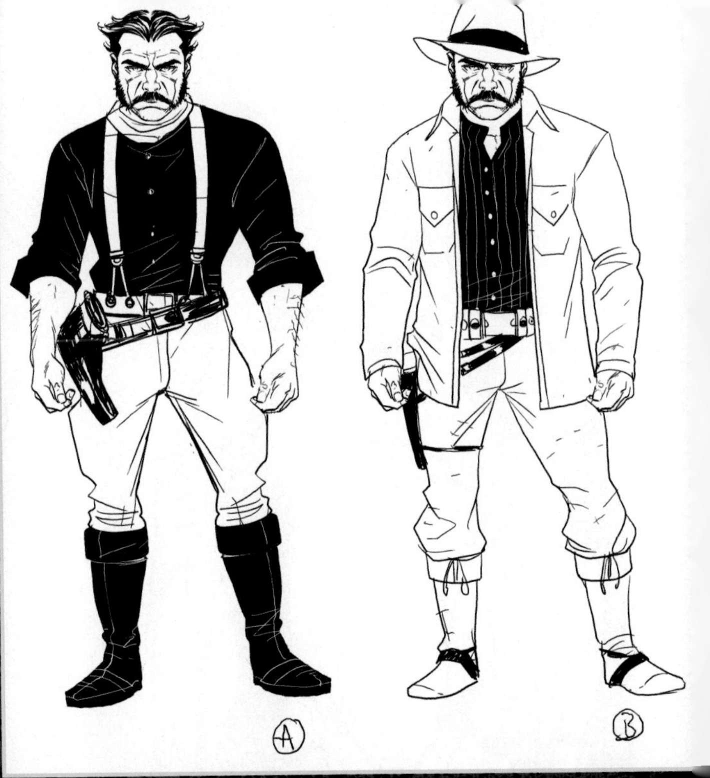
A
B

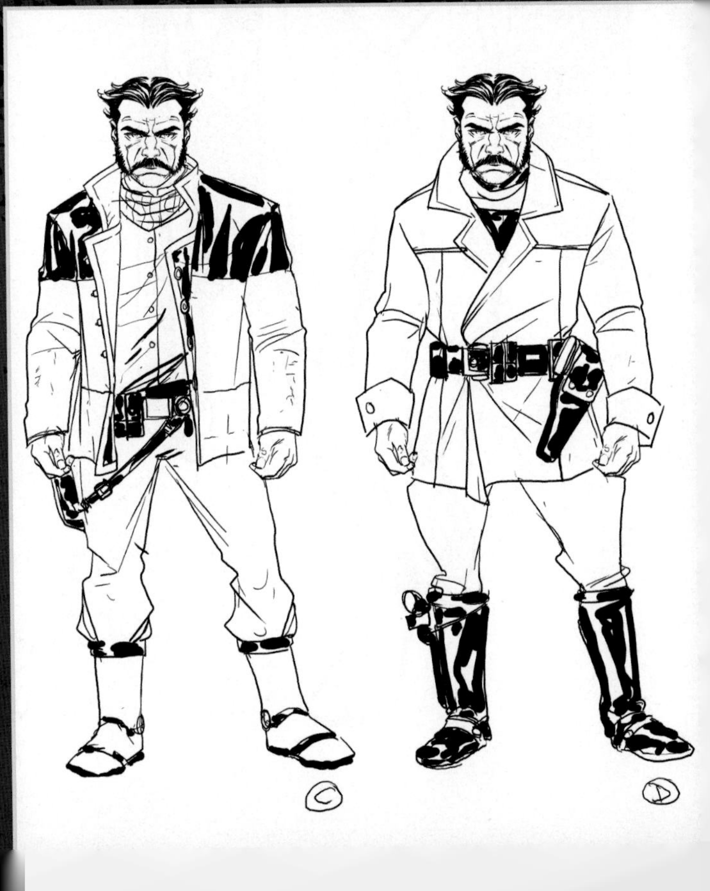
C
D

SAVIOR

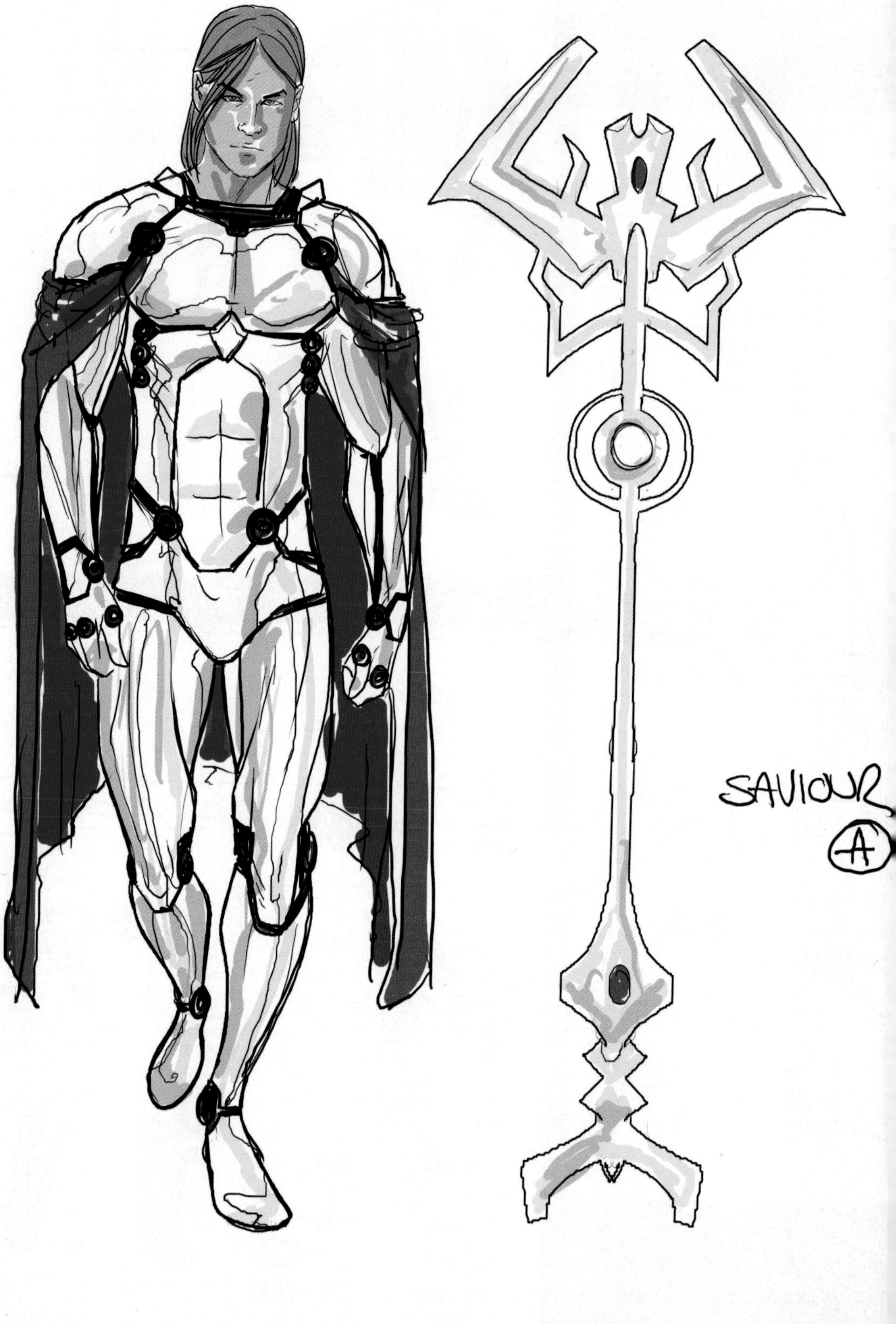
SAVIOUR

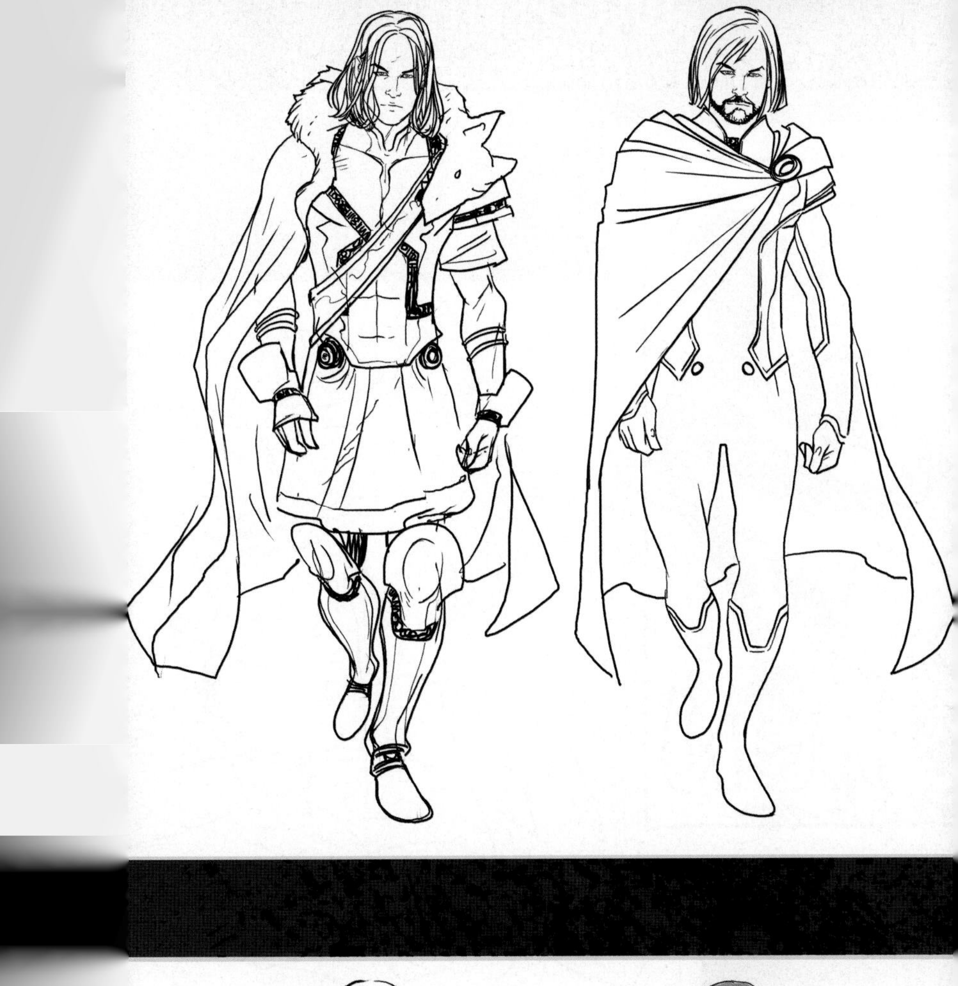

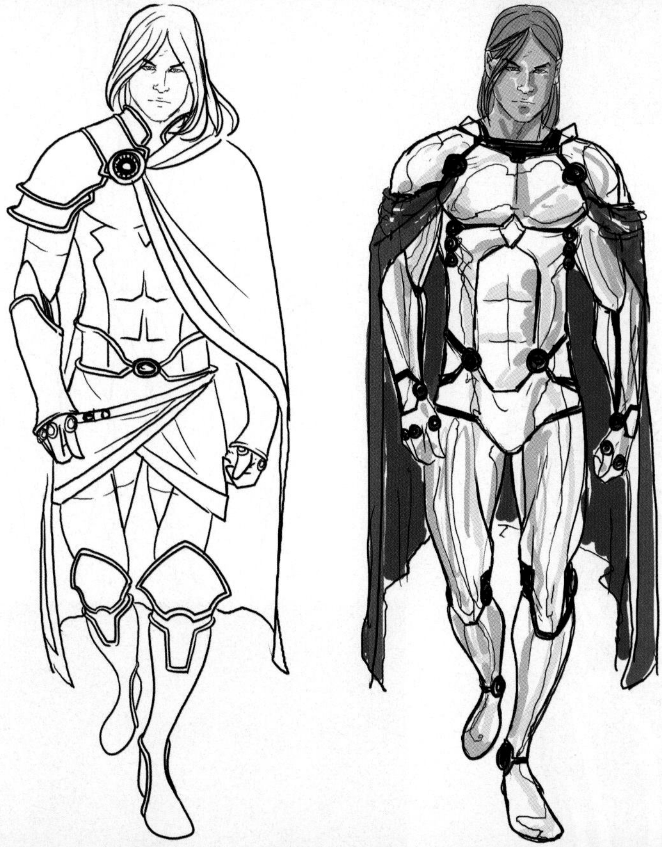

COVER PROCESS
by **Mike McKone**

#

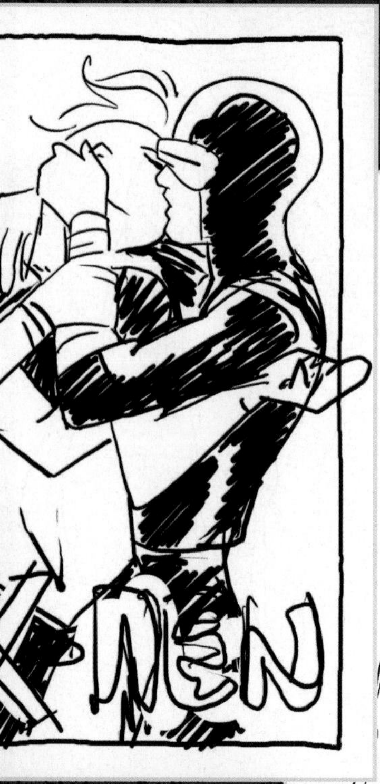

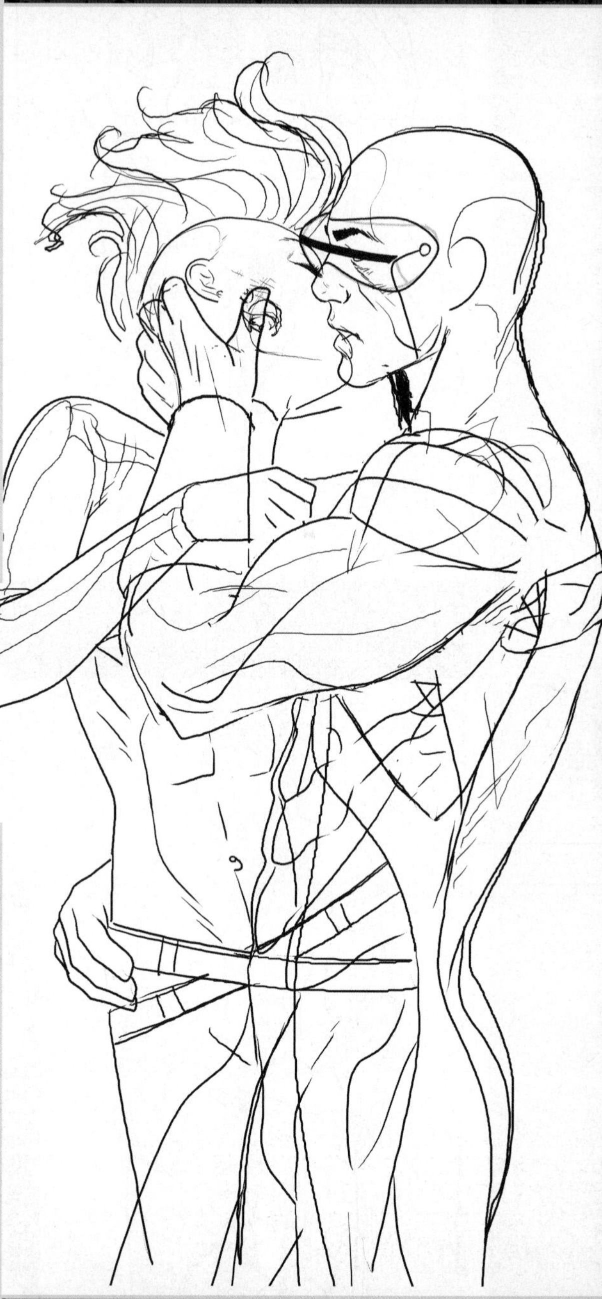

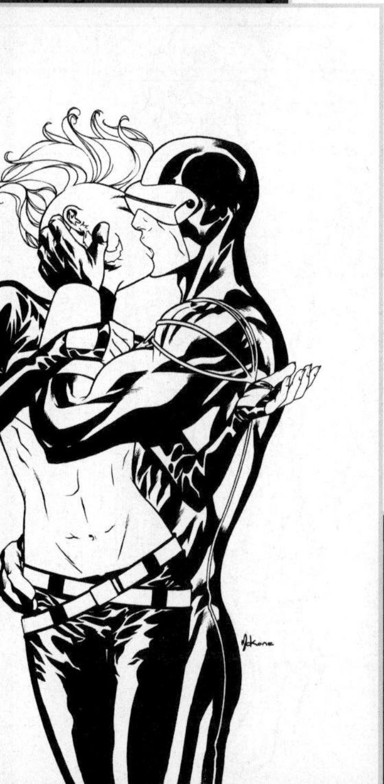

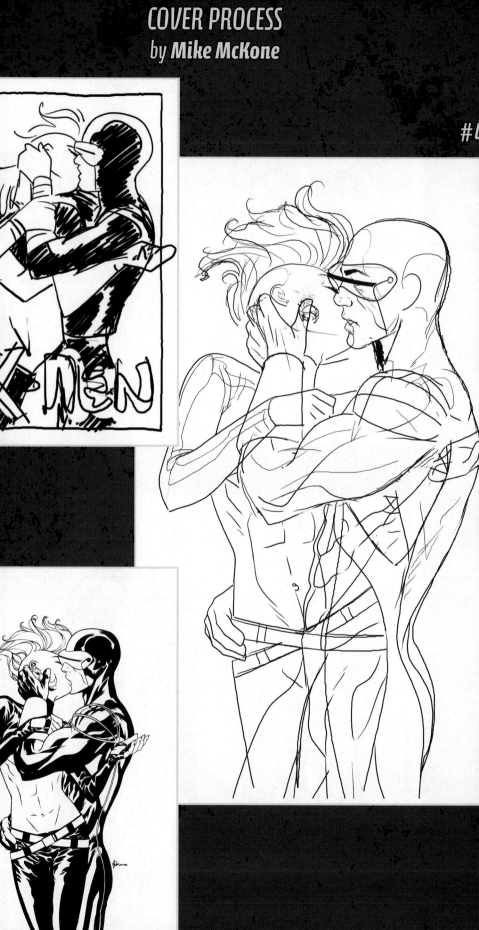

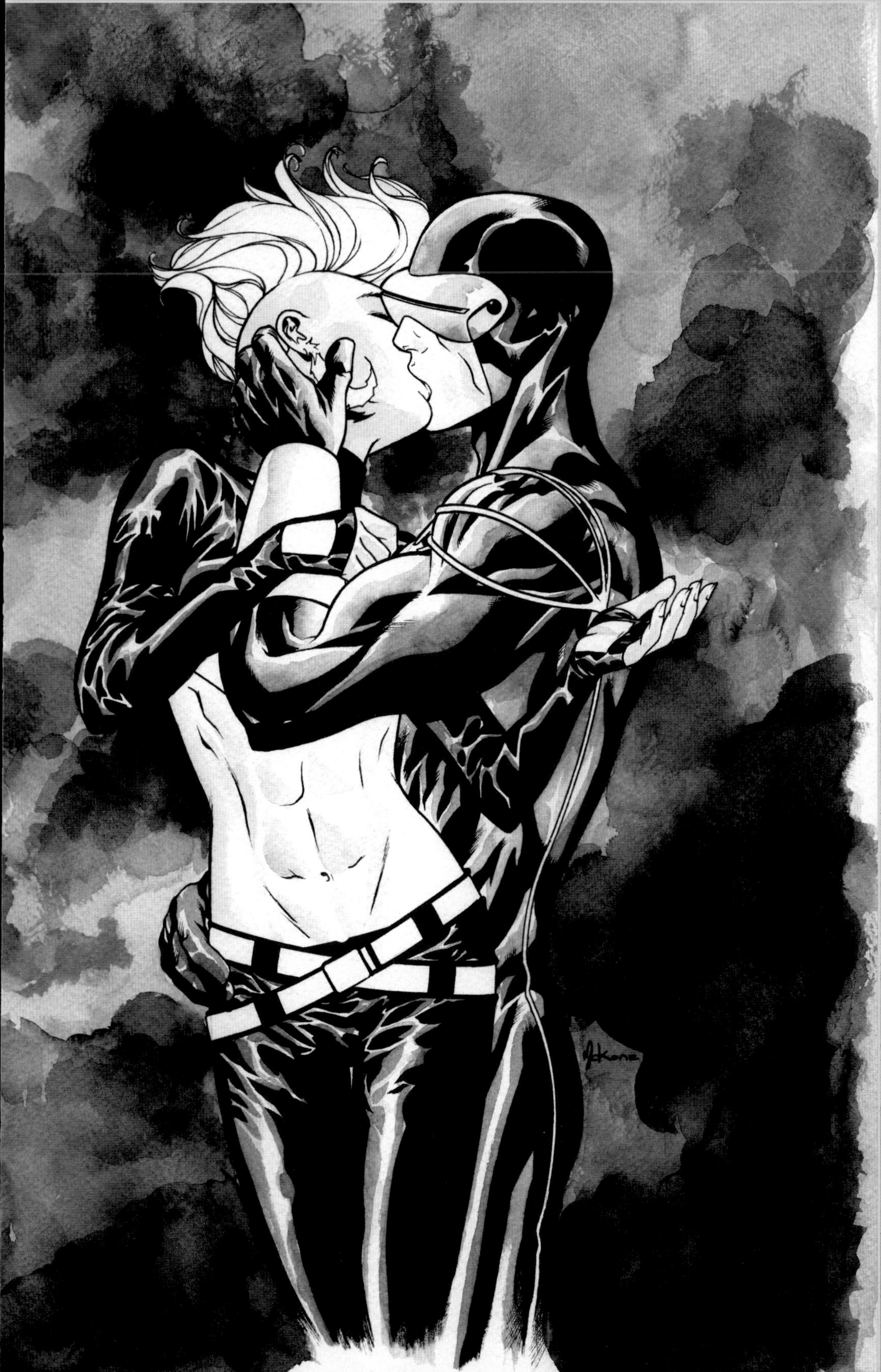

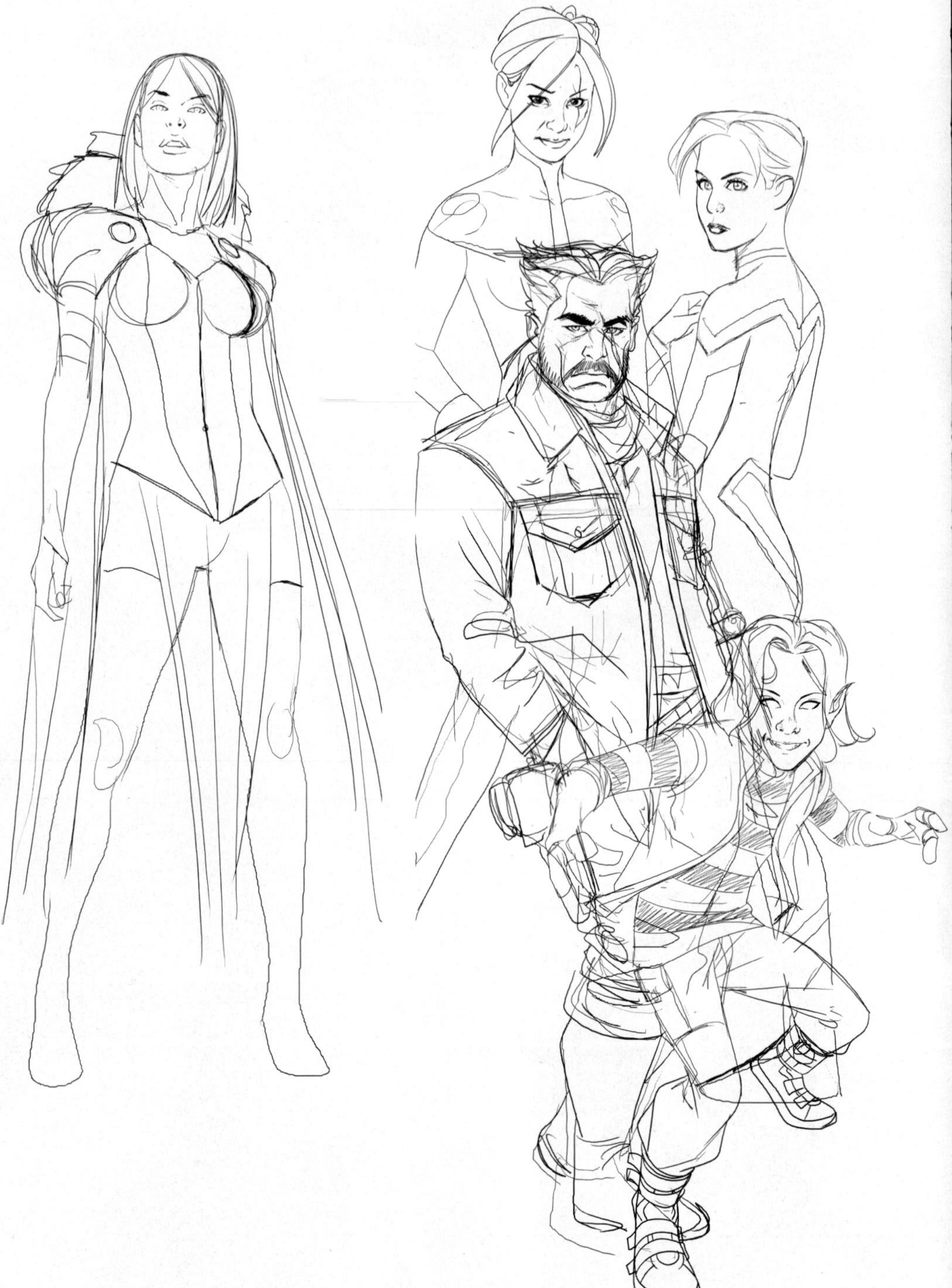

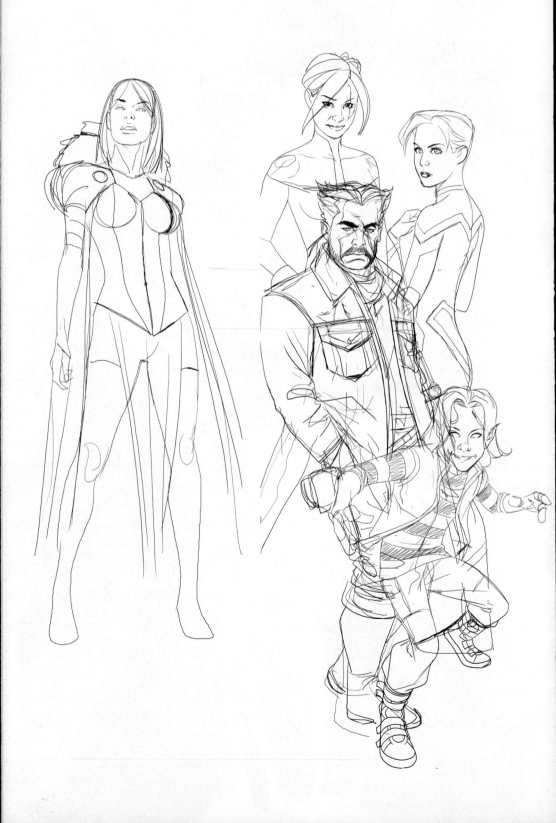

AXM 45 COVER MCKONE

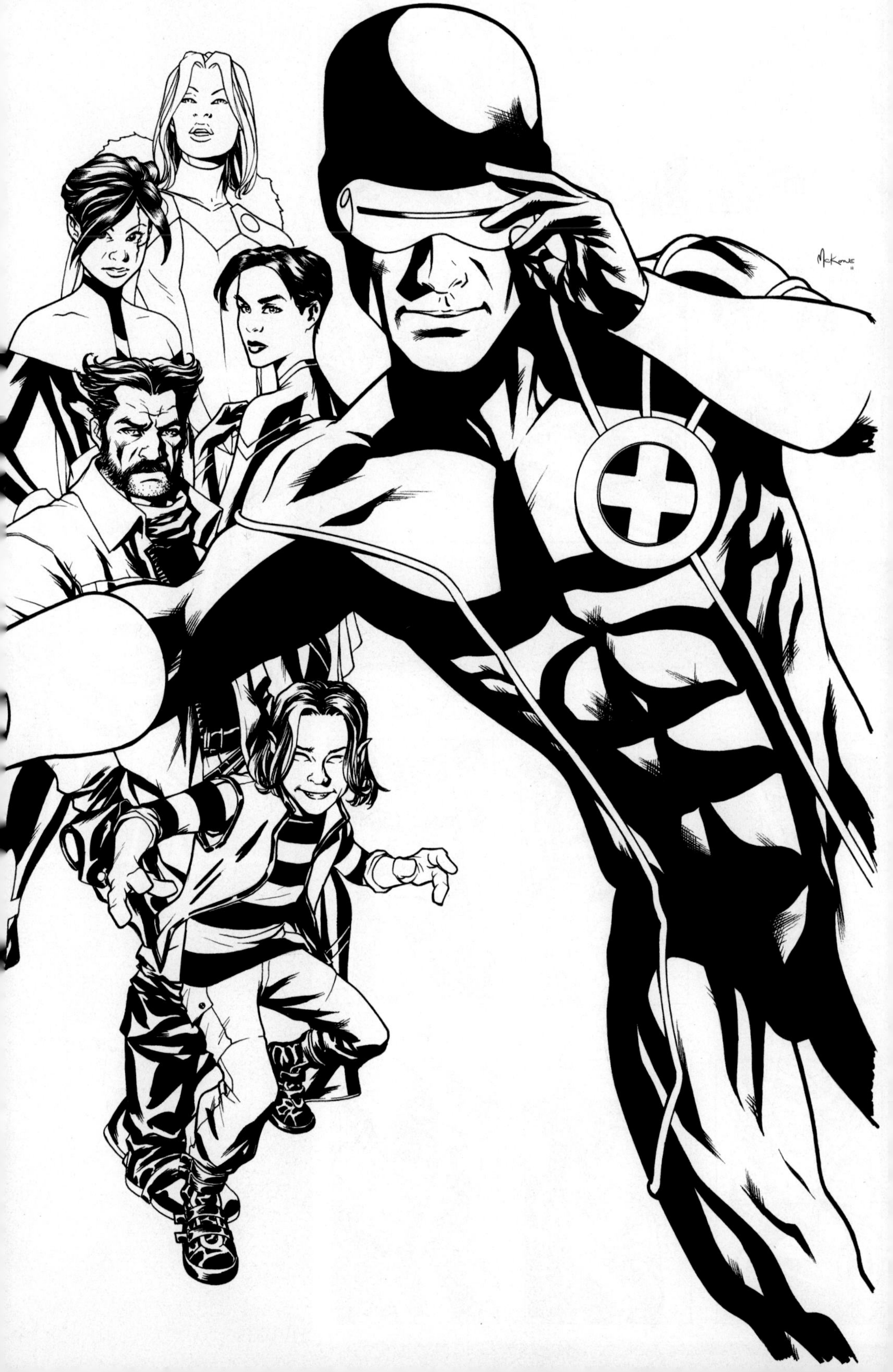
McKone

#46

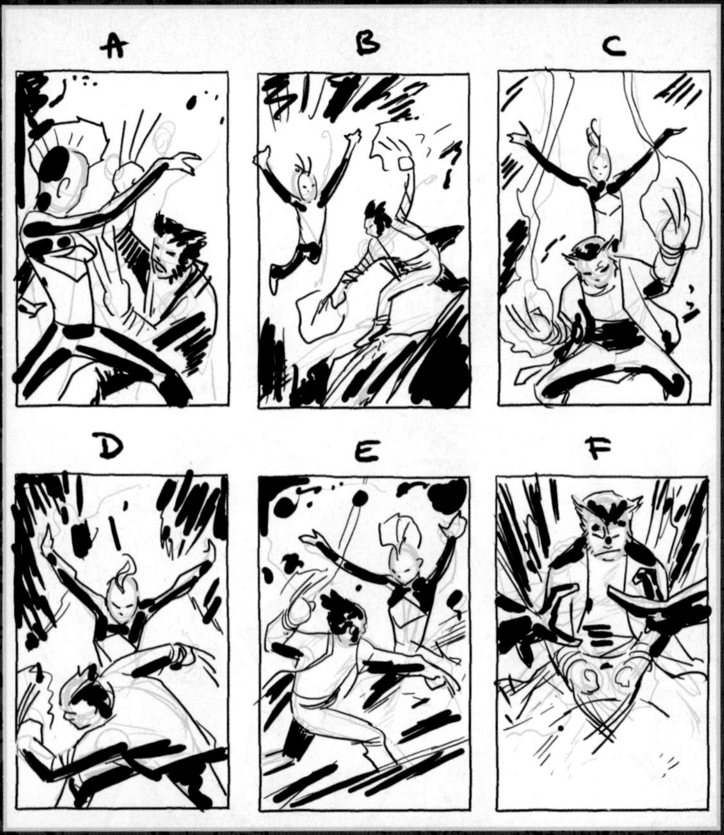
A
B
C
D
E
F

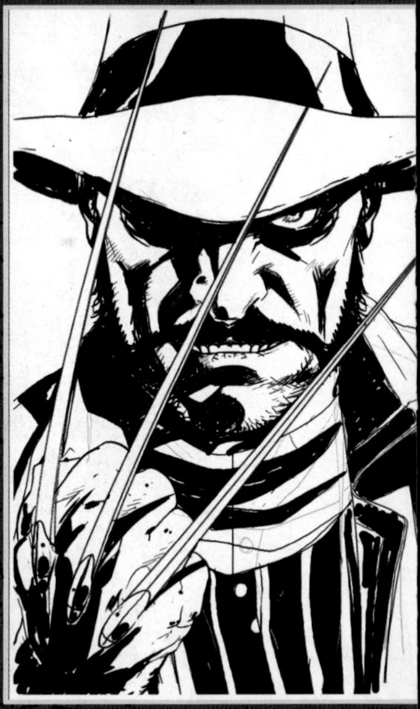

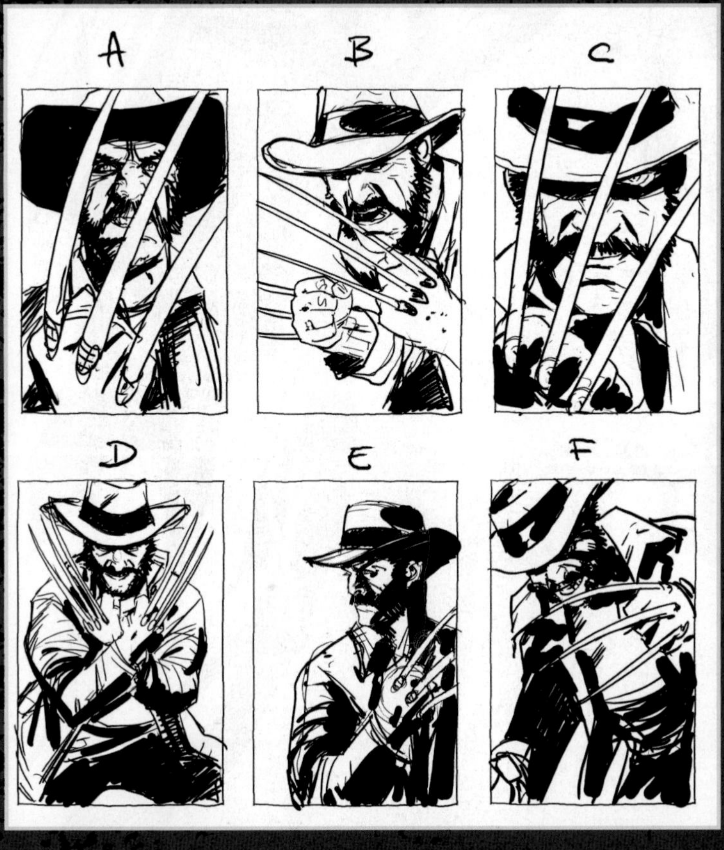
A
B
C
D
E
F

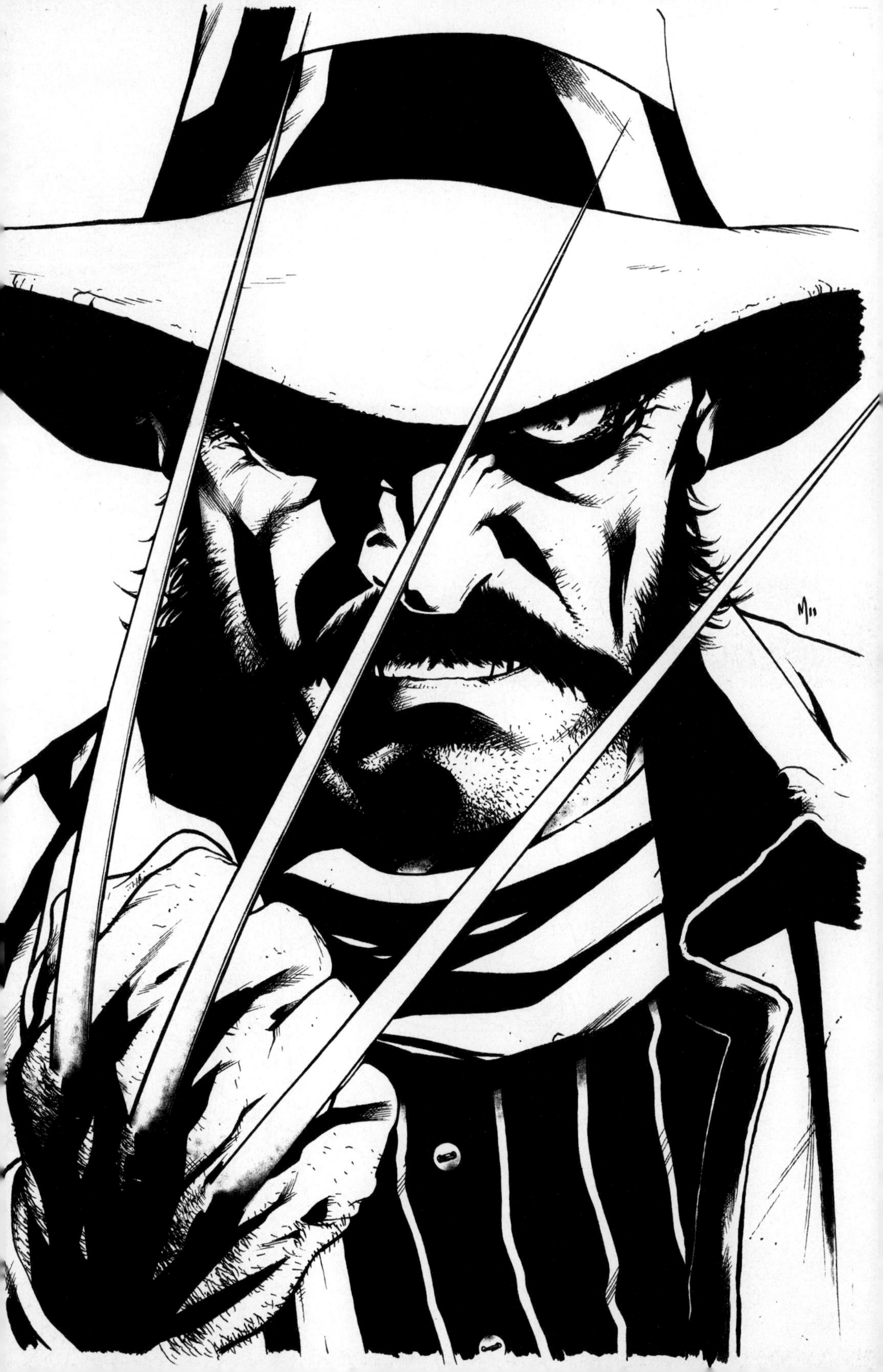

#47

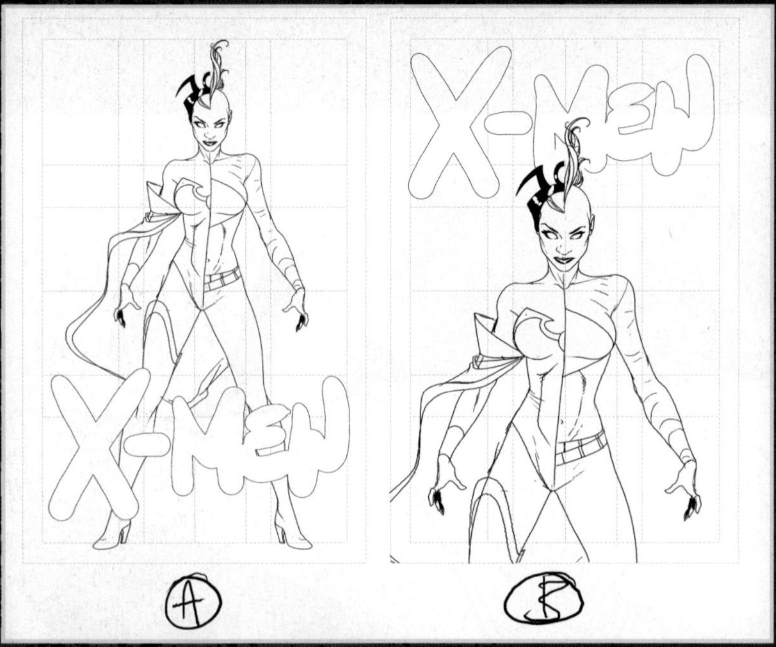
X-MEN
X-MEN
A
B

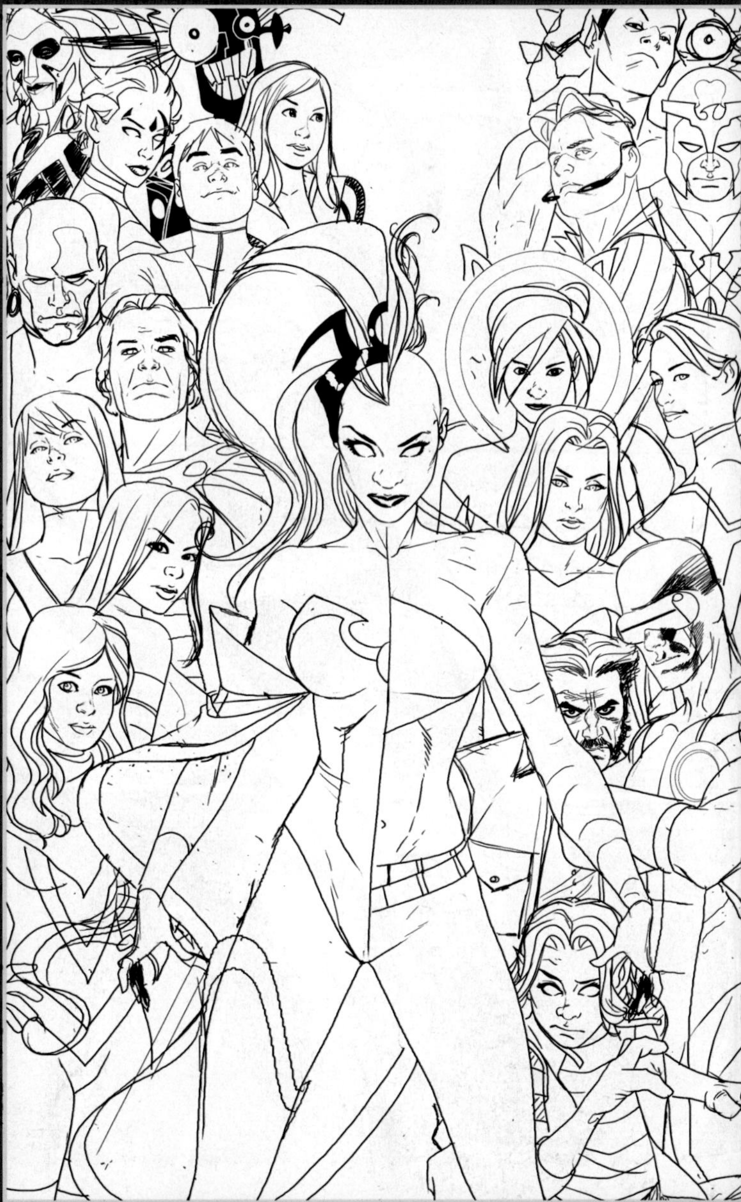

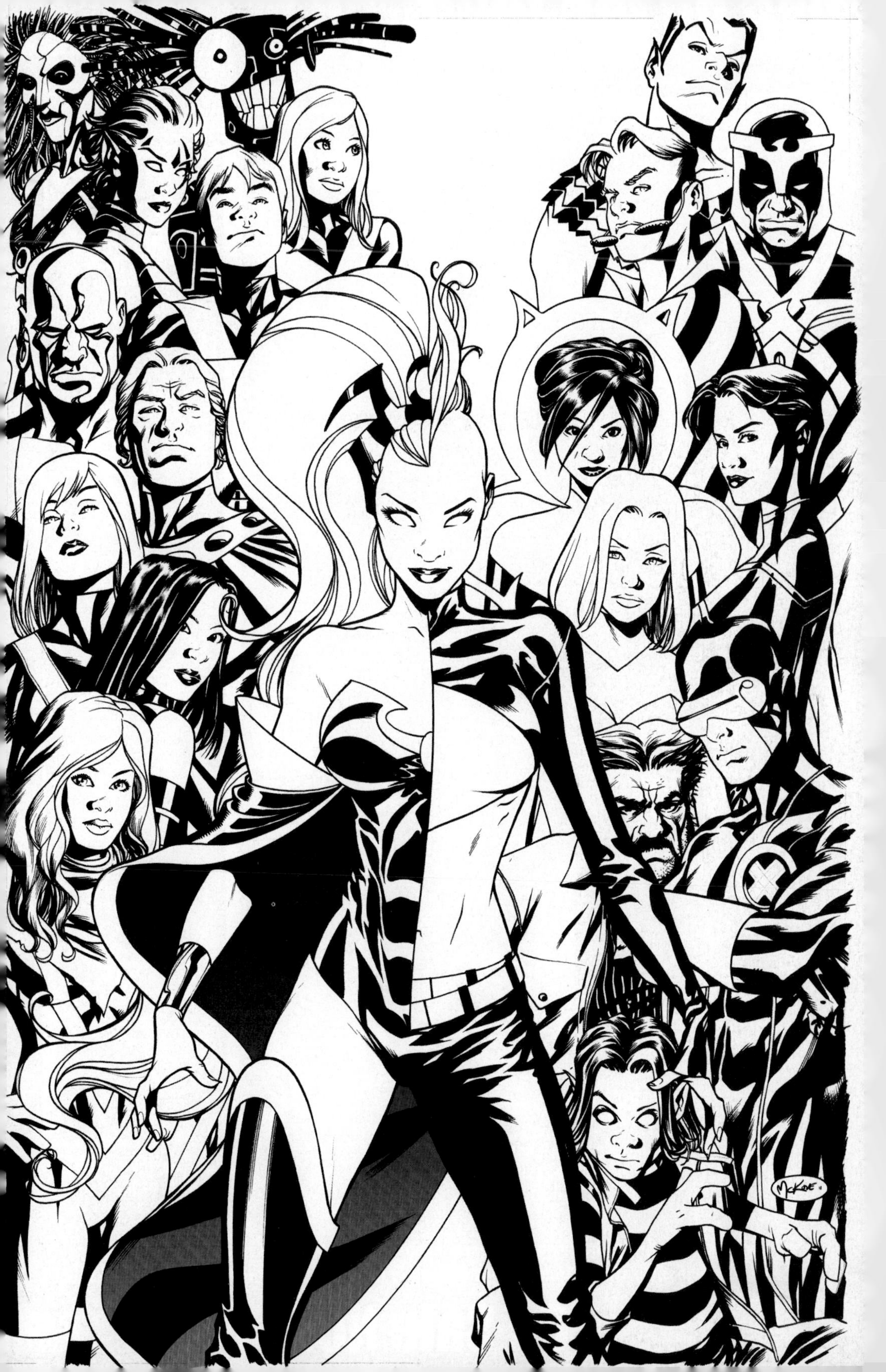

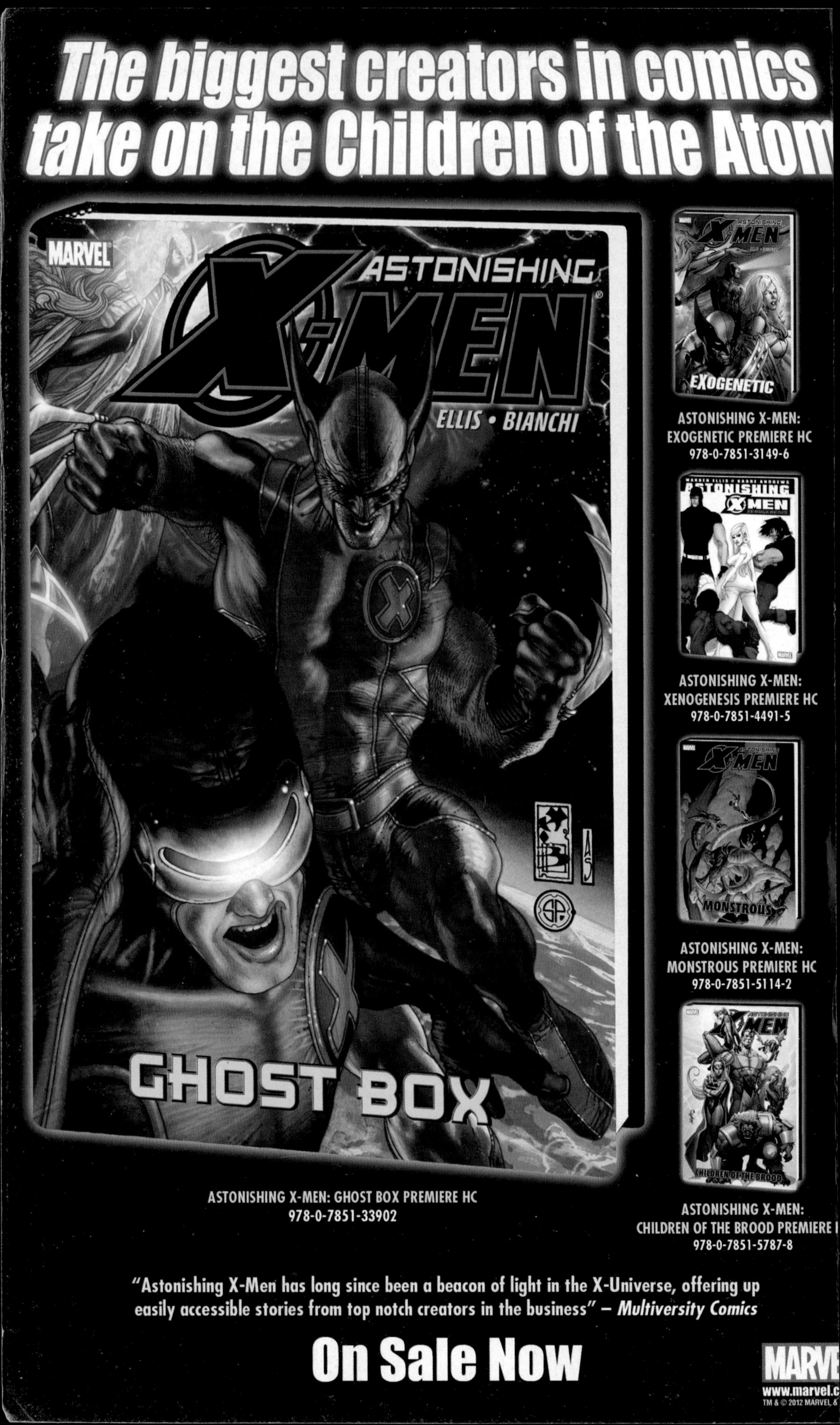
The biggest creators in comics take on the Children of the Atom
MARVEL
ASTONISHING X-MEN
ELLIS • BIANCHI
GHOST BOX
ASTONISHING X-MEN: GHOST BOX PREMIERE HC
978-0-7851-33902
EXOGENETIC
ASTONISHING X-MEN: EXOGENETIC PREMIERE HC
978-0-7851-3149-6
ASTONISHING X-MEN
ASTONISHING X-MEN: XENOGENESIS PREMIERE HC
978-0-7851-4491-5
MONSTROUS
ASTONISHING X-MEN: MONSTROUS PREMIERE HC
978-0-7851-5114-2
CHILDREN OF THE BROOD
ASTONISHING X-MEN: CHILDREN OF THE BROOD PREMIERE I
978-0-7851-5787-8
"Astonishing X-Men has long since been a beacon of light in the X-Universe, offering up easily accessible stories from top notch creators in the business" – Multiversity Comics
On Sale Now
MARVE
www.marvel.c
TM & © 2012 MARVEL &